THIRTY-ONE
NIL

ON THE ROAD
WITH FOOTBALL'S OUTSIDERS

JAMES MONTAGUE

For Mum and Dad

Bloomsbury Sport
An imprint of Bloomsbury Publishing Plc

50 Bedford Square
London
WC1B 3DP
UK

1385 Broadway
New York
NY 10018
USA

www.bloomsbury.com

First published 2014
This paperback edition first published 2015

British Library Cataloguing-in-Publication Data
A catalogue record for this book is available from the British Library.

Library of Congress Cataloguing-in-Publication data has been applied for.

ISBN: PB: 978-1-4088-5163-0
        ePub: 978-1-4088-5159-3

2 4 6 8 10 9 7 5 3 1

Typeset in Adobe Garamond by Saxon Graphics Ltd, Derby
Printed and bound in Great Britain by CPI Group (UK) Ltd, Croydon CR0 4YY

MIX
Paper from
responsible sources
FSC® C020471

To find out more about our authors and books visit www.bloomsbury.com.
Here you will find extracts, author interviews, details of forthcoming events and
the option to sign up for our newsletters.

'The Philistine with his shield bearer in front of him, kept coming closer to David. He looked David over and saw that he was little more than a boy, glowing with health and handsome, and he despised him. He said to David, "Am I a dog, that you come at me with sticks?" And the Philistine cursed David by his gods. "Come here," he said, "and I'll give your flesh to the birds and the wild animals!"'

1 Samuel 17:41–44

'It was me against the swimming pool.'

Eric 'The Eel' Moussambani

CONTENTS

	Introduction	1
1	Palestine, Afghanistan	15
2	Haiti, US Virgin Islands, Curaçao	41
3	Rwanda, Eritrea	63
4	American Samoa, Cook Islands, Samoa, Tonga	88
5	Lebanon, United Arab Emirates	111
6	Egypt, Mozambique	131
7	Antigua and Barbuda, United States	149
8	Switzerland, Albania, Kosovo	168
9	Croatia, Serbia	190
10	Egypt, Lebanon, Rwanda and Eritrea Reprised	209
11	Brazil, Nigeria, Spain, Tahiti	223
12	Romania, Hungary	246
13	Bosnia and Herzegovina, Slovakia	266
14	Iceland, Norway	281
15	Jordan, Uruguay	292
16	The Last Thirty-two	306
	Postscript	313
	Acknowledgements	321
	Index	323

INTRODUCTION

Nottingham, United Kingdom. August 2013

The Norman Archer Memorial Ground on the edge of the Clifton council estate, itself on the outskirts of Nottingham, glowed green in light and dark stripes, mown in perfect parallel lines as the first game of the football season drew close.

The pitch was guarded along one side by a corrugated-iron stand capable of hosting no more than fifty, perhaps sixty, paying spectators. A ticket cost £3. In front of it stood a wooden dugout and technical areas. The perimeter was dotted with just enough home-made wooden advertising hoardings from local businesses to keep the ground afloat financially: Michael's Fresh Bake, J. D. Plumbing & Heating and NG 11 Taxis had all dug deep into their pockets.

A hot August sun had greeted this Saturday. Not a soul had yet sullied the pitch, nor the dugout, nor the corrugated-iron stand. Metal crush barriers optimistically surrounded the pitch, even though it was unlikely there would be any need for them. Fresh netting had been pulled down tightly from each crossbar. Temporary corner flags had been pushed into the ground, occasionally fluttering in the light breeze.

In the nearby clubhouse an excitement recognised by anyone who has waited impatiently for the return of English football's metronomic presence – August to May, August to May – filled the air; a mixture of humidity, Deep Heat and hope. It was one hour before the home team, Clifton All Whites FC, kicked off their season against Hucknall Town FC in the Central Midlands Football league (South Division). This is the lowest tier in English semi-professional football, the transitional point at which the forever amateur meets a cursory, peppercorn wage. For the tens of thousands of players who dream of the Premier League, of England, of the Champions League – or simply dream of being paid enough to survive doing the thing they love most in life – this is either the first rung on a long and almost impossible ladder or its precarious last, with only oblivion below.

Jay'Lee Hodgson had arrived at the Norman Archer Memorial Ground early, as hopeful as at the start of any season during his resurrected career. Logic dictated that, at thirty-three, even if in good shape and with youthful lines shaved into his right eyebrow, the direction of the Nottingham-born striker's footballing trajectory was as clear as it was inexorable. But that logic was somewhat misplaced. Jay'Lee skipped up the steps of the squat, brick-built clubhouse and embraced his new coach, one of more than a dozen he had similarly embraced in six years. 'I'm buzzing,' he announced excitedly before he entered to join his team-mates, tossing the butt of his roll-up on to the floor. 'I can smoke five or six of these before a game but it doesn't affect me. My friend's still call me the black George Best!' He exhaled a long 'huh, huh, huh' machine-gun laugh before disappearing into the building.

This was to be Jay'Lee's first competitive match for Clifton All Whites FC, a team that was celebrating its fiftieth anniversary this season. The club had a strong local reputation for discovering top young players. It acted as a sort of unofficial feeder club for some of the bigger local teams, like European Cup winners Nottingham Forest and Notts County. The latter, founded in 1862, is the oldest professional football club in the world. Former England international Viv Anderson started here, as did the likes of Jermaine Jenas and Darren Huckerby, who both went on to play in the English Premier League.

Clifton All Whites FC may be a team that nurtures the earliest of embryonic international talent, but this season was the first time a *bona fide*, current international footballer had turned out for the team. That international team may be one of the lowest ranked in international football – indeed, it is perhaps one of the worst teams in the history of the international game – but that team, and Jay'Lee himself, was now a small but important footnote in the history of world football. In June 2011, two years and two months before the start of this new season, even before the afterglow of the 2010 World Cup in South Africa had been replaced by the twinkling distant hope of the next finals, Jay'Lee Hodgson played in the very first qualification match for the 2014 World Cup finals in Brazil, for the tiny Caribbean island of Montserrat against Belize. Not only that, he had scored twice, too.

Not many people had paid much attention to that match, played as it was between two teams ranked 206th (Montserrat, joint last) and 154th (Belize) according to FIFA's international rankings at the time. In fact, only 150 spectators had turned up to watch the game in the Ato Boldon Stadium in Trinidad and Tobago. It was to be a two-game play-off, home and away. Four other fixtures would be played at the same time in total, involving the ten lowest ranked teams in CONCACAF, one of FIFA's six confederations that represented teams from North America, Central America and the Caribbean islands.

Most of the teams came from small countries with tiny populations, made up of amateur players who spent their days as mechanics, policemen, doctors or preachers. Many of those players had never tasted victory in their entire international careers. Rather, they had become accustomed to losing matches by scores in double figures. Yet campaign after campaign, beating after beating, they continued to believe and continued to play. Alongside Montserrat and Belize the likes of Anguilla, Aruba, the Bahamas and the Turks and Caicos Islands still dreamed a remote and implausible dream. There was even room for a grudge match of sorts: the British Virgin Islands had been drawn against the US Virgin Islands. Neither had ever won a World Cup qualification match before, meaning something finally had to give. Even given the crazy odds, there was still the faintest of hopes.

Montserrat, a British Overseas Territory with a population of just 6,000, couldn't host its home match against Belize. The southern half of the island – including its capital, Plymouth – had been destroyed after the island's Soufrière Hills volcano erupted in 1995. Two-thirds of the population left. Today, the southern half remains an exclusion zone. Without a stadium that met FIFA's standards elsewhere on the island – the national coach Kenny Dyer, a forty-nine-year-old Englishman with Montserratian roots, lamented in the press before the game that the pitch in Montserrat was one of the best he had ever seen but that 'the dressing rooms weren't ready, they hadn't been painted' – the match was moved to Trinidad instead. With little money and very few international fixtures between World Cup qualification campaigns, a team had to be raised almost from scratch.

Jay'Lee hadn't been born in Montserrat. Most of the team hadn't. Instead the Montserrat Football Association decided to tap into an underexploited resource: the second- and third-generation diaspora that still existed in the home of the empire that had colonised it. But Jay'Lee hadn't been scouted in the conventional manner. Instead his call-up to international football had come in the most meritocratic of ways. 'I just went on a trial in Hackney and I got an email four weeks later from Kenny Dyer that I was in the squad and then *Bob's your uncle* ...' Jay'Lee recalled, now sitting next to the pitch as his team-mates trained in front of us, as if becoming an international footballer was as easy as applying to appear on a game show.

In a way, it was. Coach Kenny Dyer decided that an open trial on Hackney Marshes, a large area of common land home to dozens of football pitches in London's East End that filled up every weekend with thousands of amateur footballers, would procure a team that could qualify for the World Cup finals ahead of the likes of Mexico, the US and Jamaica.

'We went over to London for a local Caribbean tournament and I know a lot of pro players in the UK from non-league right up to Premier [League] and there was so many players down at the park,' Dyer said, speaking from Jamaica on Skype, the camera on his iPad zooming in a little too closely to his dreadlocked head. He looked two decades younger than his forty-nine years.

'There must have been seventy players there and I got them together. I stood up and I told them: "I am the head coach of the Montserrat national team and I am looking for players and I need to know which one of yous has parents, grandparents, great grandparents from Montserrat."' He was rewarded with silence. 'They looked at each other as if to say: "So who the hell is Montserrat!"' he laughed. 'But then one hand raised ... and then another ... and then another. We managed to assemble the best squad of players that Montserrat ever had.'

Dyer had become an accidental national team coach. A former Arsenal and Tottenham Hotspur trainee, he'd moved from club to club in England's non-league before heading to Cyprus to play professional football there. When his brother went to Montserrat, the island of their father's birth, on holiday, he started giving Kenny's number out, boasting about his professional contract in Cyprus. Eventually he was called into the squad. 'They came to England first,' he said of his first meeting with the team. 'The coach introduced himself and I went training with the boys. I knew immediately what kind of strength we had and it wasn't very good.'

With the end of his career nigh – Dyer made his last appearance for the Montserrat team at forty-six – he eventually moved into coaching and was employed as the national team coach for the start of the 2010 World Cup qualification campaign, largely because he was the only person with any professional experience. Montserrat's campaigns tended to be short: one, maybe two brutal beatings at best. Their previous World Cup campaign for the 2006 finals ended in a 20-0 aggregate loss over two matches against Bermuda.

'Would you take the job if you were asked?' Dyer asked. 'These opportunities don't come up. It's a once-in-a-lifetime. It's in my blood. It was a chance for me to try and see what I could do to develop football on the island.' But the scale of what he had agreed to soon dawned on him. 'At every football club there's a chain of command: a coach, a kitman, a physio, groundsman, right? Well, here, they never had any of it. I was rubbing my eyes saying what the hell is going on.' What upset Dyer most, however, was the dress code. 'Even when we were travelling for games, you usually all wear the same tracksuits so you look like a national team. No. They were wearing all sorts of different clothing. I said to them: "You are representing yourself, your mother, father, grandmother." They turned up in flip-flops and shorts. I had to put my foot down on that.'

Dyer almost missed his first game in charge, too, a World Cup qualifier versus Surinam in Trinidad. A disagreement with a member of the Montserrat FA meant they had flown to the game without a coach until the president intervened. 'Three days prior to the trip I got an email from the FA president begging me to take the trip. I said I'd do it. Two days before the match I went.' It wasn't a happy experience. 'They were a shambles,' he said. 'The players who travelled, I wouldn't have picked them for a Rymans Premier League game. They weren't up to international standard at all. We got beat 7-0.' It took a few moments for him to realise he got the score wrong. 'Sorry. 7-1. We weren't ready.'

In the aftermath of that beating Dyer decided to give the team at least a veneer of respectability and use his contacts from years of moving around English non-league football to find the Montserratians whose families – thanks to hurricanes, volcanoes or poverty – had been cast far and wide from their home island. Eventually that path led to Hackney Marshes, an open trial and Jay'Lee. 'He was a breath of fresh air,' remembers Dyer. 'He reminded me a little of Jermain Defoe. He was just goals, goals, goals.'

Jay'Lee recalls the makeshift park trial slightly differently. 'There was about twenty-five people there and there was a few players you could see who, er …' he pauses diplomatically when asked about the standard of some of the players at the trial. 'Let's just say you could see who was quality there and who was not. I just did my thing and hoped for the best, innit. The standard, I thought, was really good. You had some players who had played in Australia, for Leyton Orient, for Northampton, for [Nottingham] Forest [three English professional teams] and St Mirren [in Scotland]. I thought to myself I've never played at a higher level before. This is my chance.'

That Jay'Lee's chance came so late in his career, at a time most footballers are considering what to do once the game has finished with them, was rooted in indiscipline, bad luck and, finally, a tragedy that changed his life for ever. As a teenager he had a trial for non-league side Tamworth Town. The coach asked him back for a second chance but he never turned up. 'My mate who was driving said he wouldn't go,' he says. 'So I sacked it on the head and didn't play football again until I was twenty-six.'

He always had talent but growing up on one of the biggest and most deprived council estates in Western Europe provided its own problems, and distractions. 'I was doing all sorts,' he recalled with a smile. 'Fucking, women and drink, all sorts. It's what teenagers do.' Many of his friends had ended up on drugs or in prison, but it would take a bereavement to force Jay'Lee to change his ways. 'My cousin passed away and one of the last things he said to me before he died was "you should have been a footballer". It broke my heart,' he said. 'So I knuckled down and started playing football again.' He started getting fit, although he could no longer do without his ubiquitous roll-ups. That would just have to be tolerated. He started from the bottom, playing for anyone who'd take him in Nottingham's amateur Sunday leagues. Everywhere he went he scored goals. 'I played again, played on Saturdays and Sundays, moved to Long Eaton, played for Loughborough, and got a job as a personal trainer.' He was as far as he could possibly be from international football, let alone the World Cup. But there was something inside telling him he was meant for something else, something bigger. 'As a kid I remember watching the 1994 World Cup with my mum and my auntie,' he said when asked about his earliest World Cup recollections. 'I said to them: "One day I'll play in the World Cup. One day."' And then came the trial on Hackney Marshes after someone from the Montserrat FA discovered that Jay'Lee qualified thanks to his grandparents, who were born on the island. He was on a plane to Trinidad and the first qualifier of the 2014 World Cup finals, the first step on the road to Brazil. 'I'd just lost my job, too, and two weeks later I was an international footballer,' he laughed. 'It's funny how things work out, innit?'

**

International football means something. We live in an age where the economic evolution of the club game has made money omni-potent in football. International football, however, doesn't reward with money. It doesn't revere the most lucrative contracts. It doesn't tolerate transfers, except in the most limited or bizarre of circumstances. International football is luck, the throw of a dice. In theory, who you play for is largely determined before you are born. A national football team becomes the nation personified, rubbing up alongside enemies and friends in equal measure. International football, and its zenith the World Cup finals, can start wars, spark *détente*, ridicule and undermine despots or save an unpopular regime from oblivion.

The immense power of international football first dawned on me at the age of seven. I had just watched Argentina's Diego Armando Maradona punch the ball past Peter Shilton at the 1986 World Cup in Mexico. My dad screamed at the screen. I burst into tears. But the goal stood. Many valuable lessons had been learned that day, not least the fallibility of referees. Later I would learn of the importance of that goal. How Maradona had believed that God had personally intervened. How it was God's hand that smote the English. How it was retribution for the Falklands War waged between Argentina and the United Kingdom four years earlier over a tiny, apparently unimportant group of islands in the South Atlantic that had none the less claimed the lives of hundreds of Argentine sailors, mostly young conscripts the same age as Maradona.

International football meant something. It meant unity, identity and on this occasion it meant revenge. And there could be no bigger stage, other than perhaps a second more successful war, for revenge than the finals of the World Cup. But the World Cup finals are merely the tip of an iceberg. Beneath it a long battle is played out worldwide, sometimes for years in advance.

Ever since the second World Cup in Italy in 1934 (the first, in 1930, was by invitation only) the qualification process has almost perfectly reflected the world around it. But the qualification for the World Cup doesn't begin in London or Cairo or Rio. It starts in places like the Ato Boldon Stadium in Trinidad. It begins with players like Jay'Lee Hodgson and coaches like Kenny Dyer. It begins with the underdogs and the dreamers. *Thirty One Nil* is an attempt to tell the story of qualification for the 2014 World Cup finals, and, with it, tell something of the story of the world during this period. But not just through the eyes of the teams and the players who made it; rather, it is an attempt to tell the story of qualification through the eyes of those who have almost no hope of making it. The underdogs. The amateurs who begin each qualification campaign with real hope, before their eventual humiliation. The title of the book comes from the record score in a World Cup qualification match when, on 11 April 2001, Australia beat American Samoa 31-0. Striker Archie Thompson bagged thirteen goals that evening, another world record. The match became a worldwide story. Why? Because we are all fascinated by the outsider. The world of professional sport can only be viewed longingly from the stands by most people. But the outsider? He is one of us, moulded in our image, recognisable to the touch.

The business of losing heavily regularly, though, can take its toll. How does a team recover from a mauling such as the American Samoans suffered, ridiculed across the world to this day? What is it about the human spirit that forces a player to pick himself up and try again? *Thirty One Nil* tries to understand exactly that. It tells the story of qualification through the eyes of the players, coaches, fans and administrators who will probably never see or be part of the World Cup finals. It tells the story of hope in the face of realism. The journey begins in the West Bank. From there to Jordan, Tajikistan, Haiti, Rwanda, Australia, Samoa, Lebanon and beyond. It tells a story about international football's survival, about defeat amidst the mirages of victory.

And yet ... with every tournament, every cup competition anywhere in the world, there is always one team that defies the odds, the one example held aloft as proof that, no matter how far away qualification can seem, there is always a chance of being the next Trinidad and Tobago of 2006, the Jamaica of 1998, United Arab Emirates or Cameroon of 1990, Iraq of 1986, North Korea of 1966, or Zaire and Haiti of 1974. As the scramble for qualification nears its conclusion, with all the political intrigues along the way, there is one team that inevitably emerges to prove that miracles might happen. At the end, the 203 national teams that began with dreams of qualifying for the 2014 World Cup finals in Brazil will have been brutally chopped down to thirty-two. A long, bumpy journey, it began in Trinidad with that game between Montserrat and Belize.

**

The first match went by in a flash. Jay'Lee remembers the heat, the rain and the nerves. 'In the first ten minutes I did an overhead kick and hit one of the defenders. And the referee said to me: "Yellow card." And I was in bits. I thought I'd be sent off if I made another rash challenge,' he said. But it was Belize who took the lead. Yet despite the disparity in FIFA rankings, Montserrat equalised. 'I had a header that went wide of the post, I remember. And then the ball was whipped in, I hit the ball, volley, back of the net. The ball bounced down and I celebrated my goal as I always do, pointing to the sky.' The gesture honoured the cousin whose death prompted Jay'Lee to rethink his life. The game was tied 1-1 at half-time and Montserrat had a famous scalp in their sights. 'We had about fifteen chances in the first half of the first game,' Jay'Lee lamented. 'We should have buried them.' Instead it was Belize that came out stronger, stung by being held by their supposed inferiors, scoring four times before Jay'Lee scored a second goal. The match finished 5-2. Montserrat's three-goal deficit looked insurmountable until a scandal erupted within the Football Federation of Belize. FIFA suspended the Belize federation over 'political interference' in the running of the game. 'We thought we were going to get into the next round and the next stage, the group stage,' coach Kenny Dyer said ruefully. 'We actually arrived at the hotel in Belize [for the return match] and got the call saying that the game was cancelled. We stayed overnight and went home.'

As time ticked down to FIFA's preliminary World Cup draw at the end of July 2011 in Rio to determine the qualification groups in all of FIFA's confederations, Montserrat prayed that Belize wouldn't be readmitted. But, with days to go before the draw, Belize was reinstated and the match was hosted at the second neutral venue of the tie. In Honduras, Montserrat again equalised, again with Jay'Lee Hodgson scoring. But Belize ran out 3-1 winners, the tie finishing 8-3 on aggregate. 'We should have been winning 5-0 in the first twenty minutes,' Dyer said, the pain of that defeat still evident as he recalled a match that had taken place over two years earlier. 'It was very nice to hear the Belize officials saying: "We had our backsides whooped. We should have been out of the World Cup."'

After a lifetime of non-league obscurity Jay'Lee had scored all three of Montserrat's goals in World Cup qualification and had become one of his adopted homeland's all time top scorers. 'After I played in the World Cup qualifiers against Belize I went home with all my mementos, my flags and the shirt and all that and my mum said to me: "Don't you remember in 1994 when you said to me and your auntie in the kitchen that you will play in the World Cup?" And I've done it. It is a dream come true.'

Kenny Dyer won't be masterminding a future Montserratian assault on the World Cup finals. In May 2013 he left the post. He had a new challenge to face, as technical director of Portmore United FC, the reigning champions of Jamaica's Red Stripe Premier League. But it was the national team game that still reigned supreme, even if Dyer regretted the loss of its attraction to a certain kind of modern player.

'Club football has the power and TV has the power. Players' finances have taken over,' he said. 'Whereas before you played for England it meant a hell of a lot. It meant a lot more ten to fifteen years ago. It is club over country at the moment and it should be the other way around.'

But not in Montserrat. I had one final question for Dyer. What, after all the beatings, motivates a coach, a player, a kitman, a physio, to try and try again in the face of such long odds? He thought for a moment but the answer came easily to him. 'It is inside every player, although it is hard to describe. At the game with Belize when you stood in the hotel room and corridor, you could feel the buzz, the anticipation. There was a light on all our faces. We believed we could do this. And we almost did. We almost did.' A month after we spoke, Portmore United FC fired Dyer.

One day, teams like Montserrat won't exist, not in their current haphazard form. Professionalism will continue to spread uniformity. It will be a good thing that those with the talent can be paid and be treated with the respect they deserve. But without the Montserrats or the San Marinos or the American Samoas, what will be left? Without the underdog, and with it the faintest of hopes of the upset that every sports fan craves, football would be a dead-eyed and black-hearted place. World Cup qualification is unique in that respect. The Olympics has its odd shocks, it has its Eric the Eel moments, the swimmer from Equatorial Guinea who found himself at the 2000 Olympics in Sydney despite having never swum in an Olympic-size pool before. Eric the Eel is still written about today. Few remember who won the gold medal. But these, in a way, are manufactured, qualifiers handed a spot at the finals in good faith. The World Cup, on the other hand, is as brutal as it is meritocratic. In the draw for the 2014 finals, the 2010 finalists Holland were drawn against Andorra, a principality with a population of 85,000. Andorra would no doubt be crushed but, unlike in many other sports, the chance remains that an upset could still take place, that a rock from David's sling could still break Goliath's temple.

Belize made it through to the first group stage of CONCACAF World Cup qualification, along with the Bahamas (who later pulled out because their national stadium, a gift from the Chinese government, wasn't ready in time), the Dominican Republic, St Lucia and the US Virgin Islands, who won the battle of the Virgins and with it their first ever World Cup match. The first round of CONCACAF qualification had come to a close. Next it was Asia's turn, where my journey would begin in Jordan, Tajikistan and the West Bank. Palestine had been drawn against Afghanistan, a potentially politically explosive affair.

After all the hope, Montserrat were out. But the experience of World Cup qualification hadn't left Kenny Dyer bitter. Even after the 7-1 defeats, the ignominy of being ranked last in the world, the disagreements, tantrums, lost luggage, inept bureaucracy, corrupt politics, ingratitude, tiny crowds and, finally, for all that hard work, unemployment, international football was still what he dreamed of. 'The World Cup is the pinnacle,' he said, as if he was pining for an unrequited love. 'I will never play in the group stages of the World Cup. You can win the Champions League, but playing in that World Cup ... Just saying you played in the World Cup in the greatest sport and the greatest tournament in the world ... for me playing it is the pinnacle.'

**

Clifton All Whites FC finished training and Jay'Lee Hodgson was called into the dressing room for a final team talk before the first game of the Central Midlands Football league (South Division) season. His exploits in Trinidad and Honduras hadn't led to the flood of professional offers that he had hoped for, just a few trials further up the food chain that hadn't amounted to anything. Bad luck and injuries, Jay'Lee explained, had hampered his chances. Instead he had laced up his boots for whoever would have him, whoever made him feel at home. 'Every time I play football it is the same,' he said. 'I am on a pitch with my mates. Whether I am kicking it in the park or playing Belize, it is the same. For ninety minutes I just let my troubles go.'

Just over forty spectators saw Montserrat international striker Jay'Lee Hodgson score on his debut for Clifton All Whites FC. He had already set up his team's first goal, before volleying in the second at the near post. During the second half he was moved to centre-back, where he made sure Hucknall Town's strikers could not get their team back into the game. The match finished Clifton All Whites 2 Hucknall Town FC 1. Jay'Lee Hodgson limped off the pitch, the result of a clearance during the frenzied last ten minutes of the match as Hucknall Town sought an equaliser. 'It's always good to score on your debut, innit, job done,' he said of his performance. But Montserrat was never far away. He was already thinking of the next World Cup, in Russia in 2018. He'd be thirty-five by the time the qualifiers came around again. 'I'd love to play in the World Cup again, I'm waiting for that call,' he said, limping back to the clubhouse canteen. 'I hope I can stay fit and injury-free. I'm thirty-three now but there are players who play until they are forty. As long as you look after your body your body looks after you. I am just waiting for that call, waiting for that email.'

1

PALESTINE, AFGHANISTAN

Tursunzode, Tajikistan. June 2011

The white-tiled dressing room is silent and hot. A single air-conditioning unit is turned up high, fighting a losing battle against the 40 degree temperature as the players from the Palestinian national football team sit with their backs against the wall wearing green shirts and shorts. Around the neck of each man is a black and white *keffiyeh*, the desert scarf made famous by Yasser Arafat. Some choose to close their eyes, raise their hands and pray. Others simply stare at the only thing moving in the room. Coach Moussa Bezez, a French Algerian who once represented France at youth level and has been in charge of the team for two years, paces the room, careful to tread softly so as not to make too much noise. He has nothing more to say to his players after delivering his final, impassioned team talk. He opens his mouth as if to add a piece of wisdom, but he knows that his players need this moment. The silence is finally broken by the match commissioner. It is game time. The team, the squad and the coaches meet Moussa in the middle of the room. They link arms in a circle and begin to pray. 'Fil-es-tine!' shouts one of the players. The rest roar back in agreement.

Palestine's long road to the 2014 World Cup finals in Brazil begins here, in an obscure, decrepit stadium in western Tajikistan against Afghanistan. Technically it is a home match for Afghanistan. The tie was due to be played in Kabul, but the security situation was so bad that it was moved to Tursunzode, a dying aluminium-smelting city a few miles from the Uzbek border. To prove just how dangerous the situation was, two suicide bombings in Kabul and eastern Afghanistan a few days before meant that no one knew whether the Afghans would even show up. But they have. The Afghan players stand in line in the tunnel of the Metellurg Stadium. Both sets of players eye each other suspiciously. It's the first time either team has been able to see who they will be playing. They are almost complete unknowns to each other.

'Come on, guys, let's do this!' shouts Omar Jarun in an accent from the Deep South as he claps his hands. Jarun is a six-foot-five monster of a centre-back, with a blond mohawk, who hails from Peachtree City, near Atlanta, Georgia. He has never been to the West Bank and he speaks no Arabic, but his grandfather comes from Tulkarem, a small town north of Jerusalem. He was spotted playing football in the US second division after the Palestinian Football Association launched a global hunt for players among the Palestinian diaspora. Behind him stands a microcosm of the Palestinian experience. First is left-back Roberto Bishara. He is from Chile and plays for Palestino, a first division club that was built by Palestinian immigrants who fled their homes and arrived in South America following the creation of the State of Israel in May 1948. He too speaks no Arabic. Or much English.

Midfielder Husain Abu Salah is an Israeli Arab, a descendant of one of the Palestinians who didn't flee into exile. They stayed in Israel. He speaks Hebrew and holds an Israeli passport. He even spent several years playing for Bnei Sakhnin, an Arab club that plays in Israel's first division, but he decided to quit and play in the West Bank so that he could better represent Palestine. The goalkeeper, Mohammed Shbair, is from Gaza. He is a dead ringer for Iker Casillas, Real Madrid's Spanish international goalkeeper. He hasn't been home for two years. Such are Israel's movement restrictions that he has to seek special permission to leave the West Bank where his club is. Once his papers weren't in order after a friendly in Sudan and he was refused permission to return home; he spent three months in exile in Jordan.

That the Palestinians have a national team at all is a miracle; they are a national team without a nation state. FIFA recognised Palestine in 1998, one of only a handful of international organisations to do so. But then the second intifada intervened and the national team has been in limbo ever since: unable to play games at home, divided between Gaza and the West Bank and prevented by both the Israelis and the Egyptians from getting their players out of the territories to fulfil its away fixtures.

But this World Cup is different. For the past three years football in Palestine has undergone something of a revolution and has been used as a political vehicle by the Palestinian Authority to promote a recognised Palestinian entity abroad. The second match against Afghanistan will take place in the Faisal al-Husseini Stadium outside Ramallah, Palestine's first ever World Cup match on home soil. The national team is the mirage of a nation made flesh. In front of them stand the unknowns of Afghanistan, a country equally as blighted by war and tragedy.

'How do you say "come back" in Arabic?' Jarun asks his fellow centre-back hopefully, just as FIFA's official theme tune – a sugary, pompous dirge that sounds as if it has been gleaned from the *Super Mario Brothers* soundtrack – is played too loudly on the crackly Soviet-era PA system. The players walk out of the narrow tunnel and into the blinding sunlight, the pressure released like a caged bird thrown into the cloudless blue sky.

**

One week earlier

Outside the clean but functional Gardinia Hotel in Amman, the capital of Jordan, coach Moussa is sweating as he throws kitbags into the belly of the Palestinian team coach. He curses under his breath as his squad of players slowly emerge into the already hot summer's morning.

'I said 7 a.m.,' he fires at the few players who have made it outside on time with a sarcastic shrug. It's 7.30. The team doctor, chain-smoking Marlboro Red Tops, grudgingly abandons a fourth cigarette and helps him pack the coach instead. Omar Jarun is sitting on the steps of the hotel. He's been there for forty-five minutes reading his copy of the *Jordan Times*, the country's only English-language broadsheet. 'No, there's nothing,' he replies when I ask him what is going on in the world. 'Nothing that's good anyway.' He puts down the paper and goes to help.

International football, and especially World Cup football, might look like a glamorous parade of glory and five-star luxury, but not here. The Palestinians are in Jordan for a training camp in Amman before flying to the Tajik capital of Dushanbe, an eighteen-hour flight via Dubai, for the first leg of their World Cup qualifier against Afghanistan. It is the first round of Asian Football Confederation qualification, designed for the lowest ranked teams in Asia, a chance to weed out the truly appalling and unprepared from those that have a chance. Sixteen teams have been drawn for the first round, ranging from the obscure (Chinese Taipei – a political sop of a name designed to allow Taiwan to play despite Chinese objections – Macau, Timor-Leste and Mongolia) to the underdeveloped (Cambodia, Nepal, Sri Lanka, Laos) to the huge and hugely underachieving (Pakistan, Bangladesh, the Philippines, Vietnam, Myanmar and Malaysia). Incredibly, between them their national football teams are drawn from countries that represent three-quarters of a billion people, almost the same population as Europe.

For any of these teams the task of qualifying would be hard enough at the best of times. It would prove logistically challenging even with top international players and a football association with an unlimited budget. But this was Palestine, a team that had neither money, top international footballers nor a country to call their own. The problems in getting a team together were legion. For a start, each of the Palestinians based in the West Bank had to leave overground into Jordan, the only exit to the rest of the world open to most Palestinians. In the past, several players had been detained by the Israelis on their way to play a match. When qualifying for the 2006 World Cup was under way, five players were detained trying to leave Gaza and the West Bank for a match against Uzbekistan in neutral Qatar. They lost 3-0.

This time FIFA and the IOC had put pressure on the Israelis to stop this happening. Almost the entire squad got out without any problems. Almost. 'I was at the border seven hours,' laments Moussa. The coach was now packed with sleeping players and swaying through traffic to the airport. 'I tell them [Israeli border guards]: "I'm the coach of the Palestinian national team." The border guard looked at me and said: "NATIONAL team? Wait here." I did, for seven hours.' Other players weren't so lucky. Many of Palestine's best footballers come from Gaza, but ever since the militant Islamist group Hamas took control of the strip in 2007, Israel and Egypt have been loath to let anyone out of 'fighting age' just in case. In fact, Palestine's best player, defender Abdelatif Bahdari, was sent back from the Gaza border by the Egyptians, who had banned any men between the ages of eighteen and forty from crossing for fear that extremists militants might cause trouble in the semi-anarchy of post-revolution Egypt. He now wouldn't be playing in the first leg.

Others had much further to travel. At Queen Alia airport Moussa meets his left-back for the first time. Roberto Bishara, the Chilean, has finally arrived and is waiting at the departure gate. Omar, Moussa and Bishara try to make small talk, firstly about Real Madrid's recent transfer activities. Bishara looks back blankly. He doesn't speak French, Arabic or English. Omar and Moussa give up when they realise none of them can really under-stand each other. Unsure how to communicate with his new player, Moussa slaps Bishara on the arm. They stand looking at each other for a brief moment before they awkwardly both stare down at the floor. 'Good,' says Moussa finally in English, declaring their meeting over. They shuffle off in different directions.

The Palestinians are a patchwork of bureaucracy, languages and cultures. They travel on eight different passports: some have the black Palestinian Authority passport, others a special permit from Gaza for those lucky enough to get out and play in the West Bank's newly established professional league. A few have East Jerusalem ID for those from the city who didn't want to become Israelis. Several have Israeli passports. The rest come from all over the world: Chile, France, Jordan and, of course, America. At each border the team is stopped, checked, checked again and treated with the utmost suspicion. The Palestinian Authority passport is, after all, possibly the least useful passport in the world. Yet all are joined together by a common purpose: to return home, even if it is a 'home' that Omar Jarun had never seen before. 'Their first impressions were: "Who the hell is this guy? How the hell is this guy Palestinian?"' Omar explains on the short flight to Dubai. I had asked him what the Palestine players had thought about him joining the squad. He points back to his team-mates. Everyone is sitting in economy. A few have found a spare row of seats on which to curl up and sleep. 'They welcomed me in like I was one of the brothers. It wasn't like I was an outsider. No one was judging each other.'

Omar's journey from Georgia to the West Bank actually began in Kuwait, the country of his birth. Born to an American mother and a Palestinian father born in Jordan, his family fled the country before the First Gulf War, when Saddam Hussein invaded in 1990. 'I remember bombs going off. Missiles shooting off near the apartment. I remember grabbing my bear, me and my sister running to my dad's bedroom and saying: "What's going on?"' he recalls. 'The next morning my dad would come in shaking ... my mom managed to get the entire family into the US. We left everything behind. My parents had nothing.' He is a Muslim and, despite first impressions given by his apple-pie American good looks, identifies himself as a proud Arab. He prays every Friday at the only mosque in Peachtree City, in a hotel. Football, too, is in his blood. His father taught him the game in his backyard and although he always held out hope of one day playing for Team USA, when the Palestinians approached him he didn't think twice. 'In my heart I feel like an Arab, a Palestinian. I see what happens to the people over there and you know the world needs to know that the people from Palestine are stuck like rats in a cage,' he says as the plane begins its descent. 'I knew it wouldn't be particularly professional. But I could do my part. I didn't know what I could do for the Palestinian people apart from play football. So when they told me I could play for the Palestinian national team, I said yes.'

We arrive in Dushanbe at 1 a.m., but this isn't the end of the journey. A coach takes us two hours south-west to Tursunzode through the pitch-black countryside. The national stadium in Dushanbe is being renovated. There are no street lights. No one really knows anything about Tajikistan, other than that it is a former Soviet republic and that it was from here that the Soviets launched their disastrous invasion of Afghanistan in 1979, a decision that costs thousands of lives and convinced a then little-known but devout son of a filthy rich Saudi construction magnate to declare war on the heathen West. His name was Osama Bin Laden.

The hotel in Tursunzode is closed. There is no drinking water, no electricity, no internet, no food. The water runs black from the taps. One of the coaches is sent out to look for water and food and finds five large watermelons outside, enough to avert a brewing mutiny. The players take them upstairs to the kitchen and break them open on the metal tables. We all devour red chunks of melon like animals, spitting the black pips on to the floor. Downstairs, Omar sits shaking his head at anyone who will look in his direction. He has forgone his share of the watermelon. He had expected his experience of representing Palestine to be a little rough around the edges, but he hadn't expected this. 'This place reminds me of a bowling meet,' he says, looking around at the cheap Soviet-style wooden panelling on the walls. 'Some butt-fuck shack in the middle of nowhere.'

**

The taxi bumps its way back along the broken highway. It is daylight now, the morning after our arrival, and Tajikistan is, for the first time, spread out before us. It is a country whose sole natural resource appears to be water. It is green and lush: water from the mountains cascades through the towns in specially built concrete channels. Thousands of watermelons are piled carelessly on the side of the road, like severed heads collected after a bloody battle. Everything seems to be flavoured with watermelon: the chewing gum, the soft drinks, the air around the painfully thin girls who smile to reveal rows of gold teeth. The Soviet Union has left its scars, too: drab rectangular housing blocks, red and white smoke stacks reminiscent of Chernobyl and wide concrete boule-vards just wide enough to fit a column of tanks down all sit incon-gruously against the sub-tropical greenery. It is racked by poverty, too. On the side of the highway gangs of men carve bricks out of the mud, leaving them to dry in the sun.

Coach Moussa, striker Ahmed Keshkesh and I watch the alien land roll away from us. Keshkesh's presence had solved an ongoing mystery. We are travelling to a FIFA press conference, a mandatory requirement for the coach and team captain before any World Cup qualification match. The issue of who was to be captain had been a divisive one. 'In - tha - Middle - East - tha - issue - of - who - is - cap'n - is - important,' Omar had explained slowly to Roberto Bishara earlier in the day during their first training session, as if talking to a child. 'It - is - always - the - player - with - the - most - experience. Under - stand?' Bishara was silent, blinking hard.

Bishara had somehow got into an argument with Keshkesh although it was a mystery how. Having been part of the team that tried and failed to qualify for the 2006 World Cup, by rights Bishara should have been captain. He, after all, was the most expe-rienced player in the squad. But the rest of the team had disagreed and quarrelled openly about it. Bishara may have been Palestinian,

acknowledge each other's presence as they sit down. The two coaches (and the two players, for that matter) are of similar age and build. It is the first time either coach has garnered any information about their opponent. Such is the confidence among the Palestinian players that they have already started talking excitedly about Thailand, their next opponents should they beat Afghanistan. They are extra-confident given that the Afghan government has intervened to try and prevent the team from travelling to the away leg near Ramallah. 'It was clear that their players and officials would not be allowed by the Afghan government to come because they didn't want their passports stamped with the Israeli [border] stamps,' explained Jerome Champagne, a former special adviser to president of FIFA Sepp Blatter, who now worked as a consultant to the Palestinian Football Association, when we had spoken in the West Bank before the trip. Afghanistan doesn't recognise Israel and the government feared that the match would be seen as a form of recognition by the back door. The press conference meanders on. Keshkesh doesn't seem to understand what a press conference is and refuses to speak at first, before giving one-word answers to any question asked. The Afghan coach, Mohammad Yosuf Kargar, sporting a huge moustache, knows how to handle the Tajik press. He plays down his team's chances. He explains all the problems. The lack of money. The security situation in Kabul. The suicide bombings. He emphasises that Afghanistan is the true underdog here and how his team is training in conditions far inferior to those of the Palestinians. I thought of the mysterious black stuff that had oozed out of the taps of our hotel on our arrival and involuntarily shuddered at the horrors that must have awaited the Afghan team. But then he drops a bombshell. 'We have nine players who play professionally in Germany, Cyprus and America,' he casually tells the gathered journalists. They dutifully note this down. Moussa's head pings in Kargar's direction. The Afghan coach also explains how his team has been the fastest rising on FIFA's rankings in 2011, overtaking Palestine in the process. Keshkesh refuses to answer any more questions. It is enough new information for Moussa, who quickly leaves once the conference is over.

Afghanistan's captain is more talkative. Israfeel Kohistani is a softly spoken twenty-three-year-old midfielder who plays for Kabul Bank FC in the Afghan Premier League. He is missing four fingers, his thumb the only reminder of a left hand that picked up an unexploded grenade when he was a boy. 'When the Taliban came to Kabul I was eight years old, I found a bomb,' he says of the day he lost most of his hand. 'It was difficult for me but I became national captain so it hasn't affected me,' he explains, sliding his hand behind his back as we speak, as if embarrassed. I feel bad for asking about it. Still, it was tough being a footballer in Afghanistan. There was no money. Security outside Kabul was impossible. Security inside Kabul was still tenuous. 'People don't think about football like they used to,' he says. 'They are always thinking about fighting, fighting. We have difficulties with our government, they don't give us any money.' But he was here, with his team of professionals that weren't quite the whipping boys the Palestinians had expected. The big question was: would they even play both matches?

Will you make it to the West Bank for the second leg? I ask him.

It seemed improbable given the high level of Afghan governmental resistance, not to mention what the Israeli security forces would make of a coachload of Afghans turning up at the border. Israfeel shrugs. 'It is not clear whether we go there or not.'

In the taxi on the bumpy road back to the hotel Ahmed Keshkesh and Moussa Bezez sit in silence. Keshkesh falls asleep, but Moussa is wide awake. He is troubled. 'Nine professional players,' he repeats as we ricochet from one pothole to another back towards Tursunzode. 'That is more than we have.'

**

There were few benefits for the Palestinian national team being hosted in Tursunzode, but the isolation had one positive effect.

There was nothing to do in the city, nowhere a group of cooped-up young men on a rare trip abroad could cause trouble. The streets were empty during the intense heat of the day. At most you might catch a glimpse of a colourful skirt disappearing into a doorway. The factories appeared to have stopped functioning decades ago. Occasionally a shop would appear to be open, its young attendant snoozing by the till. A lone car trundled around a wide roundabout with a huge, garish green and red portrait of the country's long-time president, Emomalii Rahmon, gleaming at its centre.

The Palestinian players pack the hotel's one vaguely functioning internet café, sitting three to a chair, immersed in various Facebook girlfriends. Omar Jarun sits on his own, researching the Afghan team they are due to face the next day. News has spread that their opponents might be better than they first thought. 'They even have some players from the States,' he says, his eyes never leaving the screen as he clicks through the Wikipedia profiles of those Afghan squad members who have them. 'They look pretty good,' he concludes.

Moussa decides it is time for some fresh air. He gathers up his players and marches them out in single file for a brisk walk around the town. His charges mooch behind unwillingly in the blistering heat. They pass a gaggle of curious old ladies with gold teeth, sun-beaten skin and pink dresses sweeping the streets with straw brooms. The old ladies laugh like hyenas and hide behind their brushes. Fahed al-Fakhouri, one of the goalkeepers, seems preoccupied. 'I had a dream last night,' he explains when I ask what is wrong. Fakhouri is unlikely to play a part in either match. He is third choice, and was only drafted in after Palestine's first-choice goalkeeper (and first-choice captain), Ramzi Saleh, had been injured in the run-up to the fixtures. His dark hair and goatee give him an uncanny resemblance to Spain striker David Villa. He seems happy just to be there, until now that is. 'I had a dream that I shot someone, a man,' he elaborates.

Why did you shoot him? I ask.

'I don't know, he wouldn't let me leave.'

Fakhouri and Jarun have struck up a friendship. Fakhouri plays for one of Tulkarem's local teams. He has promised to show Jarun his ancestors' home town once the game is over. 'You will come too, yes?' he asks me keenly. I agree. The heat has now become unbearable. The column of sweating, surly players follows Moussa past one identical grey Soviet housing block after another. After a few minutes, he gives up and walks them all the way back, surrendering them to their Facebook girlfriends, three to a chair.

But the trip wasn't a complete waste of time. The outline of what appeared to be a restaurant was spotted. Later that night Stéphane, a six-foot-six French cameraman there to film a documentary on the team, and I sneak out to see what Tursunzode has to offer. The open-air bar is almost empty. In the centre a fountain gushes water as inflatable watermelons bob in its flow. We are ushered to the main table. Two businessmen inquire as to why a Russian and a six-foot-six black man are in their restaurant and their town. We explain that I am not Russian and that we are journalists here to cover the football match. They shake our hands and introduce us to the city's chief of police. Still in uniform, he has his wide-brimmed Soviet-era hat tucked under his shirtsleeve as he slams vodka shots. This is a majority Islamic country, but only nominally. The police chief explains that he had been in the Soviet army that had invaded Afghanistan. Now his job is to hold back a different invasion, one coming the other way: the opium flowing from Afghanistan, through his borders, and all the way into the veins of the West. He has a shaved head and mean scowl, which becomes harder and meaner the more he drinks. The night blurs as one shot follows another. The police chief's hat ends up on my head. He snatches it back, cursing such disrespect in Russian. We stumble through the dark, unlit streets back to the hotel and collapse into bed.

The Palestinian team greets us with silence at breakfast. Something is wrong. Moussa has a face like thunder as we gingerly ease into our seats. 'Where did you go last night?' his assistant asks. We tell him about the vodka and the businessmen and the chief of police.

'Who were you with?'

'The chief of police.'

'No, who else? Which players?'

The coaching staff had heard rumours that we had broken some of the players out of the hotel and taken them drinking and dancing at a local nightclub, carousing with the local women. Behind Moussa and his assistant, Fahed and Ahmed Keshkesh are in hysterics.

Kick-off is a few hours away.

**

The Palestinian and Afghan teams walk out of their oppressive tunnel and on to the pitch as FIFA's insipid attempt at a national anthem plays. The heat is incredible. FIFA insists that the match takes place at 5 p.m., but the stadium, a gift from the aluminium factory that keeps the city alive, is a large bowl with a running track around it. There is no shade from the 100 degrees-plus heat. A small crowd of a few thousand noisily cheer on their Afghan neighbours.

Within thirty seconds it becomes clear that the Afghans are much better than the Palestinians had given them credit for. Israfeel appears to be running the show for Afghanistan in midfield until Murad Alyan – a striker who, unlike many of his colleagues in the professional West Bank Premier League, works in a local hospital – scores for the Palestinians with a glancing header.

Ahmed Keshkesh has a miserable half. Back in the dressing room at half-time, Moussa is screaming at him in English to follow his instructions. But he ignores him, walks up to the white board that Moussa has been swiping at violently with a blue marker and tells his coach where he thinks he *should* be going instead, an almost suicidal moment of bravado. Moussa is stunned. He doesn't pull Keshkesh out of the game straight away: instead he is substituted within a few minutes of the start of the second half. He doesn't know it yet but it is the last World Cup match he will play while coach Moussa is in charge.

The Afghans press in the second half, and have their chances to equalise, but Keshkesh's replacement, Ismail Amour, somehow fires a rocket of a shot from an impossible angle into the top left-hand corner. The strike is so good, and so out of character for Amour – a talented but wasteful winger – that the bench do not celebrate until thirty seconds after he has scored, when they realise the ball is now back in the centre circle. It is one of the finest goals a player could possibly score, but it isn't caught on film. No camera records it. It is lost for ever, a memory only for the few who witness it.

The referee blows his whistle. Palestine has won its first 2014 World Cup qualification match 2-0. The players hug and dance around the pitch celebrating as if they have already qualified. Moussa is livid. He runs on to the pitch pulling down the players' arms. 'We are not through, stop this,' he shouts, trying to apply a sense of perspective, fearing the response from the opposition that arrogance can bring. Israfeel and his Afghan team trudge back to the dressing room, sweat-soaked and shattered. No one knows if this is the last we will see of the Afghan national team.

**

Chelyabinsk, Russian Federation

The Palestinian team leave that night. It is a long flight home, first to Dubai, then Amman, before a bus through the Jordan valley to the Israeli border. But Stéphane and I aren't there to witness it. Instead we are sent on a more circuitous route, flying to Chelyabinsk – a city in Russia near the Kazakh border that I haven't previously heard of, but which will later become infamous when a superbolide meteor explodes above it in 2013. From there we fly to Moscow and then to Amman, before taking a taxi for the short journey overland to the Israeli-controlled Palestinian border.

We land in Chelyabinsk in the early morning sun and approach the border in a grand, high-ceilinged arrivals hall. A collection of border guards in Soviet-style military hats stand and stare. We tell them we are journalists and hand over our passports. Stéphane once had a Russian girlfriend and speaks a little Russian. The border guards' mouths drop open. Two journalists, one British, one a black Frenchman speaking Russian, at the border of a provincial Russian city wanting to pass. Their minds are suitably boggled.

A file is produced. It is a thick blue binder with more documents than it was designed to hold. Three guards flick through, page by page, until they find a reason not to let us in. The tallest explains to Stéphane that they won't let us in because we don't have a transit visa, even though we are not staying. Worse, we are being deported back to Tajikistan, where we will almost certainly be jailed. They lock us in a room with three beds and no toilet alongside a mute Tajik teenager who has no baggage, scars on his face and toes and who has tried to enter Russia on a false passport.

Seven hours pass. Occasionally we are let out to use the toilet, but only when we bang on the door hard enough and scream for attention, and only between incoming flights. The mute Tajik teenager, his clothes dirty and torn, collapses on to the bed and falls into a deep sleep, as if it is the first mattress he has seen in years. Eventually we are taken to a man sitting at a desk. We have to pay money, he says. It isn't a bribe. Here, look, I have paperwork for you to sign, he says. It is definitely not a bribe. We pay the man sixty euros, sign a form in Russian and are escorted to a plane bound for Armenia, then Dubai, then Amman. We arrive in Amman forty-eight hours before the game.

**

Amman, Jordan

Despite the best efforts of the Afghan government, the Afghanistan national football team arrives in Amman, this time via Delhi and

Dubai, twenty-four hours after us and just one day before the match. Stéphane and I wait for them at Queen Alia airport. The players file on to the waiting bus, shattered. It is four days since their defeat in Tajikistan and the team has not trained since. Those who haven't slept stretch out on the floor of the bus as it speeds west towards the Israeli border between Jordan and the West Bank. It is Saturday, the Jewish Sabbath, and the border closes early in a few hours' time. If it closes with the Afghans on the Jordanian side then the match is finished.

Mohammad Yusef Mashriqi stays awake as the bus descends into the Jordan valley and towards the Israeli border. Like Omar Jarun, Mohammad is an American citizen, a New Yorker who used to play for the US national youth team and, he says, has a contract with the New York Cosmos. He brings up a picture on his phone: him, arm in arm with the club's new Director of Soccer, Eric Cantona. He had never been to Afghanistan until after the game in Tajikistan.

'I went to Kabul for the first time ever, it was so exciting,' he says. 'You know, my family are from Kandahar. My family didn't want me to enter Afghanistan, but they agreed in the end.'

His parents had good reason to worry. The family fled Afghanistan in 1985, before Mohammad was born, six years after the Soviets invaded. They had always been a football-crazy family – his father Tahrir used to play for the Afghanistan national team back in the 1970s and his grandfather was heavily involved in the game while a high school principal. 'My grandfather was very big in football in Kandahar, but the communists took him,' he explains. 'He was handed in by someone working with the communists. He was never heard from again. No one knows what happened to him.' Like Omar, he too dreamed of representing Team USA, and played for some of the same youth teams as Freddy Adu and Michael Bradley. But after 9/11, all that changed. 'After the 9/11 attacks I was never called back to the US national team, that was what bothered me the most,' he says with a hint of bitterness. 'Now I'm filling my father's shoes. I just wish we could play against the States in four or five years' time.'

The Afghanistan team has relied equally on a mixture of players from its diaspora and its home-grown talent, so much so that many of the team are unable to speak to each other. 'Afghanistan has thirty-two languages, but the two [main] languages are Pashtun or Farsi. I only understand Pashtun,' admits Djelaludin Sharityar, a thoughtful twenty-eight-year-old defender with long hair and a big black beard. He is for some unknown reason called 'Toto' by his team-mates and talks with a German accent, his family having fled there when he was seven years old. 'Sometimes it is a problem in the game to explain something ... but we find a way to explain to everyone what they want. The first game was a big problem, I went for the ball and shouted "my ball!". He didn't understand so we both went for it. Now I know some Farsi words to tell him.'

The bus reaches the border, and crosses over the River Jordan, more a trickle of sludge than the biblical torrent of yore. The players crowd by the windows, excitedly taking pictures of the first Star of David flag they see fluttering nearby. 'Will we get stamp, from Israel?' one of the players asks me. Three of his team-mates nod with concern.

No, I tell him. It has all been arranged beforehand. Don't worry. The Israelis won't stamp your passport.

'No,' he repeats slowly, as if I am not understanding him correctly. '*Can* we get a stamp from Israel?'

His three team-mates nod again, their faces eager; hopeful rather than concerned.

'We *want* a stamp from Israel,' he smiles, obviously aware that nine members of the Afghan national team disappeared in 2004 when they travelled to Italy for a charity match. 'We don't want to go back to Kabul.'

The Allenby Bridge crossing terminal is a hateful place. The building is innocuously designed, like a 1970s Duty Free supermarket, but is seething with resentment. Israeli teenagers carrying machine guns patrol close by as hundreds of Palestinian men, women and children wait in line. The Afghan squad stand in the holding area, watching the daily chaos unfold around them: children running around, arguments, shouting, anger. Sitting down on one of the metal benches is Toto. He looks dazed. This wasn't what he was expecting. 'This ... this is unbelievable,' he stutters. He is sitting in front of a long line of covered women, some of whom hopefully hold up American passports that will make no difference. 'They are being treated like cattle. Just to get into their own country.' He doesn't say another word for the rest of the journey. The squad is eventually led through to another room and processed out of sight from the Palestinians. Each Afghan team member passes through without trouble, even the four players who don't want to go back to Kabul. They ask for, but they don't get, their Israeli stamps.

**

Al Ram, Ramallah, West Bank

The Faisal al-Husseini Stadium is small, but it is home. Busloads of fans from all across the West Bank arrive two hours before kick-off, driving past the West Bank separation barrier that runs a hundred metres from the stadium's entrance. Banks of riot police clad in body armour and helmets, some carrying machine guns, prepare for the biggest match in Palestine's history. Its significance goes far beyond the football pitch. For the past two years the Palestinian Authority has been busy building the basics for an independent state: a strong economy, an honest, incorruptible civil service, a security force that can match any internal strife it may face, especially a football match. But part of this strategy involves sport, and especially football.

The man in charge of the Palestinian Football Association is Jibril Rajoub, one of the most powerful men in the West Bank. As a young radical he spent seventeen years in an Israeli prison for throwing a grenade at an army checkpoint. While in prison he learned to speak fluent Hebrew and, after his release, later rejected violence as a means of achieving Palestinian statehood. He rose to become Yasser Arafat's feared West Bank national security adviser and was one of the highest ranking members of Fatah. For him, the national football team is another way of showing the world that the Palestinians can take care of their own business. 'In 2006 we had no football, no competitions, nothing; now there has been a revolution in Palestine. This has a political dimension and I think having a home pitch recognised by FIFA is proof that statehood is possible. I do believe that sport can help this,' he tells me that morning, in the café of Ramallah's sole five-star hotel. He is an imposing presence, with a wide back, barrel chest, bald head and a moustache. He speaks in a low, gravelly voice. He is now a man of peace, he says, but he is not someone you would want to get on the wrong side of. 'I think this match is a clear-cut message to the international community that Palestine is capable, putting it on the map of sport for the first time,' he says. 'We will have our first ever World Cup qualification on Palestinian territory, under Palestinian Authority protection by Palestinian police. The whole participation will be ours, blood and flesh. It is history.'

Rajoub's portrait hangs high in the Faisal al-Husseini Stadium, next to pictures of Yasser Arafat with the golden Dome of the Rock – Jerusalem's iconic shrine built on the site of Judaism's Second Temple that is considered the third holiest site in Islam – in the background. Next to them are pictures of the Palestinian Authority president Mahmoud Abbas and Sepp Blatter, whose decision to allow Palestine to join FIFA will arguably be the greatest legacy of his career. Fans stream into the stands, paying their five shekels for a ticket. Hundreds of members of the press from all around the world are here, too, to watch history being made. In the Palestinian dressing room the pressure returns. The players are silent. Ahmed Keshkesh is nowhere to be seen. On discovering he was to start on the bench, he stormed out of the team's hotel and hasn't been seen since. The players sit with their backs to the wall while the team's three goalkeepers lay their training bibs on the floor and pray together. Coach Moussa again quietly paces around the room, now in shirt, tie and jacket. Finally it is game time. The team, the squad and the coaches meet Moussa in the middle of the room. They link arms in a big circle and begin to pray. This time, unlike before the first leg, the team kiss each other before going out into the tunnel. Moussa greets each and wishes them luck in their own language. He gets to Roberto Bishara. They hold each other, unable to communicate in a common language. They nod, acknowledging the awkwardness, and go in their separate directions.

The two teams line up in the tunnel. Omar stands in the middle, a full head above his team-mates, exhorting them in American English to 'talk to each other', although nobody does. The twenty-two men walk out into the baking sunlight to a scrum of photographers and TV cameras. More than fifty journalists are here from Israel alone. The match is even being shown live on Israel's Channel 5. In the stands Jibril Rajoub is watching, as is the prime minister Salam Fayyad, as they line up for the national anthems, both of which sound as if they have been written in seventeenth-century France. There are no tears of emotion.

The raucous 10,000-strong crowd roar on the Palestinians. It is a scrappy game at first, as if the weight of expectation is affecting the team's performance. But the Afghans seem sapped of all energy. Inevitably Palestine take the lead when Hussam Wadi shoots from forty yards out and somehow finds the back of the net. The Afghan goalkeeper curses himself, but it doesn't lead to an avalanche largely thanks to luck. The Palestinians hit the post three times and when Afghanistan equalise there's brief hope of an upset. But everyone is drained. The heat, the travel, the pressure, the dignitaries, all of it means that, by the end, the teams can barely kick the ball. It takes a few moments for the players and the crowd to realise that the referee has blown the final whistle. Two Afghan players collapse and are taken to hospital with exhaustion. There is barely any celebration as the Palestinians return to the tunnel. Salam Fayyad enters the silent dressing room and softly whispers words of encouragement into each player's ear, but he senses that the mood doesn't call for it. The Palestinians stay silent, as if the victors in an attritional war. But victors none the less.

**

Less than a month later, the two-match tie against Thailand has everything the Palestinians have become accustomed to: defeat, fatigue, hope and, ultimately, failure. The first game in Bangkok sees the Thais take a slender 1-0 lead to the West Bank. They are the favourites after all. But the return match is a different proposition and the slim lead makes little difference to the Palestinians. Either way, they need to score a goal. Which is what they do. The Palestinians level the tie early on with a brilliant move started and finished by Murad Alyan, the part-time striker who works as a lab assistant in a West Bank hospital. He initiates a one-two that pings quickly between three players before he himself fires into the bottom right-hand corner from outside the penalty box. The Thais score soon after, securing a crucial away goal, meaning Palestine need to score twice. Fifty-six minutes pass without any more goals. As the game enters its final few minutes the Palestinians pour forward, seemingly to no avail. But then, in the ninetieth minute, Alyan scores his second of the game, finding himself on the ball on the right-hand side of the penalty box. He somehow outmuscles and bamboozles five Thai players around him and fires low and hard across the goalkeeper into the far corner of the net. The Palestinians have four minutes to save their World Cup. They charge deep into injury time, but the Thais break away and when their striker is hacked down from behind by Ahmed Harbi, who receives a red card, the Palestine team are reduced to ten men. Datsakorn Thonglao scores from the free-kick with virtually the last kick of the game. It ends 2-2 and Palestine is eliminated.

It is a sad end for the Palestinians, and for coach Moussa, too. He will later be sacked for his brave but ultimately unsuccessful campaign. Not a single team that began in the first round of Asian qualification makes it to group stage. Nor do some of Asia's so-called sleeping giants. India, with its population of a billion people, is swept aside by the United Arab Emirates, with its population of nine million. Palestine's neighbour Jordan destroys Nepal 9-0 in one match. China scores thirteen goals over two games against Laos. Oman are awarded a place in the next round after riots in Myanmar call a halt to their second match. But one unlikely team does make it through to the final round.

Syria handsomely defeat Tajikistan over two games. The Syrian team had also travelled to the Metellurg Stadium in Tursunzode and won 4-0. Civil war is raging in their homeland but they have the best generation of players in their history and have a strong chance of qualifying for Brazil. The Assad regime in Syria prepares to welcome a rare good news story of unity in the face of war with open arms. But it doesn't happen. Syria are disqualified from World Cup qualification for fielding an ineligible player, George Murad, who once played thirteen minutes in a meaningless friendly for Sweden. Instead, Tajikistan take their place. By the end of July 2011, a full three years before Brazil, the chance of reaching the World Cup finals is over for almost 30 per cent of the world's population.

**

Tulkarem, West Bank. Fourth of July 2011

While his friends back in Georgia enjoy cookouts, drink cans of cold lager and let off fireworks to celebrate the birth of America, Omar Jarun has made different plans for 4 July this year. He is sitting in a taxi, the day after the 1-1 draw with Afghanistan, as it snakes its way around the hills of the West Bank towards Tulkarem, his family's ancestral home. Omar looks out of the window in awe at hills covered green by rows of olive and pine trees stretching out before him. If it hadn't been for the four ugly concrete Israeli checkpoints that we pass along the way we might have been in Spain or Italy or Greece. 'I ... I can't believe it,' he says, taking photos for his mum and dad back home, who text him periodically to check that he is safe. 'It's so ... green. I never thought it would be this green.'

Fahed al-Fakhouri, Palestine's third-choice goalkeeper, is as good as his word and is guiding Omar and me around the town in which his grandfather was born. His grandfather's house is still here. We pass an Orthodox Jew standing on the side of the road, dressed in heavy black coat and fur hat, ringlets curled down his cheek, squinting into the hot sun as he waits for a bus. Opposite him is a collection of Portakabins, dragged up on to the highest suitable piece of flat land. Electrical wires connecting the huts dangle dangerously above them. 'They put these here,' shrugs Fahed, almost resigned, pointing at the ramshackle collection of huts. He is referring to the Israeli settlers who view it as their duty to colonise what they call Judea and Samara. 'And then, in two, three months, they build a house and say: "it's ours". They just take it.'

Banners and murals of martyrs fly proudly in Tulkarem. In the almost continental normality of Ramallah you could be in any moderately wealthy city in the Middle East. But Tulkarem is different. A sign hangs between two white apartment blocks: 'No Peace Until We Return To Our Homes'. Every female covers her head with a hijab, even the children. Jarun Jarun meets us outside a café in an old, beaten-up blue Mercedes. He is a distant uncle of Omar's and they have never met before. He drops the keys to his grandfather's house into Omar's hand. The Jarun clan, it turns out, virtually run a small village on the outskirts of Tulkarem. Every auto shop and supermarket bears the Jarun name. But first a tour of the area.

Here is the wall – now thinned out to a wire fence – that separates Tulkarem and the Palestinians from Israel. 'If you shake it,' Jarun Snr warns, 'they [Israeli forces] will take you in minutes!' He mimics shaking it with his hand, laughing to himself hysterically. Here is the Jamal Ghanem Stadium that Fahed plays in, named after a local player who was shot dead on the pitch by the Israelis during a match in 1992. According to the Israeli human rights organisation B'Tselem he was unarmed and was shot three times in the chest after trying to hide behind the referee. In a report into the incident B'Tselem said that the Israeli military claimed 'the soldiers involved in the incident had shot at Jamal Ghanem's legs, but he had slipped, and therefore was hit in the body and died'. Omar is incredulous. 'During the game?!' he shrieks. And here is Ghanem's grave. We stand next to the broken tombstone for a few moments in silence. And here is a shopkeeper who lost his sons fighting the Israelis. Omar's head is spinning as he takes in all the facts, and listens to the story of how the old man's firstborn was killed. Outside his shop hangs a huge portrait of his son. He is holding a machine gun and wears a black headband bearing the *shahada*, the Islamic invocation: *There is no god but God, and Muhammad is the messenger of God.*

Which group did your son belong to? I ask.

'Islamic Jihad,' the father replies proudly in Arabic.

'Oh, I didn't know,' Omar recoils when I tell him later that Islamic Jihad is a fundamentalist organisation devoted to pushing Israel into the sea and replacing it with a caliphate. 'Thank God someone told me.'

Fahed takes us to meet his family. He lives in house large by Palestinian standards, festooned with cups and ribbons and rosettes he has won. Fahed's bedroom is a homage to Catalonia, its walls covered with posters and pictures of Barcelona players. In the front room his father tries to fire up the elderly TV, to show us one of Fahed's old matches, but is thwarted by technical difficulties. Jarun politely accepts his tea and sips it slowly as we talk about Tajikistan and Fahed's career. It is only now I notice the biggest portrait hanging in the room, above Jarun's head: a picture of Saddam Hussein. 'Hero,' explains Fahed's father, holding his hand to his heart. Jarun, whose family, thanks to Saddam, were forced to flee Kuwait for America with little more than the shirts on their backs, almost certainly doesn't agree. But he turns round, looks at the portrait, smiles, and compliments his hosts on their tea. He is too polite to mention his own experiences at the hands of his host's hero.

**

We arrive at the house of Omar Jarun's grandfather. It is big, two storeys high, deserted, and has vines and a gnarled but healthy lemon tree growing in the front garden, the same lemon tree that his grandfather used to pick from as a child. Jarun excitedly goes from room to room, filming scenes on a camcorder for his family back home. 'Man, there's a graveyard out back. And there's a donkey here, too,' he narrates. Jarun films the sick-looking donkey. 'It's in pretty bad shape,' he says as the camera rolls. The donkey he-haws on cue, as if aware he is being disparaged.

Numerous American politicians tell of a common trip that the Israelis have in the past organised for them: a helicopter flight from Jerusalem to the Mediterranean coast. The journey is so quick that it has seared Israel's tiny dimensions and its geographical vulnerability into the minds of their American guests. Jarun Jarun and Fahed lead Omar up on to the roof of his grandfather's house. Shimmering just fifteen kilometres away is the Mediterranean. Skyscrapers from the Israeli coastal city of Netanya can be seen in the distance. Further down the coast, Tel Aviv is clearly visible.

Omar, his uncle, Fahed and I stand in a line, looking at the contrasting horizon of both proximity and impossible distance as the sea shimmers ahead of us. After a few moments, we go back downstairs. Omar stops in the courtyard, reaches up and picks a lemon from the tree. He smuggles it into his pocket and climbs into his uncle's Mercedes, ready for the journey home.

2

HAITI, US VIRGIN ISLANDS, CURAÇAO

Port au Prince, Haiti. September 2011.

The sun is beating down on workers scrubbing the terraces of the Stade Sylvio Cator in the Haitian capital of Port au Prince. In the distance, to the south of the stadium, verdant mountains rise sharply. Closer by sits the city's Grand Cimitière, famous for its warren of elaborate tombs. But the stadium is alive with movement and purpose. Men with pots of blue, red and yellow paint, the colours of the Haitian flag, coat and recoat the terraces. The burst of sunshine is unexpected, a break from the dark clouds that have been sitting above Haiti for the past few weeks. Hurricane season has begun, a time for prayer and time to ask God for good luck.

Most years God ignores Haiti. It has long been the poorest country in the western hemisphere after years of being ruled by half-mad despots: first, François 'Papa Doc' Duvalier, a man who put close to 30,000 opponents of his regime to death, then his son, 'Baby Doc', who looted and maimed until he was finally deposed in 1986. Their most evil legacy, though, was the Tonton Macoutes, a paramilitary force that raped, tortured and murdered with impunity. Anyone who could flee the country did so. Those too poor to get out stayed and waited, surviving from one hurricane season to the next. Yet it was the ground beneath their feet that was the source of Haiti's biggest betrayal.

41

At 4.53 p.m. on 12 January 2010 an earthquake measuring 7.0 on the Richter scale reduced much of Port au Prince to rubble. By one count alone more than 300,000 Haitians lost their lives, although no one can be sure just how many perished. It left Port au Prince, already on the cusp of anarchy, in a ruinous state. Every spare scrap of ground has now become a city of tents, filled with the internally displaced. Haiti's national stadium – named after Sylvio Cator, the country's greatest Olympian, a former footballer who won silver in the long jump at the 1928 Amsterdam games – is one of those spaces. At least, it used to be. It became a slum for hundreds of families but they have now been moved on. The street vendors outside the stadium jealously gossip that the families who lived here were offered a $2,000 payment from the government as compensation for leaving. They left, of course. But they didn't go far. They simply melted into the torn ribbon of blue tents that formed outside the stadium's heavy metal front gates.

Now the authorities need the stadium back. Haiti is due to play its first football match since the earthquake: a World Cup qualifier for Brazil 2014 against the US Virgin Islands. This is important for two reasons. Firstly, anything that begins to move Haiti back to a sense of normality is to be cherished. Secondly, the World Cup offers a distraction. World Cup qualification won't put food in a child's mouth or cure a pensioner of cholera, but it fills the time. With little work to go around time is something that most Haitians have in abundance. But time also fuels rancour. Haiti's new president, Michel Martelly, a former singer, is aggressively promoting the match. He loves football, of course; all Haitians do. But a match against the US Virgin Islands, a team of amateurs who have won only three games in their history, all of them against the British Virgin Islands, is a sure thing. Martelly wants to make good on his campaign slogan: 'Viktwa pou pep la.' In Haitian Creole this means 'Victory for the People'. In the absence of any other kind of victory for the people, victory against the US Virgin Islands will have to do.

Ironically, time is now against him. The refugees have had to be moved, their presence erased by the smell of new paint. A brand new artificial pitch had to be laid, too, as the old one had been ruined by the camps. The smell of fresh paint is momentarily thick and intoxicating, but then the wind changes direction and the smell is replaced by that of burning refuse and human excrement.

This year Haiti is lucky. Hurricane Irene skirts around the Caribbean island of Hispaniola, which Haiti shares with the Dominican Republic to the east, but when it makes landfall in the United States it kills forty-nine people. The near miss is lucky for Haiti because it is not prepared for a hurricane. It is not really prepared for anything, especially not its first 2014 World Cup qualifier in twenty-four hours' time. The painters work with urgency, moving up and down the terraces in jolting movements like an early stop-go animation film.

By the main entrance to the stadium a guard wearing a turquoise Haitian Football Federation T-shirt paces nervously in front of the heavy, blue steel door. He is holding a pump-action shotgun tightly in both hands. The guard listens to the almost constant banging on the door from outside, his finger hovering above the trigger. When the banging become urgent he pulls the door open, sticks his head out and fires a volley of abuse in Creole. But this time it is the guests he has been told to expect. The team bus of Les Grenadiers, Haiti's national team, has arrived, bringing the players for training. It is waiting at the gate under heavy armed guard. A curious mob of Haitians has surrounded it. The guards eye them nervously, but they are not in danger. The bus is driven in and the guard quickly heaves the gate closed behind it. For him everyone is a potential threat.

Inside the stadium a middle-aged man with short, dark-grey hair and a moustache two shades lighter is walking on to the arti-ficial grass. He is not happy. 'It's forty-six degrees on the pitch, we just measured it,' tssks Edson Tavares, the team's Brazilian coach. It is three in the afternoon; the match is due to be played at the same time the following day. 'It's crazy. FIFA agreed to move the

43

match. CONCACAF said no. What do they know? They work out of New York and know nothing about the heat in the Caribbean.' The change in time is a necessity, but I don't say this to Tavares. Electricity is scarce in the city, too scarce for the expensive but now impotent floodlights that have been installed for the match. The team begin to run through their drills in the heat without complaint. Tavares retreats into the shade.

**

My plane lands at Toussaint L'Ouverture International Airport, named after the great Haitian revolutionary who led the first successful slave revolt. He didn't live to see the world's first black-led republic come into existence in 1804: a year earlier he had been deported and died in a French jail. The airport has been fixed since the earthquake, but only nominally. Huge fissures run from the bottom to the top of the white plastered arrivals and departures building. There are no taxis or reliable buses into the city. Too many people had been kidnapped, robbed and killed that way. A driver from an Irish NGO kindly takes me to the city. We sit in silence as I survey the full extent of the slums on either side of the road. Even in the upmarket district of Pétionville, with its nightclubs and Western-style supermarkets, the grinding poverty of the camps sits cheek by jowl with the high-walled, heavily armed compounds with smashed bottle glass and razor wire concreted into the top of the walls.

It feels obscene to be here for a football match but Haitian football is no different from virtually every aspect of Haitian society affected by the earthquake. The federation's headquarters were levelled, killing more than thirty of its staff. Its president, Dr Yves Jean-Bart, somehow survived. With a broken arm he joined the efforts to pull other survivors from the rubble. Only one was found. Faced with such devastation, football might be considered of minor importance in Haiti, but Jean-Bart, knowing the place the game has in Haiti's heart, went on to rebuild the federation and employed Tavares to achieve the dream of emulating Haiti's golden generation who qualified for the 1974 World Cup finals. They shocked the world back then, briefly taking the lead against mighty Italy before succumbing in all three group matches.

This time the draw has been kind to Haiti. Alongside the US Virgin Islands, Haiti is in the same group as Antigua and Barbuda and Curaçao, a Dutch colony a few miles off the Venezuelan coast that is playing in the World Cup qualifications for the first time. A few days after the US Virgin Islands match, Les Grenadiers fly to Curaçao's capital, Willemstad, for the second match in the group. On paper it is a nailed-on six points. The combined population of Haiti's three opponents is a fraction more than the number of people killed in the 2010 earthquake.

'I arrived in September, nine months after the earthquake. My first impression was to take my flight back to Brazil,' explains Tavares a few hours before his final training session. We are sitting in the team's hotel a few minutes' drive from the stadium. Like almost every building in downtown Port au Prince, the hotel is in a fortified compound with a heavy metal door. We sit in the hotel's rock garden, a fountain gurgling pleasantly next to us. Well-dressed waiters deliver us ice-cold water and Cokes. The slums seem very far away.

Tavares had previously been coach of Al Wasl in the United Arab Emirates and Sepahan in Iran, but he gave up any such stability for a shot at the World Cup finals with Haiti and a chance to represent a country in his home city of Rio de Janeiro. 'You don't realise how strong the situation was here,' he says when I ask him about his arrival. 'Today is a paradise compared. You can see the miserable people, tents everywhere, but if you compare with last year ... well, you could be walking the street and find the amputated legs of people, the arms of people. It was terrible, terrible, terrible.'

There was no league and no football association as such. Just the surviving football association president and his mobile phone. The question was: how do you begin to rebuild a team like Haiti?

Tavares decided that he needed new blood. He paid for his own flight to Europe. With him he had a list with the names of sixty-two professional players of Haitian descent who were playing in Portugal, France, England, Spain, Belgium, Greece, Scotland and beyond. Like the Palestinians I had met a few months earlier, Tavares realised that knocking into shape a team of purely local players was too big a job. Instead, he sought out those playing at a good level of professional football, players who had fallen through the cracks and been ignored by the national teams of the countries that had given them, or, if they were second- or third-generation immigrants, their parents or grandparents, refuge in the past. 'I rented a car to travel to five countries to persuade the players to play for their country of origin,' he says. 'Only one refused. We contacted twenty players. I was very happy. And they are here. Most of them don't speak Creole. One only speaks Italian. One only German. For me it is no problem. I can speak different languages but for the federation it was a big problem before, to repatriate the diaspora.'

The players wander around the hotel rock garden in their cliques. The Haiti-based players huddle together, speaking in rapid Creole, arms wrapped around each other as they walk. The French players sit at a table, coolly surveying the scene. Steward Ceus, the team's mountainous six-foot-six American-born goalkeeper, mooches along on his own. Tavares hopes that the professionalism of his new team will rub off on the local players. He also believes that the local talent is some of the best he has seen in the world. 'I am telling you,' he says, leaning forward. 'My forty years' experience I have never seen a country with so many talents like here. Players of fourteen years old here, if you put these guys in Manchester United and Barcelona, they would be a great player. The problem is to be a great player you have to have good food, a good environment, good training, good doctors. So here is nothing.'

I ask Tavares about his new team, whether there is any lingering resentment from the local players towards their richer, better fed, sometimes foreign-born colleagues who have never been here and don't speak the language. 'Always we have some resentment from local players,' he agrees. 'But they have to realise they are a long way from the other players. Here in Haiti they can only afford to eat one meal a day.' The problem, he says, is one of low ambition. 'The future here is to get a visa to the US and they are 50 per cent happy. Then they can go to America and sell ice cream in the street or go to the garage and clean a car. That is the future here.'

The squad for the US Virgin Islands game is full of talented new professional players, many of whom have never been to Haiti before in their lives. Some of them play in good European leagues. Jean-Eudes Maurice was signed by Paris Saint-Germain; Kevin Lafrance plays in the Czech Republic, and goalkeeper Ceus, a New Yorker born and raised, plays for the Colorado Rapids in the MLS. 'I was in college when I heard a buzz about Haiti being interested in seeing me play,' Ceus explains. 'It took a little bit of time to feel I was ready to play internationally.'

This is all new for Ceus, who grew up in New York's large Haitian community. He went to a Haitian church every Sunday, where he learned to speak a smattering of Creole. His family had watched the country degenerate from afar. All, that is, except his grandmother. She was the personal baker to former President Jean-Bertrand Aristide, a priest who had vowed to work for the poor against the interests of foreign-controlled big business after the Duvalier years. Twice president, he was twice deposed in US-backed coups. 'She was baking him cakes. She would tell me about walking amongst the staff of the palace. She travelled all around the world with him,' he recalls. Her two signature dishes, he says proudly, were pineapple upside down and Haitian yellow cake.

Ceus has learned everything he knows about Haiti, its language, its culture, its cake, second-hand through stories from his family. His mother and father would tell him about a golden age in Port au Prince of clean streets and security. This is the first time he has set foot in the country. 'It has left me speechless,' he says. 'People coming after training, before training. They crowd around the bus. My passion for soccer has always been there and

I always wished that the people around me shared that passion. For the first time it's the passion I've been looking for. It is the first time I've felt equally as passionate as the fans.' Ceus and his Haitian team-mates are swamped everywhere they go in Port au Prince. 'Everybody who comes up to us says: "Win the game to bring some joy to us,"' he explains. Tavares is now gathering his players for the trip to the stadium for his final training session, at 3 p.m., in the 46 degree heat. 'It would be huge for anyone,' Ceus replies when I ask what World Cup qualification would mean to Haiti. 'But the suffering they are going through is immense and all they are asking for is happiness through soccer. It would be immense to qualify and bring some hope to these people.'

**

As Edson Tavares stands in the shade and the workers busy themselves preparing the stadium for Haiti's big game the following day, the US Virgin Islands national team sit in the stands with a look approaching horror on their faces. The Haiti team are on the pitch below them running through what might be described as cutting edge European training methods: complex drills, one-touch passing, multiple coaches working in small teams, resistance training. The US Virgin Islands has a pile of cones and a small bag of balls. They have only brought sixteen players with them, too, three of them goalkeepers. 'We are one of the last teams left that don't have any professional players,' says the team's young, polite captain, Reid Klopp. They are all American citizens, living on what is an incorporated territory of the United States: three islands with a population of little more than 100,000 people. They all have day jobs. Klopp himself works for a Baptist youth outreach programme, some are students and a couple of the players work in construction. Basketball and track and field are by far the most important games on the islands. Soccer comes a distant third.

This is only Klopp's third competitive game. The first two were in the CONCACAF preliminary round against the British

Virgin Islands, the stage that saw Montserrat play Belize. Klopp scored in both games. 'It has that local derby feel. The islands are so close,' he says of what is probably one of the unlikeliest derbies in world football. 'We came away 4-1 on aggregate. This is the first time we've ever made it past the preliminary round. We are not getting too far ahead of ourselves. They all have pro players.'

Since their inclusion into FIFA in 1998 – the same congress that marked a massive expansion of members and saw the likes of Palestine join – the tiny three-island territory to be found between Puerto Rico and Montserrat has played only twenty-eight matches in its entire history, twenty of them defeats. Between January 2010 and June 2011, they were 200th on FIFA's rankings, making them one of the worst sides in world football. Games were hard to come by, too. They had only played six games over the past five years. Now they find themselves with six games in as many months, with a trip to the anarchy and heat of Haiti first. It is a baptism of fire. 'It is quite a shock when you drive around and you see there's extreme poverty and the other class that is beyond rich,' Klopp says of the inequalities and unhappiness he has witnessed. 'It's quite an experience. It makes you grateful for what you have.'

What do you expect to get out of the game, I ask.

'We come away from this game with a point or something that will be something. We are all really excited to be here,' he answers. Not one of his team-mates is smiling. 'There is a sense that this is one of the best teams we've put together. We have a small population so when you look at the numbers ...' Haiti, traditionally one of the region's heavyweights and one of only three Caribbean teams ever to qualify for a World Cup finals, was always going to be a tough place to play but in a few days' time the US Virgin Islands travel to Antigua where Klopp believes they 'could definitely get a result in that game'. He also knows his and his team's limitations, though. 'We are the extreme underdogs. That's one advantage that we have. No one expects us to come even close to getting a result in this game so we don't have to play with that pressure.'

When it is time for the 'extreme underdogs' of the US Virgin Islands to begin training, they start by running the length of the pitch, back and forth, back and forth. They take shooting practice next. No one manages to hit the target. Balls balloon over the goal, or end up near the corner flag. The maintenance men go about their work, painting and repainting the terrace steps in red, yellow and blue, only stopping to retrieve any balls that land close to them.

**

I cling on to the back of the motorbike as it careers through the slums. It is raining on the morning of Haiti's big day. Port au Prince's snarled, potholed and at times dangerous streets are hard to navigate. The quickest way is by bike taxi. Snapshots of life flash past us. Barefoot children happily splashing around in a foetid canal. A brightly coloured tap-tap bus jammed with people, a portrait of Brazil striker Alexandre Pato painted on the back. The still-manicured lawns of the abandoned presidential palace, its white turrets now collapsed but the Haitian flag still flying. A beautiful woman, with short hair and a smart business suit, expertly picking her way through the refuse and mud of a tented city in high heels. A hand-painted billboard, seven foot high, leant against a road sign to advertise the game. It reads: *Haiti Leve*. Haiti rise. I shout at the driver to stop. *Haiti Leve*, it reads. *Brasil Mundial 2014, Haiti v Virgini Sland* [sic]. A ticket for the match, it tells me, costs 150 Haitian gourde, around $3. At the bottom, misspelt but clearly legible, the sign reveals one of the game's main sponsors. *Courtoisie T-Vice, Wiclef Jean* [sic], *MTK*. Wyclef Jean? *The* Wyclef Jean? Sponsoring the Haiti team? I jump back on the bike and head for the team hotel. A special guest has arrived to wish the team luck, a man who can arguably claim to be the second most famous singer from Haiti.

President Michel Martelly wasn't always known by the name he was born with. He is more widely known as Sweet Micky, a singer of kompas music, a form of Creole merengue. He is one of the region's biggest stars – even appearing on a Wyclef Jean record in 1997 – and notorious for his onstage antics during his glory days, including exposing himself, cross-dressing and farting into the microphone. He was also a staunch opponent of President Aristide. But Martelly hasn't had a good few months. He's only been in office for five months after a farcical election. None other than Wyclef Jean himself fancied the job of president of Haiti. He would probably have won it too if he hadn't been banned from standing by a Haitian court for not having spent enough time in the country. Martelly finished third in the first ballot and only made the run-off after one of the candidates was disqualified because of voting irregularities. He has been unable to form a government and, to make matters worse, his nemesis, Aristide, has returned to the country after living in exile in South Africa. His presidential palace remains uninhabitable. Yet his election is the first peaceful handover of power in Haiti's history. He is more sober and restrained these days, wearing a suit and tie as he enters the hotel function room where the players are quietly waiting for him. He shakes each player by the hand, presenting them with a flag on a stick. He hands one to Steward Ceus, unaware that his grandmother used to be Aristide's personal baker.

Martelly gives a short speech, the lights of the ballroom shining off his bald head. The match is as much a distraction for him from the nasty realities of frontline politics as it is for the poor on the street. Everyone in the room stands for a rendition of Haiti's national anthem as President Martelly counts them in:

> For Haiti, the Ancestors' Country
> We must walk hand in hand
> There must not be traitors among us!
> We must be ourselves, unique master
> Let's walk hand in hand
> For Haiti can be more beautiful.
> Let us, Let us put our heads together
> For Haiti in the name of all the Ancestors.

The room is filled with the sound of wailing. Martelly is the loudest and it is clear that whatever singing talent he had has deserted him while in office. Mercifully, they do not attempt all five verses. 'I must tell you in the past we have beaten all the teams in the region,' he says proudly, almost a little offended, when I ask him afterwards whether he thinks Haiti can qualify for the World Cup. His nervous looking security guards scope the room, resting their hands on their guns, eager to take him away to his next appointment. 'We have not structured ourselves, we have not prepared ourselves,' he begins. 'We have been barely making it. I believe there's a new movement. There's a new will to show a new face of Haiti. We have natural talents here coming from all around the world. Haiti is ready to show that new face. In the past we have mainly talked about our problems and our issues. Today is an opportunity to show that Haiti can be a great nation and can be victorious.' His armed guards nod. It is time for the president to leave for the match. 'I couldn't express in words what Haiti would be like if ...' He corrects himself. 'When, not if, we qualify for the 2014 World Cup in Brazil.'

**

A riot is about to break out. It is one hour before kick-off and 10,000 Haitians, maybe more, are trying to crush through the single open door into the Stade Sylvio Cator. A police blockade has been thrown around the stadium, causing traffic chaos for miles on every side. Warped Creole rap music is being played from huge speakers at an ear-splitting level. The clouds above are dark and heavy as the crowd of supporters wait in line, as they have done since the morning. As the clock counts down, and only a trickle are allowed through the only door, they begin to get desperate and push forward in the hope of getting in. The police use their shields and clubs to beat them back. Children perched on their fathers' shoulders cry as those at the front are crushed against the blue metal gate. Those who can scramble up the walls, grabbing on to the razor wire atop them, leaving trails of smeared blood as they go. I am in the crush, too, pressed in at all sides. 'I am very happy, we will have our victory. This will be a victory for all of Haiti,' shouts Johnny, an engineer and translator from Pétionville who is waiting in line with me; he seems untroubled by the deteriorating situation around him. 'Life is very hard here,' he cheerily explains. 'With God everything is possible. But this is the reason why football can change something. I hope Haiti scores ten goals.'

It is now, amidst the fermenting riot, that the US Virgin Islands team bus arrives, as if timed for maximum intimidation. The police somehow hold off the angry crowd long enough for them to enter the stadium. The faces of the players are fixed in wide-eyed horror as they glide past, presumably believing that the anger must have been organised and directed at them. As soon as the heavy blue metal gate is dragged shut, two dozen policemen with sticks wade in to try and break up the angry mob, flailing at people indiscriminately. An army truck even tries driving through, but that does little to disperse the crowd either. They simply part like a sea, and, once it has passed, crash back together to assume their assault on the gate. Just when it looks like something quite bad is about to take place, God intervenes. The rain comes, slowly at first, before growing into a torrential downpour. It dampens the anger and the fans run to take cover.

Inside the stadium is now full as President Martelly takes to the pitch. A team of soldiers, some of them with the faces of young boys, hold machine guns and watch him from the touchlines. He is no longer in the suit and tie he was wearing a few hours ago but has donned a blue national team jersey and a red baseball cap. He receives rapturous applause from the crowd, applause that only the recently elected politician will ever recognise. Sweet Micky smiles at the reception and runs on to the pitch with a ball at his feet. He begins spinning with it and performing tricks to the delight of the crowd. A pack of journalists try to follow him, but they are not in as good shape as Sweet Micky and can barely keep up as they try to film and take photos. Eventually the president tees up the ball and boots it into the crowd.

As Martelly warms up the crowd, the Haiti national team await their cue. They are standing in the white tunnel underneath the stadium waiting to enter the pitch in the same blue shirts that Martelly now sports. The floor has been flooded by the recent downpour. The players cough and blink hard. The smell of fresh paint is so strong that it stings the eyes and burns the throat. The blue gate at the end of the tunnel eventually creaks open. 'Ayiti! Ayiti!' they shout together in Creole before they walk out on to the pitch to sing the national anthem for the second time that day. The US Virgin Islands are already there, wearing white jerseys with yellow and blue hoops, warming up by running from touchline to touchline. The crowd, rather unfairly given their status as 'extreme underdogs', viciously boos them. A band in the crowd plays incessantly. I stand behind the US Virgin Island's goalkeeper and wait for the deluge of goals. The crowd behind me is screaming. They are not being complimentary.

From the kick-off it is clear that Haiti have vast technical superiority. They create a dizzying carousel of passing and movement. They pluck one impossible ball after another out of the air from head height and distribute it to a blue shirt in a single, beautiful, fluid movement. In the thick humidity, surrounded by the terrifying noise of the crowd, the US Virgin Islands are chasing shadows. They are exhausted after ten minutes. The ball has become a mirage, visible for only a second, but by the time they have sprinted to it, it has gone. Even touching it is a rarity. When they do so it is blasted high and long. None the less, it takes eighteen minutes for James Marcelin to score Haiti's first goal. The crowd make a noise like an aeroplane crashing into a cathedral, the sound of hysteria and twisted metal. The goals keep coming and Haiti are soon 6-0 up. But somehow the US Virgin Islands hold out for the last twelve minutes without conceding. For the extreme underdog, this is a victory of sorts. The next day one of Haiti's main newspapers, *Le Nouvelliste*, puts the result on the front page: 'Haiti stomps on the Virgin Islands 6-0'. It could have been worse. Haiti hit the post three times, too. Steward Ceus, the American-born goalkeeper, is a virtual spectator until the final whistle. 'I did touch the ball once,' he says with a wink as he comes off the pitch. 'But not with my hands.'

The Haiti team lines up and walks to the steps where the president is standing, beaming with happiness. He greets each and every player, knowing that this is a rare good day. It won't have hurt him electorally either. Sweet Micky leaves in his motorcade as the thousands of people who had earlier threatened to riot before the rains came now celebrate, running down the street waiving Haitian flags as they mob his car. Several of his aides stand on the sidelines making the most of the situation. They hold big stacks of campaign stickers. They cannot give them away quickly enough. The stickers are gleefully peeled and stuck to foreheads, arms, posts and walls. They read: 'Prezidan Martelly: Viktwa pou pep la.' President Martelly: Victory for the People.

**

Willemstad, Curaçao, constituent country of the Kingdom of the Netherlands. Three days later.

Compared to the hellish pressure in Port au Prince, Willemstad is light and calm. It might as well be on the moon. The capital of Curaçao, part of the Kingdom of the Netherlands, is a UNESCO World Heritage Site. Its huge natural harbour welcomes cruise liners from the United States, depositing tourists on to its pretty quayside. Tall-fronted, multicoloured colonial houses line its perimeter. They are unmistakably Dutch and would not be out of place in Amsterdam or The Hague. But this harbour used to deposit a very different kind of visitor. Curaçao was a central hub for the Dutch slave trade. Until the mid-eighteenth century as many as half a million slaves were shipped here. They would be held on Curaçao to recover from the appalling journey from West

Africa, before being processed and moved on to the rest of the Caribbean, Brazil or the plantations of the American South. Its colonial rule over the local, Papiamentu-speaking black population was not benign. Today, in the smart old town and along the quayside, the faces are white and well fed. The shops are full of designer shoes and jackets. Oil was discovered here in the early twentieth century, enough for everyone. The stains of the past appear to have been rubbed clean.

Edson Tavares is relieved to have returned to something approaching normality. He is now in a sea-front café, ceiling fans fluttering above. 'We have a few problems concerning the organisation but it is always like that,' he says of his journey getting here. The Haitian federation couldn't afford a chartered flight for the whole team. Some left by the Dominican Republic's capital, Santo Domingo, while the rest flew to Miami and then back to Curaçao. They were all here now, awaiting what they see as their first real test of World Cup qualification. 'This was a training, it is not a match,' Tavares says dismissively of his last opponents. 'The other team was completely out of fitness. It was good for our team to get our things together. This was a weak match.' The 6-0 scoreline hadn't impressed Tavares, nor had the atmosphere generated by the crowd in Port au Prince. It was more a situation to manage than an atmosphere to luxuriate in. 'They were excited. Haitian people are very emotional,' he explains. 'It is up to us to control the emotions of the local players. We have to care about this point.'

The local players spread around the hotel do not care about the standard of opposition they so comprehensively beat. They are just happy not to have let anyone down. 'I feel really happy, so lucky,' says midfielder James Marcelin, who scored Haiti's first 2014 World Cup goal. 'I'm happy because what happened in the country to see all Haitian come to the game. It's incredible.' Marcelin is now playing in the MLS for the Portland Timbers, but he started his career in Haiti, where he grew up. For him, being back around his people in the country he grew up in is special. 'It is the only one thing we have left,' he says, 'we have soccer.' When James Marcelin or Jean Alexandre (also born in Haiti) or Jean Eudes Maurice (born in Paris) scored against the US Virgin Islands there was no division between the celebrating Haitian-born or French-born players. I look through my pictures from that day. One shows the team gathered in a circle in the dressing room, arms locked around each other in prayer. Another of Jean Eudes Maurice, after his goal, being hoisted up high by Jean Alexandre in front of the celebrating crowd. A third shows a blur of five players in the aftermath of another goal with only James Marcelin's smiling face in focus.

Defender Kevin Lafrance was born in Paris. He was approached after being discovered playing for Slavia Prague in the Czech Republic by Edson Tavares on his player-finding road trip. 'He contacted me and tells me he wants me to come to the selection,' Lafrance remembers. He hadn't thought of playing for Haiti before. 'To play in the French selection was difficult so I take my chance to play for Haiti.' Lafrance knew that this was his only chance of playing international football. For many Haitian-born players, indeed for any player from a country looking to attract players from its better organised diaspora, this was a delicate subject. Such issues were being discussed in virtually every national team in the world, from Switzerland to the US. Immigration was redrawing a new map, one of mixed races and countries and religions and allegiances. Lafrance battled with it just like millions of others did. 'I just want to help the country and the most I can do is play football,' he says of his first visit to Haiti for the match. 'It was very special when you see how happy these people were from a simple game of football. I think with the football they forget what has happened before.'

For a few moments, perhaps. But the window was brief. Yet Lafrance believes that the team needs the diaspora as much as he needs Haiti. 'In Haiti the level is not too good but I think the mix is a good thing,' he explains. 'Some play in France, New York, the Czech Republic; we are playing a good level, better than in Haiti, we can help Haiti. The road is long. I am here because I believe we can do this if we fight together for the qualification.'

**

Getting out of Haiti is harder than getting in. While the players take a circuitous root to leave the country, everybody else has to fight their way out. Literally. Hurricane Irene has shut the airport temporarily. It is open now but so many flights have been cancelled that thousands of people queue every morning, desperate to go. A bad-tempered line half a kilometre long snakes back out of the entrance of the Toussaint L'Ouverture departures building. There is no shade and the burning sun has returned as we shuffle forward, pushed on by those joining at the back. I am enclosed from all sides, my face crushed against a Haitian woman's back. A lone guard tries to manage the crush through the single tiny door, but he is simply taking money from the richer travellers so they can bypass the queue. The departures hall looks like a scene from ground zero of a future zombie apocalypse: thousands upon thousands of people screaming, crying, climbing, vomiting, fighting and collapsing. The rest of us wait, pushing and hustling one foot forward at a time. After three hours of fighting through the crowd, soaking wet and exhausted, I leave Haiti. I realise I am one of the lucky ones.

When I land in Curaçao it is dark. On the flight are several players from the Curaçao national team. They were born in Holland, professionals who played in the Dutch league but had no chance of ever pulling on the famous orange shirt. I tell them about Haiti. They tell me I should visit Campo Alegre. It is full of bars, they say, and a good place to meet girls. I take a taxi on their recommendation. Campo Alegre is quiet. Outside it looks like an ageing seaside amusement park closed for the winter. It is too early, perhaps, but I pay the entrance fee anyway. Inside row upon row of chalets circle a central bar. A huge screen is showing inter-racial hardcore porn. Offscreen, young women in crotchless underwear lead men – thin, middle-aged white Dutchmen with ruined complexions – to their chalets. Campo Alegre, I soon realise, is a good place to meet girls, but only if you're paying for them. It turns out to be the biggest legal brothel in the world. Prostitution in Curaçao is government-regulated, they argue, to protect the women involved in the trade. The US State Department disagrees and believes Curaçao to be a sex-trafficking hub. The man sitting next to me at the bar is wearing an 'I ✿ Girls' T-shirt. It costs $10 to buy one of these women, from Venezuela, Haiti, Jamaica, Russia or Senegal, but I leave for the clean streets of Willemstad, for the tall-fronted, multicoloured colonial houses. For the designer shops and the Western-style bars and restaurants. But this too is a sham. A few hours later I meet another white, middle-aged Dutchman with sunken cheeks. He lives in a crumbling block of single rooms. He is the only white man who lives here. His room is filthy: a single mattress, a plate and piles of dirty clothes are all that he owns. His hand shakes when he offers it to me. He also sniffs constantly. He lost everything after moving here, he tells me, his job, his savings and, eventually, his wife, too. He was addicted to cocaine, shipped in cheaply in both high quality and high quantity from Venezuela. There are thousands like him, he says, maybe more, now too ruined to return home. He vows to show me the side of Curaçao that no one sees. We walk no more than fifty metres, to the road that runs parallel to and behind the clean boulevards down which the tourists amble during the day. We are now in the middle of a slum. This is where the blacks of Willemstad live, in one-floor concrete blocks. The lights are on in only one of them. A constant stream of people are entering and leaving to buy drugs. There are men slumped on the street. We are eyed suspiciously, but the Dutchman speaks Papiamentu, the Iberian Creole that predominates here. He tells me that the white Dutch are hated. They take all the jobs and want nothing to do with the 'true' locals. Neither did he when he had a good job in the oil industry, but now he lives with them, on the edges of Willemstad, moving from one hit to the next. He

'Tonight we have won already. We know we are going far. We expect to see three thousand fans.'

And he is right. Three thousand fans, maybe more, fill one stand of the stadium, their songs echoing off the other three empty terraces. But their certainty doesn't last long. The first time Haiti's goalkeeper Steward Ceus touches the ball with his own hands during World Cup qualification is to pick it out of the back of his net. Curaçao have taken a shock lead. Their team of Dutch professionals have caught Haiti unprepared. Haiti equalise but Curaçao take the lead again. Half-time comes with Haiti 2-1 down, facing a fatal blow to their World Cup chances. Players from both teams are brawling on the pitch. Tavares marches on to the grass and drags them apart, shoving them towards the dressing room. The previously boisterous Haitian expats are silent. For the second half Tavares switches to a 3-5-2 formation and watches Jean-Eudes Maurice and Portland Timbers's James Marcelin dominate the midfield. Haiti score three unanswered goals and spare their blushes. The match finishes 4-2. Having survived their first scare, the players link arms and bow in front of the fans. 'Yes, sir! Yes, sir!' shouts Joseph, the fan I had met outside before the game, as he leaves the stadium. 'I tell you before the match that we will win!'

The Haiti team achieves what it set out to do. It has won its first two games. But the harder games will come later. Antigua and Barbuda is the only realistic threat to their qualification to the next round, the next group stage, where they could meet the US. A US–Haiti match in New York will be a home match for the visitors in all but name. It is the game everyone wants. Victory against Antigua and Barbuda is all they will need, against a side that has never been past the first round of World Cup qualification. Antigua is more famous for producing cricket players than footballers. They don't even have a proper pitch to play on. Instead the crunch Antigua and Barbuda versus Haiti game will be played at the Sir Viv Richards Stadium, a cricket ground named after the island's most famous son. But Antigua now has an ambitious young English coach, Tom Curtis. They also beat Curaçao in their first game, also after initially going behind. I check to see how the US Virgin Islands has fared in the Sir Viv Richards Stadium, a game that their captain, Reid Klopp, had hoped would offer them the best hope of a victory. Antigua and Barbuda win 8-1. The US Virgin Islands will go on to lose every game in qualification, including the return, home game against Antigua 10-0, and score just twice. They will concede forty goals.

In Willemstad, no one has heeded the eight-goal warning from Antigua. Tavares marches his team into their dressing room, a small concrete cube with a metal door. I walk around the back and listen to the Haiti team celebrating, their victory songs drifting through the ventilation holes drilled into the brickwork. The team bus is waiting. It careers through Willemstad's empty streets with an unnecessary police motorbike escort. Through the capital's upmarket centre they are greeted by the Haitians who couldn't be at the game; the working poor who couldn't afford the time off. They desert their posts and run into the streets as the bus passes them, clenched fists in the air, shouting: 'Ayiti! Ayiti!' The players disembark into the arms of chefs still wearing their whites, waiters still wearing their ties, warehouse workers still wearing their boiler suits and waitresses still wearing their aprons. It is a victory. For the people.

3

RWANDA, ERITREA

Kigali, Rwanda. November 2011.

No one is waiting for the Eritrea national team because no one believes the Eritrea national team will ever arrive. The Amahoro Stadium in Kigali, Rwanda, is devoid of life. Tropical rains have washed through here minutes before, but the dark clouds promise more, and the rains will wash through here again in a few minutes' time. But, for a few moments, it is safe to venture out between the deluges and onto the centre circle of the pitch.

The second leg of a preliminary African 2014 World Cup qualifier is due to take place here between Rwanda and Eritrea. Twenty-two of Africa's lowest ranked teams have been drawn for two matches, home and away. The competing countries read like a UN list of failed states and conflict zones. Somalia will not be allowed to play at home. The vicious Islamic fundamentalist Al-Shabaab militia – which essentially means 'The Boys' or 'The Lads' in Arabic – is still waging war against the embattled quasi-government in the ruined capital Mogadishu. They will play Ethiopia, a team that was once one of Africa's best. They won the Africa Cup of Nations in 1962, and dominated throughout the sixties before it too succumbed to civil war and famine. The Democratic Republic of Congo, a country the size of Western Europe that has seen 5.4 million of its citizens killed in a civil war that appears to have never really ended, begins its journey to Brazil. Chad, Burundi, Kenya, too. Yet Rwanda versus Eritrea is the most unusual of the games, and not just because Rwanda is still emerging from one of the darkest chapters in human history. It is also a rare outing for the Eritrea national team.

Eritrea is one of the worst countries in the world by almost any metric. Freedom of speech, freedom of press, torture, poverty and, of course, football. They are ranked 190th by FIFA even though they, too, were once a footballing power. Since independence from Ethiopia in 1993 following a long and bloody guerrilla war, Eritrea has done little of note on the pitch, but the Ethiopia team that won the 1962 Africa Cup of Nations was overwhelmingly Eritrean. Somewhere, talent is lurking.

The trouble isn't spotting it, it's holding on to it. Such is the paranoia of the regime in the capital Asmara that it is virtually illegal for Eritreans to leave the country. One of the only ways out is to represent Eritrea in sport. Once out, however, Eritreans tend not to return. The entire national team disappeared and claimed asylum in Kenya while at the regional CECAFA Cup in 2009. Thirteen members of Red Sea FC, Eritrea's leading club side, fled four months ago. That was the last time Eritrean footballers were allowed to leave the country. This is the national team's, the Red Sea Boys, first match away from home in two years. Or it will be if they arrive.

The stadium is vast, an unbroken bowl of steps raised atop sheer blue walls to prevent anyone from getting on to the pitch. The pitch is circled by a clay running track, the same colour as the dirt roads that meander through the shanties and slums found on the nearby hills. Amahoro means peace in the local Kinyarwanda language but the stadium has come to symbolise some of the worst, and the best, of human nature for Rwandans. Like the Afghans who pass their national stadium, where women considered immodest would be executed by the Taliban, or the Chileans who pass the Estádio Nacional, where thousands were tortured by forces loyal to General Pinochet during the 1973 coup, the Amahoro is symbolic of something more than football. During the 1994 genocide the stadium became a rare safe haven for Tutsis fleeing the massacres perpetrated by Hutu militias after a plane carrying Rwanda's Hutu president Juvénal Habyarimana was shot down near Kigali International Airport.

One hundred days of night followed. A million people, maybe more, were hacked, bludgeoned, shot, strangled, stabbed, burned and drowned to death. A lucky few found shelter at the Amahoro where the UN set up a command centre and offered protection to anyone who made it. Ten thousand, though some claim 50,000, lived within the stadium while being under constant bombardment from outside. 'Efforts by the genocidal [Hutu] *Interahamwe* militiamen to enter the stadium were blocked, though some hapless dwellers were killed by artillery rounds fired at the stadium,' writes John G. Heidenrich in his book *How to Prevent a Genocide*. 'Many others suffered from dysentery and cholera, and everyone had to endure the nauseating stench of their own accumulated filth.' The Amahoro barely survived, but survive it did. Tutsi forces led by the current president Paul Kagame reached the stadium after a three-month siege. And so began a long road to forgetting the genocide had ever happened.

The Amahoro Stadium today is spartan but clean. There is no memorial here. It's hard to imagine what this scene must have looked like in 1994. The tropical rains return. I run to the dugout and sit waiting in an empty, cold stadium for a team that may never show up.

**

A few days earlier the sun is setting over the Amahoro. It is perched on the top of a hill. Kigali is a series of dark green hills and valleys. The richer you are, the higher up the hill you live. Nearby two practice pitches are a hive of activity. One is a mud and sand rectangle spotted with rocks and broken glass. A third of the pitch is flooded but the youth team of the second division team practising here simply and skilfully flick the ball over any potentially crippling obstacles without complaint. Next to them is a state-of-the-art, all-weather field. More than 500 Rwandans stand around its perimeter in reverential silence. There is a gap every few metres from the amputees holding themselves upright on crutches. There are many amputees in Rwanda. They move silently, like phantoms, through the crowds and are largely ignored.

Only one sound can be heard over the periodic *thunk thunk* of the ball being struck: the growling, militaristic barks of the Rwanda national team coach Milutin 'Micho' Sredojević. Micho is shouting instructions to his players, the Amavubi, the Wasps. The forty-two-year-old Serbian is slightly built, with thick brown hair and a thin, drawn face set into a permanent scowl. I don't see him smile once. The players are as quiet as the crowd, as if it is the first time they have met anyone quite as intense as Micho before. Even when he is shouting encouragement it sounds like a threat.

Micho has only just arrived in Rwanda. He was employed earlier in the month after a series of jobs in African club football. He won the Ethiopian title with Saint George and took South Africa's Orlando Pirates to the semi-final of the African Champions League. He has just spent time in Sudan, too. This, however, is his first national team job. 'I want to tell you, talent is talent no matter in what country in the world. I'm happy we have the talent, but that talent needs strong matches, strong challenges,' he says quickly and precisely in perfect, heavily accented English. Training has finished and we are standing by the pitch with close to 100 children crowding around us. His players look relieved to be leaving the field and Micho's machine-gun orders. Unlike most other countries that have lived through war, spreading their children far and wide as they tried to escape, this is not a team that has called upon the diaspora for help. At least not yet. The closest they have to a foreign professional influence is striker Elias 'Baby' Uzamukunda, who left for Cannes in France when he was nineteen. That doesn't mean Micho isn't on the lookout. 'Many people ran away from the problems and became the diaspora. We need to find the solution with anyone who has roots. We need to expose the players to this. Those players are probably playing in Europe right now.'

Micho is a religious man. He talks about football and life as if he were a missionary, guided to fight on a long road by a higher power. Guiding Rwanda to qualification for the World Cup is part of his duty. 'This country had a very painful experience in 1994 and football is a way of healing those wounds it made,' he says. 'In that note I am counting myself as a servant and soldier down that road to give the medicine of healing in the right direction. Football is one special religion in Africa and we want to be preachers of that religion.' He also has experience of scouting in fifty African countries, but not Eritrea. They were largely a mystery to almost everyone, given that two generations of national team players have now fled and claimed political asylum else-where. 'We are going to a country where even Nigeria drew 0-0. You cannot go for tourism,' he says of his opponents. The team is due to fly to the altitude of Asmara, Eritrea's capital, that evening. 'Did you know, when Ethiopia and Eritrea played together when they won the 1962 Africa Cup of Nations, 90 per cent of the players were from Eritrea? It means they are very talented.'

Rwanda may never have qualified for the World Cup before, but there was one Rwandan who had been part of the finals. The Rwanda Football Federation president Celestin Ntagungira was also watching the team's final training session before the first game. Until recently Celestin was a FIFA referee. He had offi-ciated at two World Cup finals, the Beijing Olympics and three Africa Cup of Nations. 'We need young players, professional players in Europe, this is how we are organising a team who can qualify Rwanda. It is not easy,' he says. He, too, has seen the way the wind is blowing, the short cut that can take the Wasps to the finals. 'We don't have enough players in top leagues but with local players and some European players we can do better than years ago.' Unlike Micho, Celestin is loath to talk about the genocide. He is vague when I ask about his experiences of 1994. He was in neighbouring Burundi, he tells me, and returned after the troubles. Instead, like every official pronouncement in the press, he looks forward to the future.

'After the genocide we built another nation, another generation of players and coaches and referees. It's like starting a new nation. Everything was new,' he explains when I ask how the league was rebuilt. 'We have nice pitches now. A building for the federation. Football is now better than ten years ago. We have academies. I think we are happy but we have to do more to be in the top of Africa.' That progress had seen Rwanda qualify for the recent FIFA Under 17 World Cup finals. Every player had been born *after* 1994. Qualification for Brazil, he reasons, will mean even fewer people asking about the genocide. 'If Rwanda play in the World Cup all the news TV are talking, not bad things about Rwanda,' he tries to explain tactfully, although clearly including me in his rebuff. 'They will say: "Rwanda has good players, good talent" rather than: "In Rwanda, there was a genocide." I think football can change and give Rwanda a good image.'

But first there is Eritrea to contend with, a team Celestin had some knowledge of, not least because his former boss is Tesfaye Gebreyesus, an Eritrean who, back when he was technically an Ethiopian, refereed the 1980 Africa Cup of Nations final. He is also now president of the Eritrea federation. 'I will be very happy, I hope he will be proud to see me in this position,' Celestin says, beaming.

Have the Eritreans asked for any special provisions to prevent their players from running away, I ask.

His face freezes. 'This is not our business, this is for the federation from Eritrea,' Celestin replies mechanically. 'But,' he adds 'if they need our help ...'

Micho leaves with his players on the team bus and heads to the North Korea of Africa for the first leg.

**

Kigali's streets are clean, ordered and safe. Every motorcycle taxi driver (or *moto* as they are known) that swarms the capital's streets is wearing an identical helmet. In fact, they wear a helmet *and* keep a spare one hanging from the back seat. The fine for not wearing one is severe. The fine alone for not keeping your helmet in a hygienic state is 10,000 Rwandan francs, around $15, more than one week's wages for many. There is no rubbish in the gutters, no ugly mass of brightly coloured bags stuck to the thorns of tree branches and bushes as they are in virtually every capital in Africa. That's because plastic bags have been banned in Rwanda, to protect the environment and one of Rwanda's biggest growth industries: eco-tourism. The biggest fine for repeated use of a plastic bag can reach 300,000 francs. Groceries are carried in biodegradable paper bags. Nobody double-parks, or leaves their car unattended or speeds. That's because parking attendants issue tickets for the slightest misdemeanour. Yet the police and the military are barely visible on the streets. They are seen sparingly, in high vis jackets, holding speed guns or breathalysing suspect drunk drivers. These rules are accepted for the common good. There are no complaints, no protests from the guilty.

The new Rwanda is an ordered, clean and law-abiding place. It is as far from the genocidal killing fields of 1994 as it is possible to travel in such a small space of time. That transformation is down, largely, to the country's president, Paul Kagame. After leading the Tutsi forces that ended the bloodshed, he set about building a new Rwanda, based on the strict rule of law. No one talks of Hutu and Tutsi any more, nor the genocide. It is better to forget than to revisit the past, to question what your neighbour did during those frenzied months. Like pulling a thread from a jumper that keeps unravelling, who knows where it will end? The shopkeeper, the policeman, the teacher. Everyone has a story of how they suffered. But what about those who did the killing? Walking down any street in Kigali means almost certainly walking past people with unimaginable amounts of blood on their hands. But you will never know.

Within less than two decades since 1994, Kagame's government has introduced a national health service and reduced child mortality by 70 per cent, while overseeing a boom that has seen the economy grow by 8 per cent every year for five years. According to a *New*

York Times profile of Kagame, he has overseen a rise in life expectancy from thirty-six to fifty-six years and cut malaria-related deaths by 85 per cent. But he has also been accused of being an autocrat, of stifling dissent and squeezing the free press to death. One evening the editor in chief of the *New Times*, the biggest English-language newspaper in Rwanda which is seen as a pro-Kagame mouthpiece, is arrested after writing a series of stories looking at corruption at a dam project. Anyone you speak to on the streets has the same opinion. Paul Kagame has saved the country. Criticism of him and his policies is *de facto* support for the ethnic divisions that nearly destroyed the country in the first place.

**

I cannot travel to Eritrea. Eritrea does not like journalists, and especially not foreign ones. Instead, I go to a bar outside the Amahoro Stadium. Such is the paranoia of the Eritrean regime that only two Rwandan journalists are allowed to travel. One is a cameraman, another a print journalist. But no live pictures will be shown. Instead a small crowd is sitting in a bar outside the stadium listening to the radio. The single journalist in Asmara is commentating on the match down his mobile phone. It is then translated into English for me by the barmaid. I ascertain three salient facts from the game. Eritrea take the lead. Rwanda equalise. The match finishes 1-1. It is only the next day that we can see footage of the game. The cameraman has brought back the tape from Asmara. Only now is it being shown, as if live, on Rwandan state television. At a restaurant next to the stadium Rwanda's sports journalists are waiting to watch the match on the big screen. 'Most of the football teams here they were supported by people who were killed in the genocide so no teams had any sponsorship,' said Abdul Jabar Gakuba, a sports journalist with the Voice of Africa Kigali FM radio station. 'They were supported by individuals that were killed in the genocide. They had to start the league from scratch. The genocide had a huge role in the downfall of football.'

Abdul Jabar has darker skin than most Rwandans I meet. He was sixteen in 1994 and only survived because his family sent him to Uganda to study. Both his parents, his two sisters and two brothers were killed. Not a single relative, close or distant, remains. 'I have an idea how they were killed,' he says, one of the few people I will meet in Rwanda who talk openly about the genocide. 'They sought refuge in St Joseph's School, it is a priests' centre. They were there in February 1994 and they were all killed on 14 June. Two weeks later Kigali was captured. They almost survived.' The match begins on the big screen. The reception is poor and the camerawork worse. The stadium in Asmara is a sandy colour, with mud banks at either end. There appears to be only a handful of supporters watching the game. It is being held at altitude and it is clear that Eritrea are making the most of their advantage. Eritrea take the lead through Tesfalem Tekle, a twenty-year-old midfielder.

How can someone begin to forgive for a crime so heinous? Abdul Jabar talks calmly and rationally about his anger after the genocide, and his efforts to control it. He found Islam, too, which he says, helped him. 'It was very hard in the beginning. As time went by I realised I can't change anything. I need to live on. To care and provide for myself and create a new family. Now I am happy. I have a family of my own. With three kids. Many people suffered the same consequences of genocide. We must live. We don't need to keep thinking about the genocide. It happened. But we must keep on surviving. We need to earn a living. To me it was a lesson that people should not also keep thinking of the genocide.' I broach the subject of Kagame and his style of rule. 'You see how Rwandans are reconciling. In the government everyone is involved. If you are Tutsi or Hutu, if you are capable you are given a position.' It is the first and only time in Rwanda I will hear anyone use the words Hutu or Tutsi. One of Kagame's first acts as president was to ban printing whether a person was a Hutu or a Tutsi on Rwandan ID cards. 'There is no division like before. In schools we used to suffer. Tutsis wouldn't get into government schools.

71

generation of players to the next, Negash builds teams from scratch. He was coach in 2009 when the entire team absconded after being knocked out of the CECAFA Cup in Kenya. Twelve of the players ended up at the UN High Commission for Refugees in Nairobi and claimed political asylum. Negash and a handful of officials had to fly home on their own and explain to the powers that be how he had managed to lose a football team.

The incident even made it to the diplomatic level. Among the trove of dispatches among the WikiLeaks archive was this fascinating secret cable purporting to be from the US Embassy in Asmara.

S E C R E T ASMARA 000429

E.O. 12958: DECL: 12/10/2019
TAGS: PGOV MOPS SOCI PREF ER
SUBJECT: ERITREA'S SQUABBLING COLONELS, FLEEING
FOOTBALLERS, FRIGHTENED LIBRARIANS

Classified By: Ambassador Ronald K. McMullen

Things are getting worse and worse in Eritrea. The
regime is facing mounting international pressure for
years of malign behavior in the neighborhood. Human
rights abuses are commonplace and most young Eritreans,
along with the professional class, dream of fleeing the
country, even to squalid refugee camps in Ethiopia or
Sudan... 'He is sick,' said one leading Eritrean
businessman, referring to President Isaias' mental
health. 'The worse things get, the more he tries to
take direct control--it doesn't work.'

The cable then goes on to list a series of crazy incidents highlighting the deteriorating situation in the country. One of them is the fate of the Eritrea national team.

Soccer team 1-0 Regime

Eritreans are mad about soccer. Many dusty streets in
Asmara are filled with urchins kicking an old sock
stuffed with rags back and forth between goals made of
piled stones. Senior government and party officials are
avid fans of the British*[sic]*Premier League and
sometimes leave official functions early to catch key
matches. Despite tight control of the domestic media,
satellite TV dishes are allowed, probably so folks can
watch international soccer. Impressive numbers of
senior regime officials attended the World Cup pool draw
reception thrown by the South Africa embassy last week.

Diaspora websites are reporting that the entire
Eritrean national soccer team defected … If true, this
will be stunning news for the Eritrean population. Only
the coach and an escorting colonel reportedly returned
to Eritrea.(One wonders why, given their likely fate.)
(President) Isaias has previously claimed the CIA was
luring Eritrean youth abroad; if the soccer team has in
fact defected, he will undoubted try to twist logic in
some way to blame the United States.

And defect they did. After months in a refugee camp eleven of the
players were granted political asylum in Australia. One decided to
stay in Kenya. Negash Teklit now has a new team of young men to
coach, so young in fact that they look like boys. At the side of the
pitch Kahsay Embaye is watching training intently with his one
working eye. 'This team is far better than before because we have
started to work on the grassroots level,' says the vice-president of
the Eritrea National Football Federation, as if the defections were
actually a handy opportunity to try out some new blood in the
team. He is short, bald and wears a patch over his right eye. He lost
it in 1979 during an operation to take a port from the Ethiopians.

Embaye was a soldier for seventeen years, retiring only after independence from Ethiopia was secured in 1993 and President Isaias Afewerki was inaugurated. Afewerki is still in power today.

I try to broach the issue of the missing players tactfully. 'That is not a problem; as I have told you we are having so many players at grassroots level,' Embaye replies cheerily. The team, he explains, comes from the Under 17 squad. 'It is not a big deal. For a year it can touch you. But you can work with the grassroots.' I ask why he thinks the players fled. 'Ehhhh,' he stammers. 'Something must be mended. We are trying to know what is the cause. But sometimes it is a conspiracy.'

A conspiracy? By whom?

'Some people who are abroad,' he replies, meaning the perpetual enemy Ethiopia, the United States, the CIA and its allies. 'These people go directly to the UNHCR and they give them asylum. These are the tricks that are working.'

Who is involved in the conspiracy, I ask.

'I won't say that.'

So they had their heads turned?

'That is 100 per cent sure.'

I wasn't sure whether the British idiom 'having your head turned' translated well into Tigre or Tigrinya, the two most widely spoken languages in Eritrea. Given the widespread prevalence of torture in Eritrea, perhaps he took this in its literal meaning. Yet having a former revolutionary fighter with little or no footballing experience around the team seems like a strange move. Perhaps he wasn't from the federation at all. Perhaps he was there to keep his one remaining good eye on the movements of the eighteen players. Perhaps it was his job to make sure all of them were present on the flight home. At least Negash Teklit's loyalty is assured. He instructs his players to jog leisurely around the pitch for a few minutes. They meander along in their mismatched shirts in complete silence. The team trains for just a quarter of an hour, before walking slowly off the pitch. This is all we will see of them before the match.

'I prepare them from the beginning, when they were in the Under 17s,' Negash explains proudly on the side of the pitch once his players are out of earshot. 'In my country the players start their playing in the home town at age five or six and are very talented players. The only problem is body constitution.'

Body constitution?

'This is a matter of nature,' he answers. Eritreans may have once dominated the Ethiopian national team but, thanks in part to Asmara's altitude, they are better long-distance runners and road cyclists, the latter a cultural throwback to when Eritrea was part of the Italian empire. Eritrea are the current champions of cycling in Africa.

There was one image from the WikiLeaks cable about the 2009 incident in Kenya that had stayed with me:

```
Only the coach and an escorting colonel reportedly
returned to Eritrea. (One wonders why, given their
likely fate.)
```

There are no visible scars on Negash's face or his hands. He had been deemed trustworthy enough to be allowed out of the country again, a rare honour. I ask him about 2009 and that incident. 'Ahhhh, hrumph,' he exhales, mincing the correct words in his mouth for a moment. 'We have no problems with the players. Maybe some of the players are very childish to make the disappearance like that. But we have many players.' He is shrugging his shoulders now, following the party line. It was actually a good thing the selfish players left. It is not just Eritrea's problem, but one of African youth all over the world. They can emigrate from one country to another, chasing wealth. Eritrea doesn't need them. Now there's room for the new blood, new talent. 'This generation, this team, is the best,' he says a touch defiantly. 'This is a special one.' I almost believe him.

The real reason footballers and athletes defect from Eritrea at the first opportunity is much darker and more complex than envy, self-improvement, selfishness or poverty. Eritrea's thirty-year civil war with Ethiopia was led by a Marxist insurgent, schooled in the art of discipline, self-sacrifice and extreme loyalty. Isaias Afewerki led the Eritrean People's Liberation Front to victory against the Ethiopians in 1991, and his new country was recognised by the UN two years later. In power Afewerki has proved to be a ruthless tyrant. A 2011 Human Rights Watch report on Eritrea makes grim reading. It paints a picture of a country with zero civil society, zero democracy and zero accountability. Anyone who voices any opposition at all is labelled a traitor. They are thrown into jails and never heard of again. The few survivors who manage to escape tell horrific stories of journalists and opposition politicians being locked up for years in underground metal shipping containers buried in the desert in pitch darkness. When they eventually emerge, half mad, almost blind and crippled by the beatings, they seldom survive for more than a few months. Eritrea is also on a constant war footing, ready for its next inevitable conflict against its former occupier Ethiopia. National conscription is meant to last for eighteen months but, in reality, conscripts remain in the army for life, used as cheap labour for the government's many business interests, especially gold mining. 'Prolonged service, harsh treatment, and starvation wages are principal reasons for the hundreds of monthly desertions,' the Human Rights Watch report concluded. 'President Isaias said in 2010 that most deserters left for economic reasons or were "going on a picnic".'

It is this fear, of ending up in a shipping container in the desert or in the looping, perpetual nightmare of conscription, that forces thousands of people a year to flee, or die trying. According to Human Rights Watch, 'despite a "shoot-to-kill" policy for anyone caught trying to cross the country's borders, thousands of refugees pour out of Eritrea to Sudan and Ethiopia'. The UN High Commissioner for Refugees reported in 2010 that, according to one estimate, close to 2,000 Eritreans escaped over the border every month. As many as 50,000 refugees were living in Ethiopian refugee camps. One-third of them were military deserters. No one knows how many Eritreans are shot dead before they make it, or how many are vaporised crossing the minefields that ring the country.

There may be discussions on the nature of freedom in Kagame's Rwanda, but the young men of the Eritrean team – feeling the wind and the rains on their faces in Kigali as they trained – would never have tasted anything freer than this. The question was whether the temptation to leave would become too much. The Eritrean high command was confident, almost too confident, that they would return. What measures could they have put into place? Perhaps they chose players who had demonstrated only the most extreme party loyalty? Perhaps they had to pay a crippling deposit to make it into the team, a measure introduced a few years earlier that made a mockery of sport being the purest form of meritocracy? Perhaps their families were held and threatened, kept in a boiling hot shipping container under the desert until their sons, husbands or grandsons returned? No one could know for sure. If Negash Teklit knows, he is doing a good job of hiding it. He walks out of the stadium after talking to a few Rwandan journalists eager to know more about the mysterious Eritrean opponents. Embaye keeps a close eye on proceedings throughout.

Later that evening I talk to Micho. The last time I saw him he was on Eritrean national television, arm in arm with Negash in the post-match press conference. It is the first and only time I see him smile. He is holding court in front of what is left of Eritrea's press corps. 'We come to play in front of a crowd that knows where the football is!' he states jovially. 'They *really* know their football.' He is almost charming. Yet, in Kigali, the relief is palpable. 'It was like a wall had fallen on the whole country,' he says of his time in Asmara. He swipes his hand slowly over his impenetrable face, mimicking a guillotine.

**

It is match day in Kigali. Police arrive in their dozens in open-back trucks. Wearing heavy military boots and carrying long black nightsticks, they jump on to the concrete as if about to quell an impending riot. The queue outside the Amahoro Stadium is quiet and orderly. A single line of men snakes backwards in silence. In the distance the ubiquitous wasp drone of the vuvuzela can be heard from the stands. A lone amputee propels himself along the side of the queue, asking for a spare ticket, but is ignored.

Inside Eritrea's dressing room the team prepares in silence. Coach Negash is nowhere to be seen, but Kahsay Embaye is prowling around, slapping his players on the back in encouragement. He is wearing a brown suit and reflective aviator sunglasses. 'I am like Moshe Dayan!' he laughs when I compliment him on his eyewear. 'I was fighting almost all my life. Everyone was fighting at that moment, the same as the Israelis.' The war, for him, is ever-present. His skin is darker but the resemblance between Embaye and the brilliant Israeli military strategist is striking. For all the secrecy and suspicion, I am allowed to roam freely. The Eritrea team eye me with friendly curiosity. Few of the team speak English, except the team's goalkeeper and captain, Daniel Goitom. Like Negash, Goitom's loyalty has been proved. At thirty-two he is by far the team's oldest player. Eight of the starting line-up were born in 1993, the year of independence. 'It is a long journey,' he says of the trip to Kigali via Sudan. 'But I've been to Rwanda three times before.' He didn't play in the first game in Asmara. Samuel Alazar, the player lobbed by Elias 'Baby' Uzamukunda to concede that important away goal for Rwanda, did. Alazar is nowhere to be seen either.

Each time Goitom has travelled overseas he has returned. He plays for Red Sea FC, Eritrea's best club side. Four months previously thirteen members of that team defected and claimed asylum in Tanzania after a match. But not Goitom. I want to ask him why. Why did he return when his team-mates didn't? What does he have in his life back in Asmara that his team-mates did not? Maybe he is an ideological purist, a loyalist who believes the embattled rhetoric of the government that the defections are all part of a CIA plot? Perhaps life is good for Goitom, better than it would be in the

UN refugee camps he would have to live in for months before being sent somewhere alien and cold to rebuild his life? Perhaps he is scared? But I ask none of these questions. It is an hour before kick-off, before a once in a lifetime opportunity to try and qualify for the World Cup finals, so I stay quiet. 'It will be a tough game,' he says of today's opposition. 'We only have one chance to qualify for the World Cup. We have to be careful and concentrate.'

The Eritrea team, dressed in light blue shirts, is now standing in the tunnel waiting for their moment to emerge on to the pitch. Each player is assigned a Rwandan child with a cardboard 'Brasil 2014' hat wrapped around their foreheads. The Rwanda team join them. They do not speak to each other. FIFA's World Cup anthem begins and the four lines – two teams, each player holding the hand of a child – walk through a white tunnel and into the noise. It is mid-afternoon on a Tuesday but the Amahoro is almost full, and we are deafened by the indiscriminate parping of a thousand vuvuzelas. The sun has emerged and a military brass brand is marching around the pitch. The musicians are young and the green uniforms they wear swamp their slight frames as they march. Rwanda's prime minister is here and is introduced to the Eritrean and Rwandan players. Daniel Goitom and Rwanda's captain, Olivier Karekezi, exchange pennants, Karekezi towering over his slightly built opposite number. The national anthems begin. The boys and girls in the oversized jackets play the two songs. They turn the Eritrea anthem into something both jovial and dark, like a New Orleans jazz funeral. And then the match begins.

Rwanda have gone into the game with a slight advantage, having scored an away goal in Asmara. Within four minutes both captains play a role in the moment that will define both teams' fates. Goitom urged concentration in the dressing room, but makes a mess of Karekezi's shot and the ball is in the back of the net. It is the first time I see and hear Rwandans act with abandon, their screams rising and falling as the ball approaches Eritrea's goal. But Eritrea hold out until half-time. Micho has a face like thunder as he departs down the tunnel. The second half follows the same path as the first. Rwanda have all the possession. Sensing Goitom's weakness on crosses and his lack of height, they pepper his goal with shots. He is short, much shorter than any goalkeeper I have ever met before. How many goalkeepers had fled Eritrea before they turned to him, I wondered. Two more goals follow, as the weight of pressure finally tells. It is 3-0. I am standing by the Rwandan goal now, watching as the Eritreans, tall and elegant, pass the ball with grace. With a few minutes left, Eritrea win a free-kick on the edge of the penalty area. It looks almost too close for a direct shot at goal but I watch as defender Abraham Tedros curls the ball over the Rwanda wall. It crashes into the net off the underside of the bar. It is every bit as technical and brilliant as a David Beckham free-kick, one of the best goals I have ever seen. But it is too late for Eritrea. They need two more goals to progress. Rwanda are nervous for a few minutes as Eritrea try to force an unlikely comeback but the referee blows his whistle. The match has finished 3-1, 4-2 on aggregate over the two matches. The Rwandan team huddle in a circle on their knees with Micho leading them in prayer.

Rwanda qualify for the group stage with former finalists Algeria, Mali and Benin. Eritrea's hated rivals Ethiopia survive a scare against Somalia. They drew 0-0 in neutral Djibouti before taking the Somali team to the altitude of Addis Ababa and winning 5-0. Lesotho, Congo, Namibia, Mozambique, Equatorial Guinea, DR Congo, Tanzania, Togo and Kenya all join them in the group stage. But Eritrea will have to wait another four years for a chance to qualify for the World Cup finals. The players are all gathered on the centre circle, hands on hips. They look distraught. Coach Negash Teklit approaches each player, puts an arm around his shoulder and whispers softly into his ear. It is time to leave.

Negash will later admit at the post-match press conference that the better team won but will claim that the travel was a deciding factor. 'We are coming here to win but to tell you frankly we are moving out Sunday. We sat fifteen hours in Khartoum, boarding at 1 a.m. and landing here at two in the afternoon. We tried to rest but finally we lose.' He is upbeat, though. It is a young team. They will improve. There is an up and coming CECAFA Cup tournament to prepare for in a month's time. Micho, on the other hand, is not a happy man. He is sitting in the press conference room being peppered with impertinent questions. The Rwandan journalists are not happy either; with the team selection, with the substitutions, with the fact that Rwanda only scored three goals.

'Your personal opinion you can keep for yourself,' he barks at a disembodied voice at the back of the room. 'If you think that they are on the bench then come and do this job yourself. Because you are not qualified!'

'You are a very talented guy. Give me your phone number so I can later send you on a coaching course because it looks like you know when to change and who to change!' he shouts at another sarcastically.

'If I rate this performance out of one to ten, I would give two. I am at all not satisfied,' he concludes dismissively.

He storms out past the fans who have been waiting outside the gate blowing their vuvuzelas, and on to the team bus. Strangely, the *New Times* match report fails to mention any of this. 'The Wasps, who are rebuilding after a disappointing 2012 Nations Cup qualifying campaign, were too good for the Red Sea Boys much to the delight of screaming fans.' Rwanda's victory, it seems, is an unqualified, unopposed success.

**

The next day an empty bus with an Eritrean flag glued to the window is waiting outside the Red Sea Boys' hotel. The engine is running and coach Teklit is in a hurry. He is moving quickly, bringing bags to the bus and then disappearing back into the hotel. Eritrean officials, even the hotel manager, are standing outside, nervously looking from their watches to the hotel entrance to the bus. The players begin to emerge one by one. I count them as they enter and take their seats. All eighteen players are present and accounted for. No one will be absconding today. Kahsay Embaye is also watching the departure with his one working eye, satisfied that his work is done. We shake hands warmly. 'Maybe one day I will see you in Eritrea,' he offers. The bus pulls away and coach Negash waves out of the back window.

The Eritrea team returns home. I phone the airline and the office of the UN High Commissioner for Refugees. The team boards the plane, and no one has claimed asylum. Perhaps that was to be expected. Tanzania and Kenya might well have granted asylum to close to fifty Eritrean footballers in the past. But Rwanda? 'No Eritrean player would take the risk to defect in Kigali in a country where Kagame's tough rule would likely send them back to Asmara,' one former FIFA official later told me. 'If there are defections, it will take place in transit in Nairobi.'

There were some similarities between the two presidents, Kagame and Afewerki. Both had come to power at the head of revolutionary militias. Both preached order and stability over individualism and freedom. Yes, Rwanda was a freer place, but there was something strange here, too. The outward appearance of freedom, checked internally for the common good, always fearful of what its people are truly capable off. Rwanda didn't need Eritrea's brutal dictatorship. Rwanda had a more nuanced form of control: self-censorship of the mind. There are no defections in transit or in Nairobi. But then a strange thing happens. The Eritrea federation pulls the national team out of the CECAFA tournament that Negash Teklit had been so excited about. The federation claimed that it could not afford the trip, but few believe that. The CECAFA tournament is due to take place in Tanzania, where only four months earlier thirteen Eritreans from Red Sea FC claimed political asylum. The Eritrean National Cycling Federation also pulls out of the Tour of Rwanda. Eritrea has recently been crowned continental champions, too, and Eritrea's leading cyclist, Daniel Teklehaymanot, won the Tour of Rwanda in 2010. No reason was given for the withdrawal. No one knew when, or where, the Eritrea national football team would surface again.

**

Adelaide, Australia. December 2011.

Ermias Haile lives a few blocks from the Hindmarsh Stadium in the Australian city of Adelaide, the city of churches. It is the home of A-League side Adelaide United FC, and once hosted group matches during the 2000 Summer Olympics. Ermias's house is an unremarkable bungalow. It has a small unkempt yard in the front and larger patch of grass in the back, and is to be found down a quiet suburban cul-de-sac opposite a large supermarket. His shift at the factory only finished an hour ago, but he has already changed into his football kit. Five young men live in this house, cooking together, praying together, going out together, chatting up girls together and, when the opportunity arises, playing football together. 'We work at a switchboard manufacturing company,' Ermias says proudly, with the zeal of a newly arrived immigrant still marvelling at the size of his first pay cheque. 'First we were told what to do,' he says. 'Now we have started to paint boards and we get to put together the boxes.'

Ermias rarely refers to himself in the singular. When he talks it is not of 'I', but of 'we' and of 'us'. The five young Eritrean men who live here are a collective, forged together through a shared journey and a shared sacrifice. Possibly one of the biggest sacrifices any person can make: never to see your home or your family again. 'We go everywhere together,' he says of his housemates. 'We are like brothers. We take care of each other.' In 2009 Ermias left his home in Asmara to travel to Kenya. He was part of the Eritrea national team sent to the CECAFA Cup where he played as a defensive midfielder. It is a thankless position, one that involves discipline and hard work, offers few opportunities for glory or goals, but one which is essential for any team to succeed.

Defensive midfielders are the water carriers, the beating heart of the team. 'I used to play in the streets,' he says of his early years in Asmara. 'Then the coach saw me playing on the streets, he picked me and put me in the team. I was selected for the Under 17 Eritrea team and then from that I was getting better and better.'

Football used to be strong in Eritrea, Ermias says. Of course, he tells me about Ethiopia's successful 1962 Africa Cup of Nations team, how nine of the starting eleven were Eritrean. Every Eritrean I have spoken to has told me variations of the same story. But then a government decree changed everything. 'In 2005 the government decided that all players should go for army service,' Ermias says. Conscription; the never-ending cycle of war and forced labour in Eritrea that was almost impossible to escape from. 'After that football got weak and no one had interest to play soccer. And some players were getting opportunities to play overseas but they weren't allowed. It's a bit hard. But all Eritreans have to do it. That is why they decided all the players have to, too.'

Unlike any other profession, football still provided some escape from never-ending servitude. Eritrea travelled to the 2009 CECAFA Cup in Kenya with little hope of making it past the group stages. They surpassed expectations. A 0-0 draw against Zimbabwe was followed by a narrow 2-1 loss to Rwanda. But a 3-1 victory over Somalia meant that Eritrea finished second in the group, qualifying for the quarter-finals ahead of Zimbabwe on goals scored. They were drawn against Tanzania although it was clear by now that this would be their last game for Eritrea. 'I think everyone had the idea independently,' Ermias says when I ask when he decided that he was going to defect. 'From that idea everyone was waiting. We collected together and went to the game.'

With the players' minds on other things, Eritrea lost the quarter-final against Tanzania 4-0. None of the players remembers anything of that game. What they do remember is what happened next. Twelve players from the team left the hotel and arrived on the doorstep of the UN High Commissioner for Refugees and claimed political asylum. They were taken, processed and then locked together in a camp for six months. 'I don't know what to say about it, man,' he says, still suspicious of talking about his escape. None of the players wants to say too much, be too critical of the old regime. They all still have family in Eritrea. The four other players he lives with don't want to talk. They don't even want to give me their names. 'They kept us in a compound. It was just us. We were like prisoners staying all together,' he says of his time at the UN. 'Then, after six months, we came to Australia. It was hard, man. It was harsh. They don't give you anything.'

Ermias didn't choose Australia; it chose him. He didn't care where he went. Whoever wanted him first, that was where he and his team-mates would head. 'We just wanted to get out, man, because life was hard. As soon as we heard we were going out it was the best day of our lives. Just because we were starting over. All over again. It was a pretty good feeling. All we knew of Australia was the Sydney Olympic Games and the harbour. That was all we knew.' The Australian government took good care of them. Even the notoriously grumpy Australian immigration officers were cordial. They were given accommodation and money to live on. But what they craved most was to play football again. And to work. The group was split between teams in the FFSA Super League, the highest level of state soccer in South Australia. They began playing semi-pro. Ermias was picked up by Western Strikers who found him his job working in the switchboard factory. Two players, Samuel Gebrehiwet and Ambes Sium, were signed by A-League side Gold Coast United. Ermias had a trial with Adelaide United FC, but couldn't pursue it. They needed a full-time commitment but with no guarantee of a contract. He had to choose his job, with its regular income, or the chance of maybe getting a contract after a trial. He chose the certainty of the job. After all, good jobs were almost impossible to come by in Eritrea. 'We didn't have anything when we left. All we had was our kit,' said twenty-one-year-old Nevi Gebremeskel, one of the players who escaped to Australia, when we spoke on the phone before I had flown to Adelaide. He was now playing for a team called White City Woodville. 'Yes, I was scared. But life here is very good, very, very good. Everyone is happy to live. If you need to work, you can work.'

Ermias still dreams of playing pro. 'That is everyone's aim,' he says. But now it is time for him to leave. He has a practice to get to and doesn't want to be late. 'We are going to work on playing for the Super League teams, get picked, go to the A-League.' The thought of their sacrifice is never far away. I ask him whether he has ever thought about returning and playing for Eritrea, maybe some time in the future, if the political situation changes. 'Waaa,' he says, exhaling harshly. 'Ahhh, I don't think so, man. You know our situation. I don't expect to go back and play for Eritrea again.'

The players who decided to flee, who were locked up together in a Nairobi refugee camp and travelled halfway across the world, have forged a strong, lifelong bond. They have integrated with the local Eritrean population, which has softened the landing somewhat. They are grateful to Australia for saving them. Not one of the players believes that they will be the last football team to flee Eritrea. And on that they will be proved correct. But that is in the future. For now, life consists of shift work, football practice, computer games, church and the occasional night out trying to pick up Australian girls. It is as normal a life as one could hope to live, but it is a normal life they have sacrificed almost everything to have.

What is the one thing you have learned during your journey from Asmara to Adelaide? I ask finally.

'I learned that when life gives you a hundred reasons to cry, life gives you a hundred reasons to laugh. Everything is possible,' he says before opening the door and inviting me to leave. 'You don't have to give up.'

4

AMERICAN SAMOA, COOK ISLANDS, SAMOA, TONGA

Apia, Samoa. November 2011.

Thomas Rongen badly needs a smoke. The coach of the American Samoa national team is pacing around the car park of his cheap motel, bemoaning the quality and availability of Samoan tobacco. 'You can't get good smokes anywhere here, anywhere,' he laments in his loud, gravelly American accent that doesn't quite disguise the inflection of his Dutch roots. Around him players dart in and out of their rooms in the wooden two-storey buildings set within thick rainforest in the Samoan capital of Apia. It is the start of Samoa's rainy season and the searing sun is replaced by torrential downpours within seconds. But the sun is out now and Rongen looks mournfully into an empty packet of filterless Camels.

Rongen is in his mid-fifties, with a thick shock of white hair, and his stash, which he brought with him from the US, ran out days ago. On a good day he smokes with the vigour of a teenager. Stress has played its part, too, given the size of the task that lies before him: to prepare the world's worst football team for their first 2014 World Cup qualifier. 'I don't see it as an obscure job to take, I see it as a unique opportunity to do something that's a once in a lifetime gig,' he replies when asked why he took the American Samoa job. This was his first full national team role, after coaching in the MLS and taking the US Under 20 national team to two World Cup finals. He finally finds what he is looking for, a packet of cheap, dry poor quality tobacco. He piles the brown strands into a paper and rolls a thick cigarette, three times the size it should be and minus a filter, before lighting it and blowing smoke reassuringly into the air. 'I'm not slighting anyone but I'd not seen a lower standard of football in international play,' he finally says. 'I inherited this team and there were five guys literally thirty or forty pounds overweight. There was no way they could even play ten minutes if they wanted to compete at this kind of level.'

The Pacific islands of American Samoa are an unincorporated territory of the United States that has always loved football. American football, that is. It has a population of just 55,000 and produces more NFL players, and for that matter US servicemen, *per capita* than any single territory in the US. The national football team sits last on FIFA's rankings and the team's competitive record is appalling. American Samoa has played thirty matches and lost every single one of them. They have only ever scored twelve times, conceding more than 200 goals in the process. Such a record would doom a team to obscurity but that all changed after a match that made headlines around the world and turned American Samoa into a synonym for sporting annihilation.

In April 2001 a young American Samoan team with an average age of just eighteen headed to Coffs Harbour in Australia for their first ever World Cup qualifier. The trip began badly. Almost the entire senior squad was ineligible as most of the players held Samoan passports. Samoa, unlike American Samoa, was a sovereign nation with its own national team. Only one senior player survived the cull and started that match: goalkeeper Nicky Salapu. Little did he know that he was about to take part in a game that would change his life forever. It took ten minutes for Australia to break the deadlock. By then Salapu had made a string of fine saves to keep the scores level. Then came the avalanche. When the full-time whistle went Australia had won 31-0, although the manually operated scoreboard mistakenly said 32-0. Archie Thompson scored thirteen goals that evening. Both the score and Thompson's haul were world records. 'I couldn't see any reason why they would want to score so many goals,' Tunoa Lui, the coach of American Samoa, said after the match. To date the match has had nearly three million hits on YouTube.

The 31-0 debacle prompted the Oceania Football Confederation to reconsider how it should accommodate some of the most underdeveloped and underpopulated footballing regions on the planet. While Australia successfully applied to join the tougher challenge of the Asian Football Confederation, the OFC devised a four-team, round-robin pre-qualification tournament featuring its four lowest ranked sides. I had taken four flights to get to Samoa, on the other side of the world from England, travelling so far that I crossed the International Date Line.

This year the pre-qualification tournament included American Samoa and Samoa (joint last, 204th on FIFA's rankings), Tonga (second last, 202nd) and the favourites, the Cook Islands (196th). The winner would qualify for the next group stage against regional powerhouses Tahiti, the Solomon Islands and New Zealand. I was expecting to see another massacre, a host of double-digit scorelines against possibly the worst national team the world has ever seen. But then, for the first time in their history, American Samoa hired a respected professional coach to stop the rot.

Rongen was an unusual fit for the post of American Samoa coach, a job that had previously been filled by amateur locals or journeymen. He had pedigree. Born and raised in Amsterdam, Rongen was a promising defensive midfielder at Ajax but never made a first-team appearance for the Dutch club. Instead, in 1979, he moved to the brave new world of the North American Soccer League, where he played (and roomed) with his hero, Johan Cruyff, and Franz Beckenbauer. He married, stayed in the US and went into coaching, winning an MLS Cup with DC United before being hired by the United States Soccer Federation to coach the Under 20s national team. It was the USSF that had effectively loaned Rongen to the American Samoans. He exhales before quickly listing the types of problems he faced on arrival.

'Coaching education is poor,' he begins. 'There's no development ... no proper training ... they don't play on standard proper size pitches ... Transportation between the islands is poor so people don't turn up for matches sometimes ... there's no science for strength and conditioning ... the soccer IQ level is very low, lower than I've ever encountered ... diet and nutrition is poor. You won't believe the fast food places, people just shoving it down their throats. It's known for obese people ...'

He has only been with the team in the American Samoan capital of Pago Pago for three weeks, trying to knock his players into shape and impart what little technical know-how he can in such a small amount of time. Tomorrow his team will face their first test, the opening match of the pre-qualification tournament against Tonga, a team they had lost heavily to in the past. In fact the biggest hurdle to overcome for Rongen wasn't physical but mental. How do you begin to deal with a team that has been psychologically scarred by a 100 per cent losing streak? 'There are guys like the goalkeeper who played against Australia during that 31-0 game,' Rongen says. Nicky Salapu is the only survivor from that team that was mauled in Australia a decade before, but Rongen has decided to call him up and start him in goal. 'This guy,' he says, shaking his head, 'has got some major demons going on, totally driven by the thirty-one-nothing, erasing this for himself and for his family. He is so preoccupied about it, almost crazed. He gets confronted in Seattle. People say: "American Samoa? Oh, you're the guy that gave up thirty-one goals." There's some incredible scars. A lot of the guys who have lost every game. Not 2-1, or 3-2 but they'd get their asses kicked on a regular basis. So there was a defeatist attitude which I really had to change.'

As we talk, I see out of the corner of my eye a tall, beautiful woman walking past wearing a sarong, tying her long black hair theatrically into a ponytail. Rongen sees her, too. 'On the island there is a great acceptance of people who are "hes" but are actually "shes",' he explains. 'Essentially I've got a female starting at centre-back. Just imagine the abuse in England, or Spain or in Russia, the racial slurs, the sexual slurs.' Johnny Saelua wasn't known to his team-mates by that name. She was known as Jaiyah Saelua and was about to become the first transgender player ever to start a World Cup match. 'I want to travel the world and dance,' she says as she gracefully slides on to the bench opposite me. Jaiyah speaks softly and exudes femininity. Outside football she studies performing arts at the University of Hawaii. 'Anything,' she shrugs, when I ask which form of dance she prefers. 'Modern, jazz, maybe a little bit of ballet ...'

Johnny 'Jaiyah' Saelua is a member of the fa'afafine, a biologically male third sex that identifies itself as female and is largely accepted in Samoan and Polynesian cultures. So accepted, in fact, that Saelua has played for the American Samoa team since she was fourteen. 'I read somewhere that it was a record when I was drafted into the national team,' she recalls. 'I was reserve the whole tournament and I had to leave early because I was still in high school but the coach threw me on for ten minutes.'

The role of the fa'afafine in Samoan culture is a complex one. Fa'afafine means 'to be like a woman' and, although widely accepted, there are still problems. According to thirty-year-old Alex Su'a, who heads the Samoa Fa'afafine Society, there are 1,500 fa'afafine in Samoa and American Samoa. 'To be fa'afafine you have to be Samoan, born a man, feel you are a woman, be sexually attracted to males and, importantly, proud to be called and labelled fa'afafine,' Su'a says when I meet her a few days later in a café in Apia. She is wearing make-up and earrings. No one in the café takes a second look. 'The fa'afafine are culturally accepted. They have a role in Samoan society. They are the caretakers of the elders because their brothers and sisters get married, but the fa'afafine traditionally don't.' Yet homosexuality is still illegal in Samoa, and there is no legal definition for a fa'afafine, meaning that they do not enjoy the same rights. In American Samoa Jaiyah Saelua enjoys the legal freedom to be who she wants to be. But in Samoa Alex Su'a doesn't.

Yet in one of the remaining bastions of homophobia in public life, the locker room, Saelua has not encountered the kind of abuse that she would no doubt experience in the game pretty much anywhere else in the world. 'I haven't had any problems with the opposition teams,' she says, as if it would be absurd to suggest otherwise. 'My team-mates make me feel like a part of them. They don't make me feel different because I am the way I am. It is what anybody needs to feel wanted within a team. That is why I always do my best. I can't let them down. We [the fa'afafine] can do what the boys do and what the girls do.'

When Saelua is out of earshot, Rongen confides that she will start against Tonga alongside a goalkeeper who holds the record for conceding the most goals in an international match. He has no idea whether his intensive three weeks of work will make any difference. Whether his players can erase the scars of perpetual defeat. Whether they now have it within themselves finally to win a match or even just to score a goal. But the experience of living in American Samoa has already left its mark on Rongen. 'I'm an atheist, this country is very religious and spiritual,' he explains. Every day he sings and prays with his team. 'It has made me think a little more about another being out there. I try and understand their songs and sing with them. I try to pray with them.' It was more than a spiritual awakening. American Samoa had given Rongen something back. Even if his team went on to lose every game heavily, it was football as he remembered it as a child growing up in Holland, played for the love of the game with simplicity and passion. 'It is pure, it can't get any purer,' he says. 'I kick their asses up at 4.30 a.m., the guys go to work or school, back at 5.30 p.m. and I kick their asses again and they have a smile on their faces.' The American Samoa team is now in the car park, gathering for dinner in the sparsely laid canteen nearby. 'Our spoilt million-dollar babies in England and Holland they would not accept this,' Rongen says, looking at the team he has kicked into shape in front of him. The American Samoa team are quiet but intimidatingly muscular, as

Tongans have turned to a foreign coach to revive their fortunes. Unlike the American Samoans, however, they have opted for youth over experience. 'These are sort of the beliefs of the team,' says Chris Williams, at twenty-five the youngest coach in charge of a full FIFA national team. 'The word "*ikuna*" means victory.' He turns to his players. 'It means victory, yeah, boys?!' The team shyly mumble back in agreement. '"*Faka'apa'apa*", is respect. "*Mamahi'ifanou*" means pride, proud to be a Tongan and "*lelei'taha*" do your best. They chose that one.'

It had been a swift trajectory for both Williams and his team. He had played semi-pro in Australia but took his coaching badges at fifteen, spending four months shadowing the coaching staff at Scottish club Motherwell and a short spell learning the ropes at FC Copenhagen in Denmark. 'I was an Aussie Aid development officer in Tonga,' he explains of how he ended up on the Pacific island in the first place. 'And then it all snowballed from there really.' For the previous eight months he had built the team from scratch, learning Tongan as he went along. The players were all amateurs, the majority working as fishermen. Those who weren't working as fishermen were unemployed fishermen. 'There hasn't been any football development for years,' he says. 'When we started I got forty guys together from the league, well, those that could actually kick the ball, and taught them how to kick, head, pass, long pass. They've come a long way but I don't think it will hit them until they hear the national anthem.'

In the opposite room Thomas Rongen is giving a final motivational speech before the team come together and pray in a circle. Even Rongen the atheist is praying with them. 'I still don't know when the whistle blows how this team will react,' he had said before the game. 'When that whistle blows will they choke again? Will they literally give goals away?' Perhaps all the hard work over the three months, the 4.30 a.m. starts, the psychological healing, the ice baths and the prayers would all be in vain.

The two teams stand squeezed, shoulder to shoulder, in the tunnel before FIFA's theme tune is played and the twenty-two walk out into the blinding light. Jaiyah Saelua is starting her first ever match, at centre-back, and walks out to join her team-mates for the national anthems. When the referee blows his whistle, history has already been made: the first time a transgender player has ever started a World Cup match. Thomas Rongen prowls the touchline as if he is kicking every ball, barely able to sit in the temporary blue cloth dugout that has been erected for the occasion. He screams directions at each player, pulling his hand back and forth, beckoning and pushing them into position as if they were attached to an invisible rope.

Nicky Salapu is having the game of his life, acrobatically throwing himself at the feet of Tonga's strikers when they burst into the penalty area and gathering the ball. He moves to the corner of the six-yard box, counting to ten before kicking the ball out of his hands. Rongen counts along, too, a pre-arranged tactic to slow down the game. As the first half comes to a conclusion, Jaiyah Saelua finds herself in possession in the centre circle. She strikes the perfect through ball for Ramin 'The Machine' Ott – a US soldier who has taken all three weeks of his annual leave at the same time to be here – who hits the ball without much conviction from thirty-five yards out. It bounces in front of the diving Tongan goalkeeper, hits him in the face and flies into his own net. For the first time in their history American Samoa has taken the lead. All the players run screaming towards Rongen like moths returning to a flame, piling bodies up in front of him. The half-time whistle blows. Against Australia in 2001 they were already 16-0 down by this stage.

American Samoa confidently pass the ball around in the second half. Salapu is in impenetrable form, confidently gathering the ball, spraying it wide or short or long when he needs to, but always gathering the ball, walking to the edge of the six-yard box and counting ten, as instructed. The minutes tick by but no one wants to believe what is happening. The American Samoan bench grows silent, the Tongans', too. They, after all, are close to losing to the worst team in the world. Only the voice of Thomas Rongen booms out like an artillery piece. Even on the YouTube video of the game, it is Rongen's voice you can hear above everything else bellowing instructions. And then, with quarter of an hour to go, victory becomes a real possibility. Shalom Luani is clear, one on one with the Tonga goalkeeper. The ball is bouncing around after a high ball over the top of the defence. Luani reaches it a split second before the goalkeeper sickeningly collides with him. He screams, but the ball has bounced over the line as Luani lies writhing on the floor. He'll be OK. American Samoa are now 2-0 up. Tonga frantically push forward and reply with a few minutes left, a well-placed header that Salapu can do nothing about. There are goalmouth scrambles, fingertip saves. In the final, desperate minutes there's no shape, no tactics, just twenty men swarming into each other in a sort of malignant scrum. Tonga have a final chance to equalise when midfielder Timote Maamaaloa breaks through and is one on one with Salapu. Salapu saves it but the ball breaks loose and is bouncing towards the goal. Jaiyah Saelua is there, at the last, to blast the ball high into the air and away.

The final whistle blows. It takes a moment for Thomas Rongen to realise he has achieved the improbable. After thirty failed attempts, American Samoa records its first ever victory. Goalkeeper Nicky Salapu has waited a long, cold ten years for this moment, a moment he feared might never come. He is on his knees in the penalty box, screaming into his gloves at a pitch somewhere between grief and ecstasy. He only stops to punch himself in the forehead, as if to check that this moment is really happening.

To his right the manually operated scoreboard shows a score he thought he would never see: American Samoa 2 Tonga 1. The man in charge of hanging the numbered wooden slats had, in recent years, become accustomed to – indeed, he had been expected to – count out goals in their dozens. But not today. The 31-0 match had changed Salapu's life for ever. It had haunted his sleep and blackened his waking thoughts. But not any more. 'I feel like a champ right now!' he shouts tearfully. In front of Salapu his team-mates, unsure about the dynamics and the etiquette of

Salapu is still coming to terms with what has happened. 'It's amazing. Sometimes you have to pray for a miracle,' he says excitedly. He seems unsure how to express everything that is in his mind, as if he'd awoken from a deep sleep and was trying to understand the new world around him. 'For all the things that happened, the 31-0 against Australia ... in Seattle most of the players there say "are you from American Samoa, you gave up thirty-one goals". They make jokes of me. Now, we won!'

It has been a hard decade since that game in Coffs Harbour. The match had made headlines worldwide. It became a '... and finally' footnote, an amusing antidote to a news bulletin weighed down by depressing stories. 'I made twenty saves,' Salapu adds, now looking at the bright side of the 31-0 defeat. Which is true. Earlier coach Rongen had spoken of how, if Salapu hadn't been in goal that day, the score would have been 51-0. In fact, Salapu's performance in the face of Australia's uncompromising win-at-all-costs mentality had procured for him a trial at the Newcastle Jets, but it didn't amount to anything. 'That was a huge mistake,' Salapu recalls of playing the match. With two entire teams ineligible due to an administrative error, it was thought that even a team of fifteen-year-olds would be better than nothing. 'We shouldn't have taken a team,' he admits. 'I've been carrying it now for nearly eleven years. It was emotionally ... dramatic. Terrible. It was the terrible thing that happened to me. This was the worst thing ever. But things happen for a reason. Maybe that's why, to challenge us.' Some in football, though, shared Salapu's and the then American Samoa coach's disdain as to why Australia would want to keep scoring so many goals. When Craig Moore and Tony Vidmar, two of the Australians who had played in that 31-0 game, returned to their Scottish league club Glasgow Rangers, their Dutch coach Dick Advocaat was livid. When I interviewed him in 2005 he had proudly told me that he had dropped both for their next game against Dundee due to their perceived unsportsmanlike conduct.

After the game, Salapu threw himself into football in Seattle, playing six nights a week, coaching two elementary school teams while also teaching his son the basics of the game. He had also devised an additional coping mechanism. He would fire up a two-player FIFA match on his Xbox 360, choose Samoa versus Australia and disconnect the second controller so that he could fill his boots. 'I'd score and go up and up until 50-0!' he says, laughing now. In the real world, however, there was little redemption to be found on the pitch with American Samoa. The next qualification campaign for the 2006 World Cup was marginally better, but only just. He conceded thirty-four goals in four matches. The dream of appearing in a World Cup finals was never discarded, even in the face of such crushing, overwhelming evidence. American Samoa kept playing and kept getting beaten badly. But now they had won. Things were different. 'I feel like I've been let out of prison. I want my son to grow up and don't want kids chasing him around saying your dad lost 31-0 ... but if we win this tournament, we will get to Brazil no doubt! Even if we qualify for Brazil, and I don't make it there, I would die as a happy person.'

American Samoa is now in the new world. They had never won before, that was true, but they had never even *approached* a game without the almost certain belief in their own destruction. Next up was the Cook Islands, a nation of just 24,000 people who, nevertheless, were the highest ranked team at the tournament and had several Kiwi players with contracts in the New Zealand league. They were coached by a former All Whites international, Shane Rufer. His brother, Wynton, had been voted the Oceania player of the century after an incredible career in Germany with Werder Bremen where he won six Bundesliga titles and even finished joint top scorer in the 1993–4 UEFA Champions League. I'd only discovered Rufer had taken over as coach of the Cook Islands after sitting next to a polite and chatty Wynton on my flight to Samoa via Auckland. He kept a stack of postcards in his bag, with a picture of himself performing a scissor kick on the front and his name on the back. He signed one, handed it to me and told me how excited his brother was about the opportunity, especially as he had eight New Zealand-based players to choose from. The rest of the qualification group would be whipping boys. He was worried that another 31-0 might be on the cards. As we said goodbye it seemed clear to both of us that the Cook Islands would steamroller every team that was put in front of them. But it didn't quite work out that way. Later the same evening after American Samoa beat Tonga, the hosts Samoa beat the Cook Islands 3-2. Rufer was already under pressure. The president of the Cook Islands federation had spoken darkly of dressing-room bust-ups and Rufer would be fired a few minutes before the American Samoa game, pitchside, by the federation. His career in international management lasted just ninety competitive minutes.

Rongen, on the other hand, was on cloud nine. 'It feels great, it really does. I delved into the unknown so it's personally satisfying,' he says back at the motel. Before the Tonga game he had complained about the lack of press interest in the game in Samoa or elsewhere. But now his phone is ringing non-stop. Just like a decade ago, American Samoa was international news again, a very different ' ... and finally' segment to bookend a broadcast full of bad news stories. 'To get that first win and release Nicky's demons, his scars, his emotional scars, for them to get that illusive win, for the first transgender player to play a FIFA event,' he says, apologising as he breaks off to take a call from Samoan television. 'At the end of the day, there's the purity, the love and joy of the game. A bunch of amateurs who sacrificed a huge amount, losing money from their jobs, getting up at 4.30, sleeping in a room with thirty guys on the floor, no mattresses. That was pretty incredible.' There was never going to be a better time to achieve American Samoa's first ever winning streak.

**

Thomas Rongen is furious. His team are scattered around him on the sidelines of the pitch at the J. S. Blatter Stadium. They look anywhere but at him. Rongen looks like he's dressed for the beach, in blue polo shirt, shorts and cream baseball cap. But his mouth is collapsing into a vicious scowl. He paces in front of the team, twitching for an outlet. American Samoa has just drawn with the Cook Islands 1-1. It's another first for them, their first ever draw. But it could have been so much more. The first half had been all American Samoa. They were a team not reborn exactly – that would suggest a return to former glories, of which there had been none – but, rather, hewn afresh. They were unrecognisable from the sacrificial meat that had been thrown in front of their opposition over the past decade. The Cook Islands were hit by wave after wave of attacks. Chance after chance was missed. There were stepovers. *Stepovers!* Finally, the pressure was too much. Jaiyah Saelua ballooned a high ball forward. The defender missed it and Shalom Luani nipped in to poke American Samoa ahead 1-0. It was the least they deserved. For a second consecutive half Nicky Salapu had kept a clean sheet. He prowled his penalty box, imperious now, chin jutting into the air with the same arrogance that possesses the best. But in the second half they were the masters of their own downfall. The Cook Islands pumped a hopeful free-kick high into the penalty area. With no one around him, Tala Luvu placed a magnificent header into Salapu's bottom left-hand corner. The problem was that Luvu had headed past his own goalkeeper. American Samoa broke through time and time again seeking the victory that would almost certainly assure them of a place in the next round. But the Cook Islands' New Zealand-born goalkeeper Tony Jamieson was equal to everything that was thrown at him. American Samoa had snatched parity from the jaws of victory. Rongen's face is thunderous, waiting for someone to ignite his fury. And that someone is goalkeeper Nicky Salapu.

'Can we do the *haka* now, coach?' Salapu asks meekly as the team gather their stuff in silence.

Rongen checks back, barely believing what he has just heard.

'No, Nicky, we only have a *haka* if we win,' he replies. Salapu tries to scurry away unnoticed.

'Are you happy with that?!' Rongen shouts after him.

Salapu looks back blankly, puzzled, unsure of the right thing to say. This is a man, after all, who has picked the ball out of his net more than 150 times for his country. He had dreamed of one day drawing a match, but it had always seemed too fanciful, too remote. Now they had won and drawn two games in a row. It felt good.

'ARE YOU HAPPY WITH THAT?!' Rongen repeats, this time booming.

'Er ...' Salapu stammers, 'yeah. Yes.' He shrugs. He is only being honest.

'And you're happy with that?' Rongen repeats in disbelief.

'Yes!' Salapu confirms, more confidently now.

'Well, that's why you didn't win a GODDAMN thing until I got here,' Rongen spits before marching towards the team bus on his own. The rest follow submissively. Salapu doesn't say another word.

An hour later Samoa took on Tonga and drew 1-1. It meant that both the Cook Islands and Tonga had been eliminated from World Cup qualification. Chris Williams, Tonga's coach, was devastated it hadn't worked out as planned. 'Look, American Samoa carried that thirty-one-nothing defeat for ten years and we'll have to shoulder that from now on,' he says of Tonga's historic defeat to American Samoa a few days before. 'But I'm really proud of the boys after what happened a few days ago. We'll finish the tournament against Cook Islands and I'll just keep travelling the world and keep learning.'

The result may have knocked the two highest ranked teams out of the tournament, but it had set up a stone-cold classic. Samoa v American Samoa, the Samoan *Clásico*. Two different countries, yes, but the same people. Improbably, American Samoa and Samoa sit joint top of the group on equal points. To qualify for the next round American Samoa has to beat Samoa. A draw isn't enough thanks to Samoa scoring more goals. Despite American Samoa and Samoa sitting joint last on FIFA's ranking, it is only an illusion of parity. The Samoans have not played an international football match in four years, preferring to build the league and nurture its players in isolation before launching them into international competition. Some of their players have been born abroad, too, given that a large Samoan community exists in Australia and New Zealand. Australian international and former Everton midfielder Tim Cahill qualified for Samoa via his Samoan mother and made his debut for the Under 20s in 1994, at just fourteen, although his two appearances in that tournament owed more to opportunism than patriotism. 'I saw it simply as a chance to go on holiday because my grandmother was ill at the time in Samoa,' he told the London *Evening Standard* in 2002. FIFA had just blocked his chance of playing for the Ireland national team at that year's World Cup, whom he qualified for by virtue of an Irish grandparent on his father's side. 'It was a chance to go back and see her on expenses as the Samoans were paying for all my flights, accommodation and living expenses. I could not have cared less about playing for them.'

This tournament had been a boon for the American Samoans. It had given the island back its pride and had given Nicky Salapu his life back. But the Samoan team also had their own connection to that 31-0 mauling. The day after their draw with Tonga, the Samoans are training on a pitch next to the J. S. Blatter Stadium. Tunoa Lui is a very different coach from Thomas Rongen. He stands on the sidelines, quietly watching the team training in near silence. When he wants to make a point he approaches a player and speaks quietly to him. Lui was the American Samoan coach that day in Australia in 2001. It was he who was quoted afterwards saying that he couldn't see why Australia would want to score so many goals. 'It was tough going back then, I felt sorry for the boys but we didn't have our best players that day,' he says. He talks just as he coaches: quietly and politely. Like Salapu, Lui had been left with some heavy baggage from the defeat. Work was hard to come by. Why would anyone want to hire the coach who had presided over a world record loss? But what, exactly, could the coach change to stop any future blood-letting? Lui rebuilt his career in Samoa and had risen to national team coach. He felt uncomfortable even talking about the 31-0 defeat, which he describes as 'one of the worst nights of my life'. He had been badgered by the press and ridiculed all over the world. And now the international media had once again descended on American Samoa, this time for their unexpected victory and draw against the Cook Islands. It was something that his Samoan team were completely unprepared for. 'The boys are not used to this,' he says of the intense interest in the game. 'It is the first time pretty much any of them have ever been interviewed by anyone. This is a rugby nation. Football is the minority sport. I think some of them find it interesting to be interviewed. They are not used to it. They are kind of shy.'

Just how shy is made clear a few minutes later when I speak to Samoa's captain, left-back Charles Bell.

> Me: The big game tomorrow, American Samoa v Samoa. Did you ever think you'd play them for a chance to reach the next round?
>
> Charles: [Long pause] They've already done well with our games and our training sessions. I trust them on the pitch and off the pitch.
>
> Me: What do you do outside of football? What's your job?
>
> Charles: I work as a customs officer.
>
> Me: So you do drug busts?
>
> Charles: [Long pause] Yeah. People are bringing drugs into our country. So we use our canine units to stop them.
>
> Me: What's the biggest bust for cocaine you've done? Two, three, tonnes?
>
> Charles: No, just small packets.
>
> Me: What do your customs officer mates make of you playing on the national team?
>
> Charles: Yeah, they are really proud of me.

Me: So ... what's your prediction for tomorrow?

Charles: [Long pause, shyly looking at the floor] I will put all my effort into the game. The boys will all give their best tomorrow.

He couldn't wait to get away.

**

It is the morning of the match and Thomas Rongen has gathered his team in the dining hall of the motel. He's going through his tactical plan on a whiteboard, sticking up paper diagrams to illustrate the runs that Samoa's forwards will be making. He spins and points at individual players, telling them forcefully what to watch for. Rongen speaks quickly but clearly, his voice booming across the room. 'We are going to win all our battles. And if we win all our battles, we'll win the war – and this is a war – for ninety minutes,' he shouts at the room. 'Peace afterwards, respect before. The *Clásico*. It is going to be a tough affair. You are ready for this ninety-minute war. And then maybe a chance for Brazil. Maybe at first we thought about just scoring a goal. But now, you have put yourself in the position of winning this tournament. Give everything for your country. That's all we can ask.' The room shouts back in approval.

It is raining heavily outside now. It is two and a half hours before kick-off and the American Samoa team are loading on to the bus for the short ride to the J. S. Blatter Stadium. Rongen is sheltering under a tree, smoking his last cigarette of the day. 'To play for a championship? Nobody, *nobody*, and I include myself in that quite frankly, thought this would happen when I went to American Samoa, went on the field for the first session and saw the level,' he says smiling. 'I feared it was going to be a really tough task. I've been to a quarter-final and semi-final with the Under 20s, an assistant coach with the US senior team at France ['98], but this will be my best coaching job.' The same group of players now aiming for Brazil had turned up at the 2011 South Pacific Games a few months before and been hammered 8-0 by both New Caledonia and Vanuatu, conceding twenty-six goals in five games and scoring none. Now, Rongen has done all he could do. Before the first game against Tonga he didn't know how his players would react to his intensive three-week crash course in international football. They passed the test, but this is a different one. It isn't about not getting beaten, or not conceding, or scoring a goal, or even winning a game. It is about becoming champions, finishing first. 'I saw a group of men grow up,' he says, throwing his cigarette butt on to the floor. 'We've turned around a defeatist mentality, a fragile team, in this short space of time. They believe that going out on the pitch today isn't about thinking "let's not give up eight, nine or ten goals". We can walk on the field to say we're here to win the game and vie for a spot to Brazil.'

The J. S. Blatter Stadium is surrounded by dark clouds as tropical raindrops fall like bullets. A mist is rolling down the hills as water pools on the pitch. Tonga had beaten the Cook Islands in the day's previous game, giving Chris Williams his first ever victory. It would also be his last. He would be replaced shortly afterwards. But the match had seen so much rain that a team of men have been trying to drain the pitch using buckets and sticks ever since. The OFC officials even suggest at one point that the match be postponed. But with an hour to go the clouds clear and the rains stop as kick-off approaches. In the dressing room Rongen is walking in a circle, urging each player to believe they can win. Even American Samoa's governor has flown in for the match and adds his own words of encouragement. The team begin to clap their hands together as striker Rambo Tapui shouts motivational slogans in Samoan as if he was Eminem in a hip-hop battle slam. The team pray together, linking arms. Rongen is there, too, eyes closed, head bowed, before the team does a group hug and runs out for the national anthems. 'We talked about clear hearts, full hearts. Make it happen. Make it happen!' Rongen shouts as each player passes through the dressing-room door and into the tunnel. 'Let's go, boys. Grab this opportunity. The surfs out.'

The American Samoa team is lined up, with their hands on their hearts. Each player sings 'Amerika Samoa', the national anthem, but Jaiyah Saelua stands tallest and sings louder than anyone else:

> *Amerika Samoa*
> *Your name forever holds*
> *Your legends of yore*
> *Stand up and be counted.*

It is the most important game of their lives. Rongen stands on the sidelines, his hand also pressed to his heart as he listens to the anthem. The rainstorm that has threatened to engulf the stadium hovers menacingly, leaving the pitch flooded in places and the goalmouth a black, muddy mess. No one is sure whether this is a good or a bad thing. The referee blows his whistle. The American Samoa bench pray for one last miracle.

It is almost all one-way traffic. Samoa have several professionals in the side from New Zealand and Australia. Their coach is also motivated by escaping the gravitational pull of that 31-0 match against Australia. But Nicky Salapu wants to escape it more. He makes one acrobatic save after another. He drops nothing. Every kick finds an American Samoan shirt. He is unbeatable. At half-time it is 0-0. Rongen takes his team talk by the blue cloth dugout. They have to score or they are out. Jaiyah Saelua did not have a great half. 'Jaiyah, you are always twenty yards behind, it's very hard for us to defend that way. Everyone should be up with them. And then we play them offside,' he says. But he is not angry. He is talking more softly now. 'We are exactly where we wanted to be, guys.' Rongen is also about to throw his Hail Mary. 'Allow me to give you the signal when there's twenty minutes left. I'll bring on [striker] Diamond [Ott] off the bench to give us some speed and we are just going to go for it. We are exactly where we are supposed to be.'

American Samoa do go for it. Rongen brings on their pacey striker, Diamond Ott. He gives his signal and the team push forward as the skies darken. It is a risky move but nothing is getting past Nicky Salapu today. Then comes the moment that could change everything. American Samoa make a rare attack. A through ball splits the Samoan centre-backs. Diamond Ott is quicker than anyone else on the pitch and reaches the ball, just as Rongen had planned. He is one on one with the Samoan goalkeeper. Ott slides the ball past him. Time slows as the crowd and the bench wait. For a brief second it looks as if it is in, but it hits the post and bounces clear. Several American Samoa players fall to their knees, knowing they won't get a better chance than that. And they don't. Instead, Samoa break away and score in the ninety-second minute with one of the last kicks of the match. Nicky Salapau was seconds away from his first clean sheet. Samoa win 1-0 and American Samoa's dream is over.

The heavy rains finally roll in almost as the referee blows for full-time. American Samoa do one final *haka*. They have lost, but Rongen has no complaints, not this time. After all, they have come further than anyone could have imagined. Rongen's contract ended the day they were knocked out. It would have been crazily optimistic to hand him anything else. But he will move on to pastures new, his love of the game reinvigorated. 'I'm so proud of what this team has accomplished. That win that rebounded around the world. I could not be prouder of a group of guys that came from nowhere,' he says as the team sings behind him. 'How can you not believe?'

Rongen is dragged into the crowd by his team, as they beg him to lead the chants of 'Amerika Samoa'. Jaiyah Saelua's tears are indistinguishable from the rain. 'I'm disappointed but we still did so well and I am looking forward to seeing the future for American Samoan soccer.' The match, however, could be the last time she takes to the pitch. 'This has been a life-changing experience for me,' she admits. 'But I don't know if soccer has a place within me after this tournament. I just want to focus on dance school.'

In just a few days the world's worst team has been transformed. They didn't make it to the next round of World Cup qualification. But who knows what would have happened? Samoa's coach Tunoa Lui pointed to the sky, to God, when the final whistle blew. He had shared the burden of that 31-0 drubbing with Nicky Salapu and had also found redemption in an unlikely comeback. But it didn't last long. Lui's reward for qualification was to be replaced for the 2012 OFC Nations Cup, Oceania's version of the European Championships. The semi-finalist qualified for the final round of World Cup qualification, but the winner would also make it to the following year's Confederations Cup to play the likes of Brazil and Spain. Samoa played Tahiti in the opening game and lost 10-1. Of those ten goals, nine were scored by four members of the Tehau family, three brothers and a cousin who all played for Tahiti. Tahiti would go on to win the cup and secure an unlikely place in the Confederations Cup. Samoa would go on to lose 9-0 against New Caledonia.

Back in Apia the American Samoa team circle their coach. 'We started together, we finished together,' he tells them. 'You can walk off the field with your heads held high. Be very proud for what you have done for your country. I am so proud of you guys.' The team come together and chant 'One, two, three, American Samoa!' as Whitney Houston's 'I Wanna Dance With Somebody' is played over the PA system. They break away. Thomas Rongen, Jaiyah Saelua, Nicky Salapu and the rest of the American Samoa team walk back to the coach as the rain falls harder than ever.

huge street protests that forced Syria to end a twenty-year custodial occupation. It is six years since Israeli jets destroyed parts of Beirut to counter the threat of the Shia militant group Hezbollah; four years since Hezbollah took over Beirut in a show of force to let the Lebanese government know who was really the boss; and three years since a parliamentary election that laid bare just how divided this country had become.

Yet Beirut's beautiful people continue to party. The *New York Times* had recently announced that the city was *the* must visit destination of the year. Gemmayzeh, once a snipers' alley in the Christian district of Ashrafieh, is now a mile-long procession of cocktail bars. On the other side of Martyrs' Square, the ground zero of the civil war that split Christians to the north and Muslims to the south, upmarket restaurants and nightclubs have proliferated in an area where Yasser Arafat's Palestinian Liberation Organisation had its headquarters before the Israelis forced them into a Tunisian exile in 1983. And now tens of thousands of Syrians are pouring into Lebanon to escape the heinous death toll in their country's own civil war, recalibrating Lebanon's precarious sectarian balance. A state that could barely offer the basics to its own citizens is creaking under its new responsibilities.

These problems would be insurmountable in most countries but in Lebanon unity is a rare commodity. Flags of the various militias that hold sway on the streets and in the parliament are more prevalent than Lebanon's own flag. Nothing has been able to rise above and offer a mirror to the country that could prove that Lebanon is more than the sum of its parts. Nothing, that is, until Theo Bucker returned to town. Bucker is sitting in an upmarket hotel suite overlooking the miserable, cold, windswept vista of Martyrs' Square as the rains flood the streets below, listening to a song written in his honour. The coach of the Lebanese national football team nods politely, if a little awkwardly, as an aspiring Lebanese singer explains why she felt compelled to come to his room, unannounced, with a MacBook under her arm, and her producer in tow, to play him a song she had written about a sport she had barely given a second thought to until recently. 'It came to me one night in a dream, all of the names of the players,' she explains to him, as the song, a bland but inoffensive Lebanese pop number, wafts through the room. 'I felt inspired after that last victory,' she giggles a little too hard. Bucker smiles mechanically when reminded of *that* match, a 2-1 victory against South Korea. It was a result that had something of a profound effect on a country, and a city, he had fallen in love with ever since marrying his Lebanese dentist.

It has been a long time since the Lebanese national team has tasted any victory at all, let alone inspired the affections and songwriting talents of the country's famously beautiful people. For five years instability, assassinations and lingering sectarian squabbling have seen matches in Lebanon's domestic league played behind closed doors. The government feared that clashes between groups of supporters aligned to different religious groups might spark a new civil war. The national team, too – made up of Shia, Sunni, Orthodox Christian, Armenian, Maronite Catholic and Druze players – couldn't lift the weight of Lebanon's history, nor rise above the hatreds. By the time the 2014 World Cup qualification campaign had come around, the Cedars – named after the national trees that still periodically cover the slopes of Mount Lebanon – were one of the lowest ranked teams in the world. When Lebanon qualified for the first group stage after beating lowly Bangladesh 4-2 on aggregate – the same stage that saw Thailand just squeeze past Palestine – Lebanon were the lowest ranked Asian team left in contention.

Bucker had been in charge of the Lebanese national team before and had recently won the Lebanese title with Al-Ahed – a team that enjoys strong support from Hezbollah – but answered the call when his adoptive country came to him again. After a 6-0 mauling against South Korea in the first game, things didn't look good. But then something strange happened. They started winning. And then came *that* victory, the victory which was now inspiring a song being played to him in his hotel suite: a 2-1 home win against 2002 World Cup semi-finalists South Korea in the return fixture.

The victory took place in front of 60,000 fans at the Camille Chamoun Sports City Stadium after the government decided that the fans could return to watch football, for free. The stadium was a few hundred metres from the Shatila and Sabra Palestinian refugee camps, site of the 1982 massacre where as many as 3,000 men, women and children were butchered by a Lebanese Christian militia as Israeli forces looked on. The Camille Chamoun Stadium had itself become a refugee camp during the worst years of the civil war. The former head of the Lebanese Football Association would hang a photograph behind his desk to remind him of darker times; of the pitch, then just mud and gravel, covered in shredded pieces of fabric that had been fashioned into tents.

The stadium had now been restored to its former glory and the South Korea game gave Lebanon hope of reaching the World Cup finals for the first time in its history. With it came a rare outburst of national pride. The national flag – the red and white horizontal stripes with the green cedar at its centre – had been flown in the stands, rather than the yellow standard of Hezbollah or the white of the Christian Lebanese Forces. And that, it seems, was largely down to Bucker. 'Since I met my wife I see myself as half-Lebanese,' Bucker says loudly and theatrically, once the singer and her producer have gone to get a drink. 'Lebanon football before I arrived wasn't under the carpet. It was buried deeply under the ground. It was not existing at all.' He is sixty years old with a thin face and a mop of reddish-blond hair. He speaks English with a heavy, rolling German accent, shouting every other word to accentuate the important points. Bucker was right, of course. Football was almost dead in Lebanon before he arrived. The league mirrored the sectarian divisions that had led Lebanon towards civil war in the first place. Each club had a distinct religious identity entrenched by the patronage of politicians who would help fund them. Teams like Ansar and Nejmeh would be supported by the Sunni Hariri family, first by Rafic Hariri and then, after his death, by his son Saad, who would also become prime minister; Safa were supported by the Druze; Racing

Beirut were aligned with the Orthodox Christians. And then there was Al-Ahed, who had won three of the four last championships and had strong links with Shia guerrilla group Hezbollah. Al-Ahed's shirts were even sponsored by Al-Manar, Hezbollah's very own TV network which is itself considered a terrorist entity in the US. In those circumstances a five-year spectator ban was probably inevitable. 'The Lebanese are tired of all the problems of the past,' Bucker says dismissively when I ask about his own time as coach of Al-Ahed. The team provided most of the players for the national team, eight from the last squad. But Bucker doesn't want to talk about Al-Ahed, or Hezbollah, or the divisions of the past, only the national team and how it is transforming the capital before his eyes. 'The Lebanese people are happy that this team is uniting them,' he says. 'Now they have a very good reason to come back to the stadium. I believe it is very good for the nation. They have found something which is really uniting them. There's a deep love for football in the country. But before they had no home to dedicate their love. Now they have a home, now they can support their own team.'

Bucker had played in Germany for Borussia Dortmund and FC Schalke 04 before ending his career in Saudi Arabia. In 1985 he began coaching in the Arab world, a journey that would take him everywhere from the huge crowds and passion of Egypt to Libya, where the Gaddafi family ruled football with an iron fist. That journey first brought Bucker to Beirut in 2000 during the high point of Lebanese football when the country hosted the Asian Cup and built a host of brand new stadiums across the country. It had been a decade since the end of the civil war but the Lebanese economy was booming thanks largely to Rafic Hariri, a billionaire tycoon who had made his money in Saudi Arabia's construction industry. Lebanon had not performed well at the finals, but hosting an event so soon after the civil war was an important marker for the country's reconstruction. Bucker was returning under very different circumstances, at a time when religious and political differences were sharper than ever, and vowed to lead by example. 'All the Lebanese players are not stupid, they understand,' he says gruffly. 'You select players in the fair way, not because my father, my brother, know somebody, not because they are Christian or Druze or Shia. I don't care if someone is a Christian or a Muslim. There is no old or young. There are only good and bad football players. I tried to make them faceless, without any number.'

Unsurprisingly, Bucker's sectarian-blind approach to team selection led to a dramatic rise in form. After doing the bare minimum and scraping through against Bangladesh, and then the 6-0 loss to South Korea, Lebanon recovered, beating the United Arab Emirates and Kuwait before that famous victory against the Koreans in Beirut in the last game. All Bucker needs now is a point in their final game against the United Arab Emirates in Abu Dhabi and they will be through to the final group stage of Asian qualification for the first time in their history. 'To beat them and beat them with good football? Well,' Bucker says with pride of the South Korea game. 'It wasn't luck. We deserved to win. We were equal in every way.' This was down to his own football philosophy, he explains, one which, if every club just listened to him without question, would bear immediate fruit. For starters he has dispensed with formations and positions. He believes only in attack and defence. 'I made the job very easy,' he says. 'I need around me a president and manager able to grow a kind of disciplined system. And if they work with this system, I GUARANTEE,' he shouts, 'I GUARANTEE I will get immediate success. One hundred per cent. But the PROBLEM,' he shouts again, 'in the Arabic world is that when someone is UP, he is drowning. As soon as his head is out of the water he is speaking like he is the founder of football. Now people are really learning.'

For Bucker football is a simple game. You eat well, you sleep well and everyone – from the kitman to the federation president – does exactly what he, Bucker, tells you to do. With his Lebanese wife by his side at every match, Bucker has been building a team representative of the nation, even if he has largely called on

Al-Ahed, the most controversial team in the league, for most of his players. The likes of winger Ahmad Zreik, who he persuaded to give up working in a restaurant in the United States to return home and play for Lebanon, and Mahmoud El Ali, who had ably led Lebanon's attack during qualification and had been the best player on the pitch against South Korea, were transported from Al-Ahed straight into the national team.

Al-Ahed is a fascinating club. Their stadium is to be found deep in Dahiyeh, the Hezbollah stronghold in southern Beirut which was heavily bombed by Israeli jets during the Second Lebanese War in 2006. During one visit to Al-Ahed's ground in 2007 I had spoken to several leading figures at the club. Outside the main office a picture of Al-Ahed's 2005 Lebanese FA Cup-winning squad was hanging on the wall. In the centre, beaming through a grey-flecked beard from under a black turban, was Hassan Nasrallah, Hezbollah's leader and arguably Israel's public enemy number one. 'From the pictures around me I'm guessing he is close by,' Bucker says of Nasrallah during his time in charge of Al-Ahed. 'But I never met him.' That might be down to the fact that, since the 2008 war with Israel, Nasrallah has had to sleep in a different bed every night to avoid being assassinated. Still, Bucker denies that he was forced to sign and play only Shia players – a charge levelled by Ahed's opponents, who also make unfounded claims that Shia players on opposition teams throw matches at the order of their spiritual leaders to ensure that Al-Ahed win the title – even if the vast majority of the team's players come from that community. What was important for Bucker was talent and unity. The former had always been there. Bucker was convinced of that. The latter, not so much. Now the team had brought a spring to Lebanon's step, inspiring patriotism and song. The Lebanese pop singer and her producer leave. They are off to shoot a video with a film crew just in case Lebanon do make it to Brazil. Bucker has one last training session in Beirut before taking his team to Abu Dhabi. Lebanon has a huge expat population in the UAE, and the match is expected to be a sell-out for the Lebanese. The notoriously fickle Emirati home support is unlikely to turn out in numbers given that the home side has already been eliminated, after losing every single game in the group. But first there is one more round of the Lebanese league to negotiate. On the wave of football euphoria sweeping Lebanon following the victory against South Korea, the government and the Lebanese football association have finally yielded and allowed fans back into the stadiums for league as well as international matches. Religion, they hope, can be forgotten for ninety minutes. 'If you believe in some religious direction, fine,' Bucker says before I leave, heading back into the freezing storm. 'But you have to respect my way of thinking. I hope everyone is smart enough to see this. Name or belief is not scoring.'

**

Tripoli, Lebanon. February 2012.

Tripoli's Olympic Stadium is a shadow of its former glory. The stadium used to be the pearl of Lebanese football, a modern steel and white canvas construction on the shores of the Mediterranean. The waves can be heard lapping on the scrubby beach nearby; snow-capped Mount Lebanon can be seen in the distance. The stadium was built when Lebanon hosted the 2000 Asian Cup. Then it represented the new hope for Lebanon, a mirage that was ended by Rafic Hariri's assassination in 2005. Now the Olympic Stadium has fallen into disrepair. I had taken a bus north from Beirut for the last round of league matches before Lebanon's vital match against the UAE. Hezbollah's team, Al-Ahed, have travelled north to Tripoli, too. Tripoli is a turbulent Sunni enclave. The city had seen periodic clashes in recent years, firstly following an Islamist uprising in the nearby Palestinian refugee camps. There are twelve Palestinian camps in Lebanon, housing a quarter of a million refugees in abject conditions and harbouring seething resentment at their treatment by the Lebanese. Then there was the

Syrian civil war, which had exacerbated the tensions between the Sunnis and Tripoli's Alawite community, the Shia sect to which Bashar al-Assad belonged. Even in the new era of footballing détente, with the fans finally allowed to return, a match between Tripoli and Al-Ahed is still a potential flashpoint. The federation decided to move the match away from the smaller stadium in the centre of the city to the Olympic Stadium on the outskirts to try and minimise any confrontations.

The stadium looks like a place where football hasn't been played for five years. The army seized it for use as a base for its manoeuvres against the restive Palestinian refugee camps in the north of the country. Concrete blockades the size of cars and rolls of razor wire block every path to the stadium hundreds of metres away from the entrance. Hundreds of troops stationed in APCs and carrying machine guns patrol the streets outside, checking the IDs of everyone who approaches on foot. Men with heavy body armour and mirrors on the ends of long poles check the undersides of cars for bombs. Inside, everything is in disrepair. The toilets haven't worked for years, nor have the lights. Almost all the windows are smashed, every room filled with rubble, refuse and water. In the dark a dozen men each lay down a small rectangle of carpet and pray. The pitch, ringed by a dark red running track, is a mess of green and brown. The grass has been destroyed by the helicopters that regularly land here. More troops with machine guns, walking in pairs, patrol the track. The rains have flooded the pitch and the stands. It is only half an hour before kick-off but both penalty boxes are ankle-deep in water. Two men with coffee cups frantically scoop as much muddy water from the penalty areas as they can.

'Look at the pitch. It is a farm, yes? It is the worst pitch in the world. Everything is bad,' explains Khodr Arja, a sixteen-year-old Tripoli fan who cannot remember the last time fans were allowed into the stadium. He is sitting in the one covered stand along with hardly more than one hundred other fans. The final attendance for the return of Lebanon's fans to the country's football stadiums is 108. 'It's new and we are happy to see it,' he admits, 'but the federation is not helping the audience to come here. They don't support us. You have to pay 5,000 [Lebanese pounds, around £2, for a ticket] and these are poor people. It should be for free.' But even a few dozen fans marks progress of a sort. The last Lebanese league game I had attended was three years previously, at the climax of the 2008–9 season. Nejmeh, a club funded by the Sunni Hariri family, snatched the league title from Al-Ahed in the last game of the season. The final round of matches took place against the backdrop of tense parliamentary elections. On the one side was the anti-Syrian March 14 movement made up of Sunnis and most of the Christian parties, and on the other the pro-Syria March 8 movement, backed by Hezbollah. Despite fans from both sides being barred from attending their respective matches, a crowd of Nejmeh fans aligned politically with Sunni prime minister Saad Hariri and the March 14 alliance attacked the Al-Ahed team bus. I had watched as the crowd grew to a mob, beating the players and smashing the bus windows. The driver managed to escape, but only by careering the bus down the street, crushing passing cars as it went. It was a miracle no one was killed. Back then it was hard to see how the fans could ever return the stadiums. 'We don't see many fans but it's better than nothing,' shrugs Ali Hijazy, a young, bespectacled football journalist with Al Jadeed TV who is eating sunflower seeds in the freezing stands. 'The football was miserable. Politics is a great reason why Lebanese football was bad,' he says caustically. Bucker, he explains, can't fix the country himself, but he's made a decent start. 'The politics is still here in Lebanese society but Theo Bucker is working with the national team, with no politics or religious views,' he says, admiration in his voice at Bucker's accomplishments. 'The Lebanese national team is doing the job that no politician can do. It is like a revolution in Lebanese football.'

On the pitch the Al-Ahed team train amid the soldiers in the mud and cold. The team had dominated the Lebanese league in recent years for the same reason any team dominates any league in any country: money. Hezbollah operated a virtual state within a state in Lebanon, funding reconstruction projects with the help of money from Iran – its spiritual, political, economic and military ally – and donations from wealthy individuals. Al-Ahed had the best facilities, the best youth team development and the best coaches in the country. 'Football without the fans is not football,' says Al-Ahed's coach, Mohammed Sahel. 'Players cannot enjoy playing football. It is a show. You need the spectators.' He looks up with disappointment at the few dozen fans in the stands. 'Lebanon is a small country in football, but the last result [against South Korea] means people around the world will pay attention to Lebanese football players. It means they have quality.' Sahel singles out two Al-Ahed players in particular who he feels would make a name for themselves on the world stage: twenty-one-year-old winger Ahmad Zreik and striker Mahmoud El Ali. 'Mahmoud El Ali, after his performance in the last game, he is a big star for the national team,' states Sahel, before taking his players off the pitch and past the machine gun-wielding troops guarding the tunnel.

The match is an excruciatingly bad goalless stalemate. Both penalty boxes are so muddy that the ball simply comes to a halt in the puddles if it is passed along the ground. The only incident of note in the entire match is a penalty for Al-Ahed. Mahmoud El Ali steps up to take it, but the ball slows to a trickle on the viscous pitch and the goalkeeper easily gathers it before it can cross the line. Al-Ahed's other star player, Ahmad Zreik, is cursing under his breath as he leaves the field. He's used to better than this, having spent five years working in his uncle's Lebanese restaurant in Michigan and playing college soccer before Al-Ahed called him. 'Look at the field. It is not for soccer,' he says, pointing to what has now degenerated into a wholly brown rectangle of wet earth. 'I left here to go with my family to the US. But then the team [Al-Ahed] call me many times.' Zreik was one of the beneficiaries of Theo Bucker's new regime, and was put straight into the national team just a few weeks after returning from Michigan. 'Every day I worked fifteen hours in my uncle's restaurant, starting at 7 a.m., coming home at 10 p.m.,' Zreik recalls. His brief turn in college soccer attracted some interest from a few bigger teams but the training, the studying and the hours in his uncle's restaurant were too much for the money he was getting. 'I only go [to the US] to work to get money,' he says honestly. 'They [Ahed] gave me the same money I took there. I'll take the same money and I do what I love. I love soccer so I did that. It's good for me.'

Zreik wasn't too concerned about the wider social or political benefits that a united and successful Lebanese national team might have on the country. For him it was about escaping, getting to Europe and playing in the best leagues in the world. The best way for that to happen, he reasons, was to get to Brazil. 'The World Cup is very good for the players,' he says. 'If the players go [to Brazil] they get to play in the Emirates and other leagues. It is very good for the Lebanese player. Playing the next round [of World Cup qualification] means lots of people come and see you. It will give our players a very good chance to move abroad.' First there was a final training session with the national team and then a friendly with Qatar in Doha en route to Abu Dhabi. 'That was my dream when I was ten years old, you watch the World Cup and dream to play in the World Cup,' he says, even if the money, the rewards and the potential route out of Lebanon towards the glittering lights of European football were a more powerful motivator. 'This is the first time we have any professional football. Any player can play here and make a lot of money,' he says. But they might not stay for long. 'If you go to the World Cup,' he says, the light now fading and the cold becoming unbearable, 'I don't think any national team player will stay in Lebanon.'

The next day Zreik joins Bucker and the rest of the Lebanese squad to prepare. Even defeat against the UAE wouldn't be a disaster if other results went their way. Kuwait would have to beat South Korea in Seoul, a highly unlikely outcome. Still, Bucker, Zreik and the rest of the team are taking no chances. They talk of beating the UAE, and possibly topping their group, which would give them a much more favourable draw in the next round. If they are to beat the UAE, they will have to do it without a warm-up match. Overnight, the Qataris pull out of their scheduled friendly, a commonplace occurrence when you are at the bottom of the international game. The players arrive at the Safa club stadium in Beirut in low, blinding sunshine, the cold and mud of the previous day's game in Tripoli a distant memory. Bucker screams instructions to his players as he runs them through their paces. When training is finished he gathers the players to the dugout, banishes the two other journalists who had come to watch the session from the pitch and gives his last pep talk on Lebanese soil. But his loud Germanic bark can still be clearly heard from the car park, echoing around the empty stands. 'YOU are the IDEAL for Lebanon and Lebanese football,' he shouts. 'THINK: if you can't respect each other, how will other people here respect YOU?'

**

Abu Dhabi, United Arab Emirates. February 2012.

Abu Dhabi is coloured red, white and green but not, as it usually is on an international fixture, with the colour of the Emirati flag. It is the day of the UAE v Lebanon World Cup qualifier and the streets outside the capital's Al-Nahyan Stadium are filled with Lebanese fans of every religious and political persuasion. Everyone, it seems, is holding or wearing a Lebanese flag. Female volunteers are even stationed on the pavements to paint the Lebanese flag on to the faces of supporters. There are as many as 100,000 Lebanese expats in the UAE and 350,000 across the Persian Gulf. The civil war has spread its sons and daughters far and wide. One estimate suggests as many as fourteen million Lebanese have settled abroad, the vast majority of them in Brazil. 'It's an amazing feeling when we are all together supporting our team,' explains Ahmed and his wife, Roula, Lebanese expats from Abu Dhabi, as they take in the patriotic scene. Around them thousands more file into the stadium. Nearby, one man is struggling to hold a full-sized, and full-weight, replica of the World Cup which he had himself cast out of metal. 'If we qualify to the mondial, to the World Cup, it will be in Brazil so there are eight million Lebanese living in Brazil. We will fill all the stadiums there!' The turnout for the game was incredible but it also proved to be another example, after the South Korea game, of just how much the political classes in Lebanon had failed to engender any real and lasting feeling of identity beyond narrow religious sects. 'They [the politicians] have to learn from this otherwise it is no use,' Ahmed says. 'They have to learn that we are Lebanese. We are not religious. There is only one Lebanese flag.' Hundreds more surge past in a blur of red and white. 'We are all the same. We are one hand. In all circumstances,' Roula adds, before they too join the crowd.

It wasn't just Lebanon's expat community who had filled the stands. Nearby, Lebanon's team hotel is being deluged by fans and dignitaries, also draped in red, white and green, waiting to have their pictures taken with the team. Several politicians from the rival anti-Syrian March 14 and pro-Syrian March 8 factions are here, too, eager to show their support for the team and distance themselves from the sectarian backbiting that has brought the country to the brink of war so often. One politician in particular has good reason to resent being in the same room as the opposition. At twenty-nine, Nadim Gemayel is the youngest MP in the Lebanese parliament, but his name is tightly entwined with the past. He is the spitting image of his father, Bachir, who was briefly Lebanon's president elect. Under Lebanon's confessional political system, the position of president is always allocated to the Christians, the prime minister to the Sunnis, the speaker of the parliament to the Shia, and so on. But in 1982 Lebanon was under occupation by both Syria and Israel and in the grip of anarchy. Before Bachir could be sworn in he was assassinated when a bomb exploded at his Phalange party headquarters. Nadim was four months old. Among many Christians in Lebanon Bachir is still revered. During the 2009 parliamentary elections I walked through the streets of one Christian district as the results were announced. Street hawkers were selling T-shirts and pin badges, not with any of the current generation of political figures on them, but with a black and white, pop art profile of Bachir – handsome and young – taken a few months before he was killed at the age of thirty-four.

'We are all gathered, we are all united under our flag. This is a success for our team, a success for our country and not any one sectarian group,' Nadim says as we wait in the hotel lobby for a glimpse of the team. The national team offered both groups the chance to be on the same side for a change. I ask him about Ahmed and Roula, the supporters I had met outside, and the fans I had spoken to at the dreary 0-0 draw between Tripoli and Al-Ahed a few days before. They had all told me the same thing. The politicians should learn from the team, from the players and, in particular, from Theo Bucker. 'Yes, maybe, I think that's a good point. It is something that as politicians we have to take into consideration,' he agrees. 'We have to emphasise in another way to bring this into politics. This team went through all the sectarian complications and now they are here united all together holding the Lebanese flag.' He pointed to a smaller group of men in dark suits, the majority of whom wore large beards. 'There is a lot of members of parliament, from [the Shia political party] Amal, from March 14 and March 8, six or seven deputies. We are all united today to support our Lebanese team, this is clear.'

With two hours to go before kick-off, the members of the team emerge one by one into the packed lobby. They push through the fans, politicians and businessmen – both Christians and Muslims – as they congratulate them, ruffle their hair and place scarves with the Lebanese flag around their shoulders. Bucker emerges last – congratulated by everybody within arm's length of him – wide-eyed as if arriving at his own surprise birthday party.

**

Abu Dhabi's Al-Nahyan Stadium is a microcosm of the host's ambition, and also of its demographic reality. It is named after the

Abu Dhabi royal family that also rules the country's seven emirates. Twenty-foot-high colour portraits of the founder of the modern UAE, Sheikh Zayed, and the country's current president, Sheikh Khalifa, have been raised over the stands. Sheikh Mansour, the man who bought and transformed Manchester City, is a member of the Al-Nahyan family, too, brother of the president no less. Yet the stadium is small, reflecting the tiny crowds that most UAE league matches attract, and is attached to a luxury mall and a five-star hotel. The stadium is bereft of Emirati supporters; just a handful are here, wearing their traditional white national dress, the *dishdasha*. While one half is empty, the other is crammed with 10,000 Lebanese. Every Lebanese player holds his hand to his heart as the national anthem reverberates around the stadium.

Bucker's one selection headache is who to play in goal. Safa goalkeeper Ziad al-Samad had been first choice, but had suffered constant criticism in the press for his lack of height and his excess weight. Even though he had let no one down in qualification, Bucker replaces him with Abbas Hassan, a former Under 21 Swedish international who plays for IFK Norrköping in the Swedish first division. He is tall, handsome, slender and confident. He acts and *looks* like a good goalkeeper. Within twenty minutes, however, Hassan is picking the ball out of his net after an awful error. When the UAE captain Basheer Saeed floats a fairly tame free-kick over the wall, Hassan somehow manages to palm the ball into his own net. The crowd shrieks. His team-mates hold their heads in their hands. Hassan lies for what feels like an hour face down on the grass. Luckily, Mahmoud El Ali, the Al-Ahed striker who has been singled out by his club coach as the star to watch, bursts through and equalises before half-time. The bad news is that the Emirati goalkeeper hits him with such force that he ruptures a cruciate ligament, is stretchered off the pitch and out of the game for six months. It will turn out to be El Ali's last ever Lebanese national team goal, but not because of the injury he sustained.

Ahmad Zreik plays his part, too. With the UAE 2-1 up, it is his pace that finds the space for him to cross for another Al-Ahed team-mate, Hassan Maatouk, to equalise. Both of Lebanon's goals have been scored and made by players trained on pitches allegedly paid for by Hezbollah. The second half goes badly for Lebanon. They concede twice but, with South Korea scoring late on against Kuwait, it doesn't matter. When the referee blows the final whistle the team know they have made it to the final round of World Cup qualification for the first time in their history even after losing 4-2. The dream of reaching Brazil – thanks to the number of expatriates living there virtually a home tournament if they can somehow qualify – is still alive. Yet the team look devastated as they leave the pitch. By the full-time whistle most of the Lebanese fans have left. Those who stayed are booing the goalkeeper Abbas Hassan loudly as he walks past.

Lebanon reaching the fourth and final round was perhaps the only shock in 2014 Asian World Cup qualification. Iraq, like the Lebanese, had also managed to construct a successful multi-confessional team that had thrived. The Brazilian legend Zico was now in charge of a team that had some experience of victory. The Lions of Mesopotamia famously won the 2007 Asian Cup, the Asian equivalent of the Copa America or European Championships, when the country was in the darkest days of its civil war. Tens of thousands took to the streets of Baghdad to celebrate a victory for a team comprised of Sunni, Shia, Kurd and Turkmen. Hundreds of celebrating fans lost their lives as insurgents targeted anything and anyone who celebrated unity rather than sectarian division. Now, though, Zico had taken Iraq into the next round, hoping to emulate the 1986 team that made it to Mexico, although not the circumstances that surrounded that success. It would later emerge that the 1986 team had been terrorised by Uday Hussein, Saddam's sadistic eldest son, who controlled the team and the federation by fear, torturing players who underperformed or 'embarrassed' him. Unfancied Jordan had joined them in the next round at the expense of China, another billion people who wouldn't see their country at the finals. All the usual suspects eased through: Japan, Australia, Korea and Iran. Qatar, who had been awarded the right to host the 2022 World Cup before qualification began, had also made it. But only just.

Former England coach Peter Taylor had taken charge of the Bahrain national team in the aftermath of a revolution in the tiny Persian Gulf kingdom. With a population of just 1.3 million, Bahrain had come within a goal of becoming the smallest nation ever to qualify for the World Cup finals when they lost to New Zealand in an inter-continental playoff in the run-up to South Africa 2010. But, in 2011, the Arab world rose up in a series of pro-democracy and freedom protests. The Arab Spring had toppled Hosni Mubarak in Egypt and brought down the presidents of Yemen, Tunisia and, of course, seen Colonel Gaddafi lynched in Libya. In Bahrain the majority Shia population rose against the minority Sunni monarchy, but the protests were crushed. Among the protesters were several leading sportsmen and women, including key players in the national team: brothers A'ala and Mohamed Hubail and Sayed Mohamed Adnan, the cultured midfielder who missed a crucial penalty in Wellington when the match against New Zealand was still 0-0. The Bahraini authorities punished them for the insubordination. They were arrested and jailed. The Hubail brothers later alleged torture and they were banned from ever again playing for the national team. When interviewed by ESPN's investigative programme *E:60*, Peter Taylor seemed to have no idea who these players were. 'I knew nothing of the politics of the situation. I was just a coach, in charge of the football team. That was it,' he would later tell me on the phone, pleading his innocence, when he was back in the UK.

Even without Bahrain's key players – even if he didn't know he was actually missing his key players in the first place – Taylor had managed to keep the team's interest in World Cup qualification alive until the last group game. The problem was that to progress he needed Iran to beat Qatar in Tehran, and for Bahrain to beat Indonesia by nine goals. The game in Indonesia, despite the country having a population of 238 million people with an almost religious devotion to English football, was in chaos.

Endemic corruption and an unsanctioned breakaway league had meant that the majority of seasoned Indonesian internationals were not picked. They had lost every game in qualification and the Bahrain match did not start well when their goalkeeper was sent off after three minutes. The referee awarded four penalties, two of which were saved, and Bahrain went on to win 10-0. Bahrain would have made it, too, if it hadn't been for an eighty-fourth-minute Qatari equaliser in front of 90,000 fans at Iran's Azadi Stadium. That game finished 2-2 but the result in Manama was so suspicious that FIFA launched an investigation immediately after the match. 'We did nothing wrong,' Taylor pleaded after the game. 'There is no need for us to speak to FIFA. At the end of the day, the game was played and we did as well as we possibly could and played the strongest team we could.' Taylor seemed to be completely oblivious to the fact that match fixing might have taken place, especially during a World Cup qualifier. His competitive nature was disarmingly honest, too. 'We should have won by more than ten,' he added. 'We missed two penalties.'

Match fixing and corruption couldn't have been further from Theo Bucker's mind as he sat in the dugout of Al-Nahyan Stadium in Abu Dhabi watching his dejected players trudge off the pitch. They had qualified but it didn't taste like victory. Bucker was livid. 'We were not focused and were scared, we scored OWN GOALS!' he shouts incredulously as we both sat on the bench. His eyes were focused, not on me, but disapprovingly on his players. 'This was the aim we had from the beginning and when we started talking about this out loud people were laughing at us,' he says of the team's progress, for the first time showing a little happiness about Lebanon's historic qualification to the next round. 'Then we started to play good matches and win matches. We have to calculate that sometimes our progress is going in waves, up and down. But we have to recognise the trend. The crowd is one of the points I was counting on, it was an atmosphere like at home. Which is why I couldn't understand.' Bucker looked confused at first, then suspicious, as he tried to figure out

6

EGYPT, MOZAMBIQUE

Cairo, Egypt. February 2012.

Smoke still hangs over the bedraggled custodians of Tahrir Square. The haze has been here for months, a blend of smoke from the fires lit to burn rubbish and keep people warm at night, the stoves used to heat food and coffee for the merchants who do business here and, occasionally, the tear gas and fireworks that follow the periodic confrontations with the authorities. Flags are flying along the steel barriers between the street and the pavement; of Egypt, Palestine, Libya, Tunisia, and of the Free Syrian Army. The 25 January revolution is little over a year old now. The former president Hosni Mubarak, the dictator who had ruled Egypt with an iron fist for three decades, has gone, replaced by an army council and the promise of free and fair elections. A million people stood here, demanding their freedom, fighting the police. They celebrated in similar numbers when Mubarak stepped down, was arrested and then thrown into a Red Sea jail. His forced departure was watched by a mesmerised world. The Arab Spring had claimed Tunisia's president, seen Colonel Gaddafi lynched in the streets and, now, sent Mubarak to jail. But for those who still clung to Midan Tahrir, Freedom Square in English, a new Egypt is just a promise. A ragged crew of activists, refuseniks, street kids and hawkers belligerently remain. 'Revolutions have never lightened the burden of tyranny,' George Bernard Shaw wrote. 'They have only shifted it to another shoulder.'

Scepticism and optimism surround Tahrir Square. The walls around it are covered in graffiti denouncing SCAF, the Supreme Council for the Armed Forces – led by Field Marshal Tantawi – which now rules Egypt. The words on the walls in Arabic and English denounce the police and the army, America and Israel. Syria, too. One wall has a stencil image, repeated dozens of times, of the Syrian president Bashar al-Assad, a Hitler moustache and side parting superimposed on his features. A tent has been set up on a patch of ground nearby highlighting the war currently raging in Syria, a gruesome exhibition of photographs showing the corpses of dismembered women and children alongside cartoons decrying the world's inaction.

One flag, though, is flying more than any other, even more than the Egyptian flag. It is red, with a shield and an eagle; the flag of Al Ahly Football Club. Cairo, Egypt and Africa's most popular team has become an integral part of this revolution. At least, their supporters have. The Ahlawy, the team's ultras group, had long been an anti-authoritarian irritant to the police when Mubarak was in power. During the revolution they had played an instrumental role in Tahrir Square, an army 15,000-strong that swung the balance when the activists and the Muslim Brotherhood fought the police during those famous battles a year earlier. Their flags and their songs had become revolutionary flags and revolutionary songs. I had watched smaller protests break out around the square. It was the Ahlawy with their flares and organised chaos that had formed the nucleus of the protests.

They had made their sacrifices, too. A few weeks earlier a football match took place between Al Ahly and Al Masry in the Suez city of Port Said. Al Masry had sprung a surprise, unexpectedly winning 3-1. At the final whistle Al Masry's fans had stormed the pitch and attacked the thousands of Ahlawy who had travelled for the match. The sole exit out of the stand had been locked, the floodlights turned off. When they were turned on again, seventy-two Al Ahly fans were dead. The incident had raised many questions. Why had the gates been locked? Why were the floodlights cut? Why did so many young men die? The Ahlawy blamed the police and the army, payback time for their role in defeating the state in Tahrir Square. I had spent the past few days with them as they marched in their tens of thousands in Cairo and Alexandria, demanding justice and commemorating their fallen comrades.

Bob Bradley had been there, too, at one of the marches, showing his respect for the dead. A few miles out of town, in a smart hotel far from the anarchy of central Cairo, the coach of the Egyptian national team is trying to piece that team back together. He is easy to pick out in the lobby, the one man in a room who always looks as if he's waiting impatiently for a train to take him somewhere else. 'All the skills you have tried to hone over the years,' he says as we sit down. 'This is a test of all of them.'

Bradley speaks with measured intensity, chewing over every sentence before he delivers it. He hadn't expected an easy ride in charge of the Pharaohs. He has been in the job for six months now, having been let go by the US national team despite qualifying for the 2010 World Cup, where they reached the knockout stages, making it to the final of the 2009 Confederations Cup and winning a Gold Cup, too. He'd been hired in Egypt's post-revolutionary squall, where football was just another battlefront for the revolution. The league had been postponed because of the instability, and then suspended due to violence, thanks largely to the security vacuum, and then restarted. Olympic qualification had been cancelled too. When Bradley arrived the league had just been suspended again. He had been in the job for six months now and not yet taken charge of a competitive match. His first, a friendly against Brazil in Qatar's capital Doha, ended in a 2-0 defeat, but he saw enough in the squad to realise that the team could go far. 'I knew they had a group of players that had been the nucleus that won the Africa Cup of Nations in '06, '08 and 2010, and that [previous coach] Hassan Shehata was a good man,' he says when I ask what he knew of Egyptian football before he got here. Bradley had met Egypt's previous coach when the US played them at the 2009 Confederations Cup. Shehata had been Egypt's most successful coach, winning three Africa Cup of Nations in a row. But he had been seen as being too close to Mubarak and the previous regime and had to go. 'The way they thought of it in Egypt, this was their golden generation,' he says. 'I ended up coming here, speaking to the people. The bottom line is you're now trying to size up the situation from a football perspective, building a new team. The dream is the World Cup in 2014. But obviously there's a lot more to it.'

A lot more to it. The US had planned a friendly against Egypt in Cairo two weeks after the January revolution. It was cancelled and Bradley watched the revolution on TV from afar, not knowing that a few months later he would be sacked by the US team before heading to Egypt himself. He adapted well to the chaos of Cairo and settled down to life in Africa's largest city. Most of the city's wealthy abandon central Cairo the first moment they can, to escape the gridlock and the pollution. Bradley was different. He and his wife moved into an apartment on Zamalek, an island on the Nile, in the heart of the city. He walked around the streets speaking to fans who begged him to play Mohamed Aboutrika, Egypt's legendary forward who was a hero to millions across the world because of his piousness and desire to stand up for the poor and disenfranchised. Bradley tried to blend in – as much as a white, bald American with piercing blue eyes could blend in. He read, asked questions, tried to understand. 'When I took the job it coincided with some of the protests that turned violent,' he recalls. 'I'm one that asks questions. I asked: who goes to Tahrir Square? Is there a real agenda? Are there people there planted by others to create problems? You start to recognise the different levels of each situation. You also get a real sense how football is part of all this revolution. Clearly the football and politics in different ways are totally connected.'

He would soon see how closely linked the two were. On 1 February 2012, a few weeks earlier than our meeting, Bradley was travelling to the Cairo International Stadium to watch the second half of Zamalek, the other half of Cairo's footballing duopoly, and Ismaily play in the Egyptian league. The league had started again after a forty-day suspension. 'That day Masry and Ahly was in Port Said but it's a couple of hours away,' he says. 'Some people told us that there might be some trouble at the game. But let's get it clear. We heard the fans didn't get on. We watched the first half on TV. It was a competitive game. Before we left there were a few things that were concerning. Fans running on the field, fireworks. We went to the Cairo Stadium and there's a TV in the lobby area. We see the third Masry goal and the whistle and see fans running on the field, and the Ahly players sprinting off the field.'

It was in the next fifteen minutes that the young supporters of Al Ahly were killed. Eyewitness reports and medical records show that the majority had been crushed to death in a tiny exit tunnel under the stadium. The door had been locked. One supporter had left early to use the bathroom. When he returned the gates were shut fast and his friends crushed on the other side. He tried to break the lock with a stone, but the gate collapsed on him. He was the first to die. Others had been stabbed to death or thrown off the top of the stands on to the concrete below. As news of the tragedy filtered through, Zamalek fans began setting fire to the stadium. Bradley quickly left. 'By the time we go into the federation it's clear that this was not a typical case of fan violence,' he says. 'There was one incredible question and answer on Egyptian TV with the captain of Masry. He didn't play but talked about what they saw. He says something to the [Masry] supporters and the supporters didn't recognise him and he's thinking: "these aren't our supporters".'

The Port Said massacre stunk. The police and the army were nowhere to be seen. The gates had been locked and no effort was made to prevent the Al Masry fans attacking Ahly's supporters or the players, who fled to the dressing room where the dead and dying were being brought. 'You know the story?' Bradley asks. I didn't. 'Here's a young fan in a locker room. The fan says to Aboutrika: "Captain, I always wanted to meet you."' The fan died in Aboutrika's arms. In the immediate aftermath of the match, Aboutrika and several other Al Ahly players retired from football. SCAF blamed football hooliganism for the deaths, but no one was buying that. For Bradley the tragedy meant two things. 'First and foremost our thoughts and prayers are with the young people who lost their lives,' he says, looking at his hands as he speaks. 'Young people who, in a group as the ultras, played a big role in the revolution. To think young, talented, intelligent people lose their lives at a football match blows you away. You think of the people who were in the stadium that night.'

Secondly, it also meant he didn't have a national team to coach. The up and coming Africa Cup of Nations qualifier against the Central African Republic, which was to be his first competitive match in charge of Egypt, was cancelled. He was at this five-star resort, not out of choice, but because the training camp for the game was due to take place there. Bradley decided to gather what players he could anyway. But the players of Al Ahly made up the vast majority of the national team: perhaps eight or nine in any starting eleven. They were emotionally shattered by Port Said and the bloodshed they had witnessed first-hand. And, besides, no one knew whether Mohamed Aboutrika and the others would ever choose to return. 'I spoke to them and at this moment those players need time,' Bradley says. 'Right now we have left them and little by little we will find the right time and the right way.'

In the aftermath of Port Said the league was cancelled and the Egyptian FA resigned. There would be no football in Egypt for a while. Yet, in the weeks that followed, the Ahlawy took to the streets. They protested in Tahrir Square. Their numbers and their legend grew rather than diminished because of Port Said. Bradley and his wife, Lindsay, joined them on the streets, marching alongside the Ahlawy in a rally to Sphinx Square. 'We would go to Sphinx Square as a sign of respect for those who lost their lives and a sign of respect for the families,' he recalls. 'In a moment like that I think it's important you are with the people. It was a simple sign of respect and a simple sign of being with football people, knowing this was a senseless tragedy in a country that is trying so hard to move on and a country we have grown to love.'

The fallout from Port Said would last longer than anyone could have predicted. SCAF's original explanation for the tragedy – mindless violence – was rejected by the Egyptian public. There was too much evidence, too many suspicious circumstances and coincidences. The Ahlawy believed they had been punished for their role in the revolution. The fans of Al Ahly had fought the police in the four years before January 2011, fought them on the barricades in Tahrir Square and, now, vowed to protest and prevent the league from restarting until they got justice for those who had died. Bradley, too, believed that Port Said was more than just fan violence. 'People are protesting because they want the handover to civilian rule to move faster,' he says of his time speaking to people on the streets during those marches. 'And then something happens in Port Said and now there are camera reports that the gates are welded shut. One of the first things you see is the police doing nothing. When I ask opinions of people, they say the military in their own way is trying to say: "Fine. You want us out so this is what it is going to be like without us."' We've been talking for over an hour now, and he is no closer to an answer. 'There's been a number of protests that have turned violent since the revolution and if Port Said is part of bringing about this change then I think it will prove even more that this was not just fan violence,' he says. 'The flipside is I don't think you can come here and be the national team coach and be oblivious to all this, have your head in the sand when you have players and a team that are so deeply involved in all these things.'

The team. Bradley was here to build a team. Now, because of the revolution and because of Port Said, he had a much more important role to play. To pick up the pieces and build a team that wouldn't just make it to the World Cup finals in Brazil, but could show a divided country a positive reflection of itself. 'A national team, to be successful anywhere, has a connection to the people. Now more than ever here,' he says. 'Everyone has a dream for the World Cup. So that responsibility, what it means when we step on the field, is making sure that we're representing what these people are all about.' The World Cup, Bradley hopes, will be his own small contribution to the revolution. 'Everyone you talk to says: "we must go to the World Cup,"' he explains. It is time to go. It is late. Bradley is taking a training session early in the morning and I have to catch a bus back to central Cairo. We shake hands. No one knows when football will return to Egypt, nor whether the price of watching those young men die in Port Said will be too much for Al Ahly's players to pay. Maybe it will be too much for Bradley as well.

It is another four months before Egypt are due to play their first 2014 World Cup qualifier against Mozambique. Egypt have been drawn in a group alongside Guinea and Zimbabwe. The winner of the group will then contest a two-leg play-off against one of the other group winners. African qualification is long and gruelling. Transport infrastructure is non-existent between some countries. The distance and heat of central and southern Africa are a problem, as are the poor facilities, food and water. It is a long way from New Jersey, Bradley's home, and a long way from the world-class facilities that the US men's national team is used to. Back then Bradley had a well-oiled organisation behind him, engineering marquee friendlies against the world's best. Now he is arranging his own matches anywhere he can, calling in favours and trying to give his players some kind of practice. He has arranged two friendlies, one in Lebanon and the other in Sudan. With the league cancelled it is the only football any of his team can get.

The Mozambique game is due to be played in Cairo but that is unlikely given the instability. Will Bradley last that long? Anything can happen between now and then. A presidential election had been planned, coincidentally at the same time as the Mozambique game. Egypt might go up in flames. 'When you're a leader in any way, when there's a tragedy, how you react, respond, this is important,' Bradley says as we part. 'We are trying in a small way

TOP Tursunzode, Tajikistan, June 2011. The Palestine national team wait in the tunnel before their first Brazil 2014 qualification match against Afghanistan.

ABOVE Al Ram, West Bank, July 2011. A packed Faisal al Husseini stadium watch the second leg of Palestine versus Afghanistan. It was Palestine's first ever home World Cup match.

RIGHT A member of the Afghanistan national team sits dejected after their 1-1 draw with Palestine.

ABOVE Port au Prince, Haiti, September 2011. A hand-painted sign advertises Haiti's first home match – a World Cup qualifier against the tiny US Virgin Islands – since an earthquake devastated the country killing hundreds of thousands of people.

LEFT An armed guard working for the Haiti Football Federation patrols the entrance to the Sylvio Cator stadium before Haiti's final training session.

BELOW It was a cakewalk for Haiti, who 'stomped' on the US Virgin Islands 6-0 in front of a frenzied crowd. Haiti would finish second in their group and miss out on Brazil.

RIGHT Kigali, Rwanda, November 2011. Ball boys waiting in the Amahoro Stadium for Rwanda's qualification match against Eritrea.

RIGHT The marching band, dressed in oversized uniforms, wait for their cue to play the Rwanda and Eritrea national anthems.

BELOW Rwanda and Eritrea's captains exchange pennants before the game, which saw Rwanda progress to the next round. Most of the Eritrea team would later defect and claim political asylum abroad.

LEFT Zagreb, Croatia, March 2013. Ultra nationalist Croatian fans gather in Zagreb's main square before their team's match against archrivals Serbia. All away fans were banned for both games in Zagreb and Belgrade.

LEFT Žilina, Slovakia, September 2013. A young Bosnian ultra shows off his tattoos before his team's 2-1 victory against Slovakia. The Dragons would go on to qualify for their first finals since independence.

BELOW Bucharest, Romania, September 2013. Fans of Steaua Bucharest arrive at Romania's national stadium to confront supporters of Hungary, their historical rivals. Riots broke out throughout the city.

ABOVE Rio de Janeiro, Brazil, June 2013. Riot police regroup after firing tear gas, rubber bullets and flash grenades at protesters angry at the cost of hosting the World Cup.

RIGHT Belo Horizonte, Brazil, June 2013. Two protesters are treated for tear gas blindness by volunteer medics after violence broke out during the Confederations Cup semi-final between Brazil and Uruguay, taking place nearby.

RIGHT As many as 50,000 people had marched on the stadium. Buildings and cars were set on fire. The sign says 'Deaths in hospital queues and money for the cup. Democracy.'

BELOW After nine hours the police regain the streets, arresting protesters and looters alike.

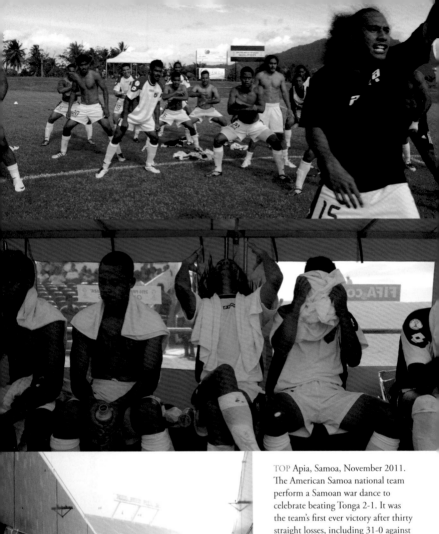

TOP Apia, Samoa, November 2011. The American Samoa national team perform a Samoan war dance to celebrate beating Tonga 2-1. It was the team's first ever victory after thirty straight losses, including 31-0 against Australia in 2001.

ABOVE American Samoa's star player was Jaiyah Saelua (centre). She became the first transgender player to start a World Cup match.

LEFT Tampa, Florida, United States, June 2012. The Antigua and Barbuda national team are rained off the pitch during their final training session before the tiny islands took on the United States at the Raymond James Stadium.

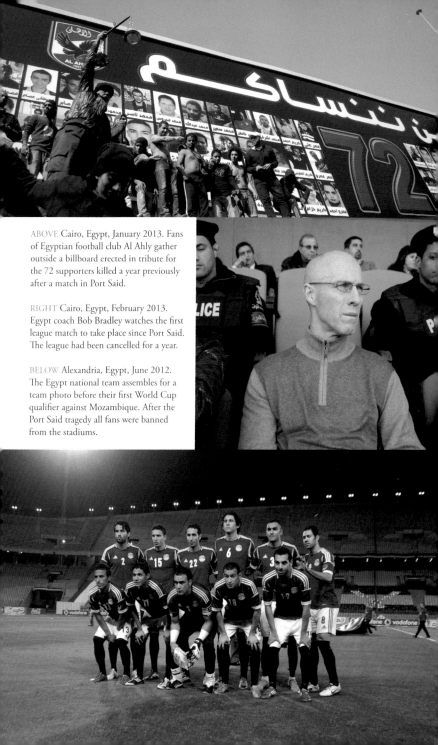

ABOVE Cairo, Egypt, January 2013. Fans of Egyptian football club Al Ahly gather outside a billboard erected in tribute for the 72 supporters killed a year previously after a match in Port Said.

RIGHT Cairo, Egypt, February 2013. Egypt coach Bob Bradley watches the first league match to take place since Port Said. The league had been cancelled for a year.

BELOW Alexandria, Egypt, June 2012. The Egypt national team assembles for a team photo before their first World Cup qualifier against Mozambique. After the Port Said tragedy all fans were banned from the stadiums.

Excited fans with their tickets before the match: Palestine versus Afghanistan (*above*), United States versus Antigua and Barbuda (*left*), Norway versus Iceland (*below left*), and Romania versus Hungary (*below right*).

to help the Egyptian people. When we are with the national team we set an example.' I ask him, finally, how he would like to be remembered when his time in charge of the Pharaohs comes to an end. 'That we qualified for the World Cup in 2014, *Inshallah*,' Bradley replies. 'That would fit in such a significant and important way with everything that has gone on. It's what the people talk about. It's what they dream about.'

I take the bus back to Cairo, past the rows of trucks full of armed soldiers, past the graffiti-covered walls denouncing the military, past the groups of dozens of small, bickering protesters and back to Tahrir Square, and the flagsellers, where the Al Ahly eagle and shield is flying highest. The World Cup seems very far away.

**

Alexandria, Egypt. June 2012.

The Borg el Arab is a white elephant. It is Egypt's biggest stadium, isolated in the desert on the outskirts of the northern port city of Alexandria. As many as 86,000 fans could come and watch a match here, as they did when the 2009 Under 20s World Cup was hosted by Egypt. The Egyptian army's stadium had been built especially for the occasion. Inside, the stadium is still immaculate, with a running track around the pitch. High up in the main stand is a large viewing platform, a huge, bulletproof glass box built especially for Hosni Mubarak and his wife, Suzanne, so that they could watch the opening game of the tournament without fear of assassination. No football has taken place here since then, yet the stadium has been dutifully maintained by the army. The grass is cut and watered regularly and the seats swept of dust and sand from the desert storms that pass over it. But a match is at last due to take place here in a few days' time. Egypt is about to play Mozambique in its first 2014 World Cup qualifier. It is four months since I met Bob Bradley in Cairo. He is still in his job and is finally about to set out on the long road to Brazil.

Egypt remains in a state of chaos and the match has been moved from Cairo to the Borg el Arab Stadium in Alexandria. Not because it is the biggest, or the best, or to give the maximum number of fans the chance to see their heroes in a country where the league is still suspended after Port Said. All the supporters have been banned from attending any home games, which is just as well. FIFA had also punished Egypt for a series of security lapses during the last World Cup campaign. The match is also taking place during Egypt's first free and fair presidential elections in the country's long history. A field of revolutionaries, religious figures and former regime politicians ran in the first round, with the top two qualifying for a run-off a few weeks later. Mohamed Morsi, the candidate of the Muslim Brotherhood – the Islamist organisation banned by Mubarak for fear that it would destabilise the country with its fundamentalism – won the most votes. He would stand against Ahmed Shafiq, a military figure who had served in Mubarak's government but who was running on a law, order and security platform.

The Mozambique game is being played slap-bang in the middle of the first and second round of voting. Given that the league remains cancelled, and that the ultras of Al Ahly, the Ahlawy, are still a potent protest force on the streets, it was decided that the match should be moved to Alexandria. An empty Borg el Arab suits everyone, it seems, except the fans, the players and Bob Bradley. At a nearby hotel, the only building anywhere near the stadium, Bob Bradley is waiting finally to take charge of his first competitive match with his Egypt team. It is almost ten months since his appointment. The hotel is so isolated I've had to flag down a passing truck and beg a lift. 'It has been incredibly difficult to find the right way to think about Port Said,' Bradley says after we greet each other. 'Playing for the national team is a bigger responsibility than ever now. The memory of the tragedy is being carried with some of them in a strong, positive way. In other cases, those terrible memories are still nightmares. The idea of getting to a World Cup now burns inside all of them.'

Bradley spent the months that followed Port Said trying to keep his players occupied with matches he'd managed to arrange. 'When all of a sudden there's no league, players are unsure of their careers or being paid anything at all,' he explains. 'We've been to Qatar a couple of times, Dubai, Sudan twice, Lebanon. We've played so many different teams, many African teams.' Egypt were winning matches, too, eleven out of the thirteen Bradley had organised.

Slowly, Bradley brought the Al Ahly players back into the fold. Mohamed Aboutrika and others reversed the decisions they made right after Port Said to retire. Although the league was now finished, Al Ahly still had some competitive games as they had qualified for the African Champions League. The club had vowed to win the competition in honour of the 'Port Said martyrs'. Aboutrika had returned to the team and played a crucial role, as he always did, in their progress. He came on at half-time during a match with Stade Malien, from Mali. Ahly were 2-0 down on aggregate and heading out until Aboutrika scored an incredible second-half hat-trick. 'We respected what the players had experienced,' Bradley says. The key to Egypt's World Cup successes, though, was Aboutrika. 'He's an incredible man, intelligent, high character, respected at the highest level in Egypt, in Africa and the Middle East,' Bradley says with pride. 'When we talked to him, the possibility of getting one more chance to go to the World Cup was something that meant so much to him. You could see in Aboutrika's eyes this meant so much for him.'

The World Cup had become something of a sore point in Egypt long before the revolution. Egypt had qualified for two finals in the past, both hosted by Italy. In 1934 (where they qualified by beating British Mandated Palestine, a forerunner of the Israel national team) they played only one game in the finals, losing 4-2 against Hungary. At Italia '90 they were drawn in the same group as England, Ireland and Holland. It was a dire group which produced few goals yet Egypt had drawn against both the Dutch and the Irish. In Egypt's final group match a second-half Mark Wright goal handed England a 1-0 victory, eliminating the

Pharaohs in the process. For all their recent World Cup qualification failures, over the past decade Egypt have dominated African football. Al Ahly have won six African Champions League titles, the national team have won four Africa Cup of Nations titles since 1998 and yet they cannot turn their continental domination into winning a place at football's biggest event. Qualification for the 2010 World Cup in South Africa was a case in point. Egypt was drawn in the same final group as Algeria. There has been bad blood between the two countries ever since a crucial qualification match in Cairo for Italia '90. Egypt won but the so-called 'death match' was marred by riots on and off the pitch. The Egyptian team doctor even lost an eye in the melee.

The two met again at the Cairo International Stadium in 2009. Egypt had to win 2-0 to force a play-off, which they did, but the circumstances were brutal. I had been in Cairo in the run-up to the match and watched as the state-run press whip the population into an anti-Algerian frenzy; watched Algerian fans being attacked by gangs of men; saw how the windows of the Algerian team bus were smashed on the way to the hotel, injuring several players, and then reported – and taken as fact by every Egyptian I met – that the Algerian players had injured themselves. 'The Algerians are scared, that is why they want to humiliate Egypt,' they would tell me. Almost everyone I had spoken to knew someone who knew someone who knew the Egyptian bus driver who had driven that coach and said that the Algerians had smashed the windows, then cut themselves in order to have the match cancelled. The problem was that a FIFA representative as well as a French film crew from Canal Plus had seen the whole thing. But that didn't matter; the lie was told and believed. It was now impossible to erase. Mubarak met with the team before the game, his sons and heirs apparent wrapping themselves in the Egyptian flag and the presumed reflected glory of the national team. The noise during the match was frightening. When Egypt won 2-0 riots broke out around the stadium and around the world between Algerian and Egyptian fans. But Algeria would have the last laugh. In the play-off in neutral Sudan, Algeria won 1-0. They, and not the greatest Egyptian team of all time, would go to South Africa.

The circumstances in which the game against Mozambique is being played could not be more different. Mubarak and his sons have gone, under arrest and awaiting trial. Before, political arguments were unheard of on the street, lest you were overheard by an informer or a policeman. Now the country discusses, argues and sometimes fights over its political views. You see it in Tahrir Square and elsewhere: groups of people arguing their point of view. Sometimes it ends in a fist fight but mostly they agree to disagree and go their separate ways. The Egyptian squad is no different. 'I still ask a lot of questions and listen to the discussions that go on,' Bradley explains of the politics within the group. Some are well known for their piety: Mohamed Aboutrika kneels and kisses the grass every time he scores. Others, like former Borussia Dortmund striker Mohamed Zidan, have been pictured kissing Mubarak's hand in the past. 'You see the players in discussion with the team staff. I try to listen and in recent weeks, as the election got closer and the run-off, I can tell when a political conversation takes place because it has a very different tone. When we're in camps you can't try to talk about football all the time.' Bradley stops to explain himself. 'I call it football now, not soccer,' he says a little embarrassed.

Bradley now has a full team to choose from, even if their preparations have been the stuff of nightmares. The Ahly players are back and others have emerged from overseas, too. There is Mohamed Salah, a young winger who has just started to make a name for himself at Basel in the Swiss league, and Ahmed Hegazy, who's just moved to Fiorentina in Italy. There was also Adam El-Abd, a twenty-seven-year-old defender who played in English football's second tier for Brighton and Hove Albion. 'Yeah, it 'as, to be fair,' he replies in his south coast British accent when I ask whether it was always a dream of his to play for the Egyptian national team. 'It's been one of my dreams to play for the national team because my dad is Egyptian and he's the one that taught me football and he's a very proud man to see me get a call-up.' El-Abd was born in England and raised in English football. He is a no-nonsense central defender with a shaved head and what looks like a broken nose. When he made his debut in a friendly against Cameroon, one Egyptian fan edited a show reel of El-Abd's contributions to the game and uploaded it on YouTube. It wasn't what Egyptian fans were used to. They had been raised on pace, cultured movement and delicate, technical interplay. This was a video of crunching tackles and long clearances booted high into the stands. But that is what they wanted. As one Egypt fan told me: 'Egypt needs a little English steel in the back.' Not that El-Abd intimidates off the pitch. He speaks with a friendly, almost Beckhamesque politeness. 'It was a great moment to make my debut and I enjoyed it,' he says of the Cameroon game, although he doesn't speak his team-mates' language yet. 'Arabic? Yeah, it's difficult, I'm learning as I go,' he says. 'But football is a universal language so it's not difficult to pick it up. I've learned a few phrases.'

Which is the most useful one you've learned, I ask.

'*Ta'ala*,' he says quickly, pronouncing it 'tar-ar-lar' in his heavy English accent. 'Which means "come here".' Despite making his debut for Egypt under Bradley, El-Abd can't play in the Mozambique game. He has heard that morning that his Egyptian passport won't be ready in time. 'Not going to happen. Got passport issues,' he says. 'I came out here two weeks ago and was aware it could be a problem. One of the delays is that I'm a dual citizen so exempt from military service.' But he will sit and watch the game from the bench and prepare himself for the next round of World Cup matches. He, too, watched back home as the revolution unfolded and hopes that the national team can play its part. 'Yeah, we got relatives who are out and about amongst it,' he says, referring to the protests in Tahrir Square. 'It's all going off. But it's good for the country. It's on the up.' El-Abd might never have represented England, but Egypt needs him. They had no one else quite like him. 'The dream is to play in central defence and make it to the World Cup,' he says. 'But first I've got to get a passport.'

Bob Bradley has also been picking up the odd Arabic phrase as he has gone along, but he has heard some words more than any others. 'I don't know much Arabic but I know *muntakhab*, national team, and *Kas al Aalam*,' he says, 'World Cup.'

**

The Borg el Arab Stadium may be miles from anywhere, but the military are not taking any chances. My taxi can't get anywhere near the stadium. It is late in the afternoon and as the sun sets a line of military personnel, wearing white shirts and white trousers, stretches out beyond the horizon on both sides. A coachload of journalists are trying to get in but are being prevented by an army checkpoint; every passport and ID is examined. The Borg el Arab is a handsome stadium, in a very modern way; a huge bowl that has seen perhaps half a dozen football matches in its short life. The seats in one stand have been painted in the colours of the flag, with EGYPT spelled out in gold in the middle. It is Friday, the Islamic holy day, and match officials are spreading whatever fabric they have to pray in the concourses, in the cafeteria and by the side of the pitch. The Egyptian journalists join them. Several hundred police officers in riot gear protect the pitch and the tunnel from no one in particular. Adam El-Abd is sitting in his training gear in the Egypt dugout, looking for all the world like an Englishman. He is slurping on a cup of milky tea as the substitutes join him.

A military band marches on to the grass before arranging itself into two perfect squares in the centre circle. The two teams enter the pitch to nothing but the sound of FIFA's irritating anthem, before lining up for their own national anthems. Bob Bradley stands to attention as the full military band plays. In front of him his players all sing proudly. 'We can't count on the fans to pull us through,' he had told me before the game. 'But if the stadium was big enough, every single person in Egypt would be there with us.' Despite the sterile environment, Egypt slowly and efficiently constrict Mozambique. I am standing by the touchline with the photographers, closer than I'd ever been to a World Cup match before. Aboutrika glides silently around the pitch like a bow-legged ghost. He finds space where he should have no good reason to find it, appearing behind an opposition player, receiving the ball and feeding it to a team-mate before any Mozambique player knows he's been there. Bradley stands close to the action, arms crossed, observing with the intense air he has become known for. The first half finishes goalless, but Egypt don't panic. In the second half Ahmed Hegazy, Fiorentina's young centre-back, heads the ball across goal to his fellow centre-back, Mahmoud Fathalla, who slides in to give the Pharaohs the lead. Fatallah falls to his knees and kisses the grass. His team-mates do likewise, including Essam El-Hadary, Egypt's goalkeeper, at the other end of the pitch. He gets up and points both his hands to the sky, to God.

The second goal follows shortly afterwards. Mohamed Zidan is fed the ball through the centre and shoots. It hits the inside of the post, rebounds off the Mozambique goalkeeper's head and into the empty net. It should, by rights, be an own goal, but Zidan kisses the ground, too. FIFA somehow still chalk it up as his goal. The match finishes 2-0. Bradley embraces each and every player as they come off the pitch. 'It feels good,' he says as he walks to the tunnel, letting his players go first. 'It's the first game, so you always want to get a good start. This is an important first step. There were a lot of positives, many positives.' The Egyptian news media descend chaotically on Bradley's post-match news conference. He has been praised by journalists for his grace under fire, for marching with the Ahlawy after Port Said, for donating money to the families of those who had died in the tragedy, for visiting a children's cancer hospital and donating money to them, too. One Egyptian journalist chases after him, calling him Captain Bob. It is a nickname that will stick with him throughout the campaign. Pressmen, players, taxi drivers, bakers and doormen will all shout after Captain Bob. 'This first win in World Cup qualification was for all the people of Egypt,' he tells the packed press conference a few moments later, dedicating victory to the nation. 'We talked before the game to look into the stands and to see ninety million fans,' he says. 'We knew they were all with us here tonight.'

The victory against Mozambique, the birthplace of the late Eusébio, one of the greatest players of all time even if he did decide to represent Portugal, was routine. The match in Guinea's capital Conakry nine days later was anything but. In front of a packed crowd, and in sweltering heat, Guinea went into half-time 1-0 up. But Mohamed Aboutrika scored with a brilliant volley at the start of the second before scoring a penalty shortly afterwards when Guinea's goalkeeper was sent off. It looked as if Egypt would start their campaign with two wins out of two, but a brilliant last-minute solo goal by Alhassane Bangoura, a striker who plays for Rayo Vallecano in Spain's La Liga, seemed to have earned Guinea a point. A point away from home would have been an acceptable result for Bradley, but in the fourth minute of injury time, Basel's talented winger Mohamed Salah broke free on the right and his cross shot beat the goalkeeper. The referee blew his whistle and the match ended 3-2 to the Pharaohs. Bradley and the bench celebrated together. 'It had been a tough place to come,' Bradley would later tell me. 'The heat was incredible and the country was so poor. Kids would be hanging through windows of the dressing room. We'd passed out what we could for them, pens, bottles of water, anything.'

Back in Egypt I took a bus to the capital and left on a flight the next morning. Later that day Hosni Mubarak was sentenced to life imprisonment. A few weeks later it emerged that Mohamed Zidan, the former Borussia Dortmund player who 'scored' the second goal against Mozambique, would never play a role for Egypt again either. The Egyptian FA alleged that he refused to play for Egypt when called up for the next round of fixtures, the home and away Africa Cup of Nations qualifiers against the Central African Republic that had been postponed in the aftermath of Port Said. They slapped on him a life ban from the national team, accusing him of preferring to travel to China to inquire

7

ANTIGUA AND BARBUDA, UNITED STATES

Bradenton, Florida, USA. June 2012.

Peter Byers and Olson Forde are standing on the edge of a man-made lake, squabbling like children over who gets to hold the fishing rod. The two players for the Antigua and Barbuda national team are still in their training kit and have retired to the lake to fish, but not for relaxation like the other surprised fisherman at the upmarket IMG sports academy and gated community complex near Tampa, Florida. The men around them have all stopped and put their rods down to watch the melee unfold, which is largely good-natured. Byers is Antigua and Barbuda's top scorer in 2014 World Cup qualification while Forde is the team's reserve goalkeeper. They have had enough of the low-calorie, super-healthy, high-performance, nutritionist-approved meals they have been served since they arrived in Florida a week ago in preparation for their next World Cup qualifier. This match is slightly different from the previous six that Antigua and Barbuda have won, largely at a stroll, destroying Caribbean island teams with impunity as they did so. In a few days they will be involved in what must be ranked as one of the greatest mismatches in the history of sport. Not that Byers and Forde look nervous or preoccupied with anything other than going after better food. They have borrowed a rod, line and a hook and are now fishing for their dinner.

'I'm from the ghetto in Antigua, I know what to do with the fish,' laughs Byers, showing a large gap between his teeth, after winning the battle for the rod. Forde has given up his claim and is now advising Byers where to cast his line. Behind the two players sits a plastic bowl half full of bluegill fish. They flap disconsolately, gasping their last breaths. 'We're gonna steam 'em up,' Byers explains, gesturing to the fish behind him, when I ask what he's going to do with them. 'I'm used to catching fish bigger than me!' he boasts, listing his greatest triumphs. Blue marlin, swordfish, tuna. His rod dips as another bluegill nibbles at his hook. Byers yanks it hard and reels in quickly, landing the fish on the grass. But he isn't satisfied with his catch and gently unhooks it. It's too small to eat, he says, and he throws it back into the lake. It will live to fight another day.

Bradenton is an unassuming town of some 50,000 people a few miles south of Tampa, yet it is something of a Petri dish for the United States Soccer Federation. Since 1999 the USSF has run an Under 17s residency programme here for the brightest and best American talent. Players like Landon Donovan and Michael Bradley have graduated from Bradenton. It was also here that a thirteen-year-old Freddy Adu was brought when his prodigious, but, in the end, unfulfilled talent was first discovered. The rest of the sprawling complex of upmarket condos, tennis courts, American football fields, baseball mounds, soccer pitches, manicured lawns, golf carts and lakes are usually given over to wealthy summer school kids looking to hone their sporting skills. Or, if you could afford it, you could simply purchase a condo and live within its gates, guarded around the clock. A house would set you back anything up to $3 million. It isn't a place in which the Antiguans would normally train. It isn't a place that the Antiguans could normally afford. And it certainly isn't a place where international footballers are seen fishing for their supper. According to Joe, an elderly former baseball pro who moved to Florida for some peace, quiet and fishing, and from whom the players have commandeered their rod, it is the first time he's seen an athlete fish for his dinner in the lake. He warns the players that bluegills are not the only creatures that lurk beneath the water. Alligators live here, too. I take a step back from the edge. Byers and Forde don't move. 'Alligators?' Byers snorts dismissively. 'We ain't afraid of nothing.'

Just as well. Antigua and Barbuda, with a population of 81,000 people, will play the United States (pop: 312 million) in a few days' time. The match will take place in the vast Raymond James Stadium, built for the sport that most Americans regard as the truest form of football. Its open stands are home to NFL side the Tampa Bay Buccaneers, perhaps most famous for being the first love – if that's the right word – of the Glazer family that owns Manchester United. It is a stadium that holds almost as many spectators as the entire population of Antigua and Barbuda.

When the bowl is full of fish, Byers and Forde hand back the rod and thank a slightly bemused Joe before taking the haul back to their shared apartment in a building overlooking the lake. Within a few minutes the place is full of smoke. The fish have been doused in pepper sauce and Byers is now frying them one by one in the pan before dishing them out with a spatula on to the plates of four expectant team-mates. Byers serves himself last, sits down at the table and, holding a fried bluegill in both hands, tears at its blackened skin with his teeth, occasionally pausing to pour more hot sauce on to the fish. He stops suddenly and looks up. 'Don't tell coach,' he says, and returns to the catch of the day.

**

In the next building, the 'coach' has no idea what his star striker is up to. The man in charge of Antigua and Barbuda is Tom Curtis, a young Englishman in only his second coaching job. The US, on the other hand, is being coached by former German international Jürgen Klinsmann. Klinsmann has won the World Cup and European Championship as a player and has coached both Bayern Munich and the German national team. Curtis's main claim to fame was being part of Third Division Chesterfield's memorable FA Cup run to the semi-finals in the mid-1990s. If the US qualifies for Brazil it will be the seventh time they have made it to the finals. It is the first match for the US in the 2014 competition while Antigua and Barbuda began their campaign a year ago and have never got close to even considering themselves World Cup material. Until now. A series of incredible results against bigger opposition has seen them reach the penultimate round of qualification for the first time ever. When the draw for the group stage was made, the US was first out of the hat, alongside Guatemala and France '98 finalists Jamaica.

Tom Curtis appears nervous when we meet for the first time. 'Come in, come in,' he beckons, inviting me into his apartment a stone's throw from the lake from which I have just seen his star striker pull his dinner. There hasn't been much interest in Antigua and Barbudan football over the past two decades, which might explain his nervousness. Or perhaps his air of apprehension is as a result of his experiences with Britain's sporting press, who took a fleeting interest in him fifteen years ago. 'It was a crazy time,' he had told me earlier. 'The high point of my career, no doubt. Until now, that is.' Curtis is thirty-nine now but looks no different from the blond, wiry midfielder who could once be seen scampering up the wing for Chesterfield. That team – which also featured a teenage future England international in Kevin Davies – produced one of the competition's great performances by an underdog in the modern era. Curtis had only been training with the club part-time as he studied for a degree yet he became a key part of Chesterfield's success, scoring the deciding penalty in an earlier round to knock out former European Cup winners Nottingham Forest, then in the Premier League and coached by Stuart Pearce. He was destined, it seemed, for great things. But they never really arrived. Curtis played at lower and lower levels until he finally hung up his boots last year while playing for the non-league Loughborough University team.

It was at Loughborough that Curtis found his true calling, coaching the team until he was head-hunted by the Antigua and

Barbuda FA to coach not just its national team but also the island's only professional outfit, too: the Barracudas. It was a brilliant first job for a new coach. The Barracudas would give him a day-to-day coaching role. The Antigua national team job was a win-win situation. Both teams were made up of locally based stars and British-born players. Strong ties remain between the two countries but the biggest improvement in the team has come from the home-grown players. The Barracudas now play in the USL Pro League, the third tier of American soccer. Previously players would have jobs in factories or on fishing boats while training in the evenings. Now they can focus full time on football. 'The Barracudas is the only Caribbean side playing pro outside the region,' he says when we sit down. He is still a little guarded. 'The purpose of the Barracudas is to develop the national team. A lot of thought has gone into it.' But he soon discovered one major impediment to developing his players: the Caribbean islands didn't have a single football pitch between them. 'We don't have any football-specific facility,' he admits. 'We play on cricket grounds, the Sir Vivian Richards Cricket Stadium, which was built for the 2005 Cricket World Cup. We train at the ARG, which is a world-famous cricket venue. We don't have good surfaces to be able to train but still we've produced a competitive team.'

Antigua and Barbuda is a cricket country, a colonial legacy left by the British from whom independence was won in 1981. Despite Antigua's size it has produced some of the greatest cricketers the world has ever seen, players like the peerless Sir Viv Richards, Richie Richardson, both of whom would captain the West Indies during their dominance of international cricket, Andy Roberts and Curtly Ambrose, arguably the greatest fast bowler of the modern era. Football has always been cricket's poor relation in Antigua and previous football World Cup qualification campaigns were littered with beatings and concluded in failure. This qualification campaign was to be different. For eighteen months, Curtis explains, the Barracudas had given his players a taste of professionalism. Initially it was tough. Time-keeping was a big issue. Curtis is big on time-keeping. 'You can't just plonk someone into a professional team and expect them to have a professional life straightaway,' he concedes. 'Many of these guys have only been pro for six months so it's not easy to slip into. But they produce great athletes. Look at the cricket.'

Antigua and Barbuda were not meant to get out of their group. They had never been out of the first round before. In qualification for the 2010 World Cup in South Africa they played Cuba home and away, and lost 8-3 over the two games. This time they had been drawn with the US Virgin Islands, Curaçao and, the favourites, Haiti. Nine months earlier, after I had watched Haiti smash six goals past the US Virgin Islands in their first qualifier of the campaign in Port au Prince, the players, officials and the Brazilian coach Edson Tavares had all told me that the crucial matches that would decide who won the group, and so clinch the single qualifying spot for the next round, would be when Haiti played Antigua and Barbuda home and away in the final two matches of the group. It would, they reasoned, effectively be a two-leg play-off.

Curtis's team came racing out of the blocks, winning the first four games in a row and scoring an incredible twenty-six goals in the process, including 10-0 and 8-1 victories against the US Virgin Islands. Haiti scored seventeen goals in their first three matches, but then it all went wrong against Curaçao in Port au Prince. They could only manage a 2-2 draw, and that was after going 2-0 down in the first half.

The crunch meeting came when the two met in Antigua's capital, St John, in November. The dropped points meant Tavares's Haiti team had to avoid losing or they were out. Tavares set his team up for a draw, in the hope that Antigua and Barbuda would wilt in the final game in the cauldron-like atmosphere I had experienced for myself at Port au Prince's Stade Sylvio Cator.

The match took place, as every home game had to, in a circular cricket ground. A football pitch had been painted out in the centre of the Sir Viv Richards Stadium but two cricket wickets could be seen clearly in the middle of the field. There were only a thousand fans in the stadium to witness Haiti's near-total possession. Their dominance was to be expected, given that almost the entire starting eleven were professional players from France, Belgium and beyond. Only five of the team that started in the match I had seen in Port au Prince against the US Virgin Islands did so against Antigua. Tavares had accelerated his acquisition of foreign-born and foreign-raised players, and a new raft of the Haitian diaspora, some of whom had once played for the France and Switzerland Under 21 teams before switching allegiance, had been recruited. Gone was Steward Ceus, the huge New York-born goalkeeper who had begun the campaign, replaced by Johnny Placide, who once played for France Under 21s. When I had spoken to Tavares about his controversial recruitment from the diaspora he had talked excitedly about Placide. 'He is one of the best goalkeepers in France,' he told me. 'We are trying very, very hard to get him.'

Antigua and Barbuda survived the first half but as Haiti's desperation grew they threw men forward, giving Tom Curtis's side the better chances. And then, in the eighty-third minute, striker Kerry Skepple – who had once played a handful of games in the Finnish second division – hit a tame shot from outside the penalty area. Somehow Placide managed to misjudge the ball. It hit his right glove, slipped through his hands and into the goal. It was a dreadful and decisive error. When the full-time whistle was blown, the Haiti players lay, face down, all over the pitch. They had been eliminated, and it was, according to the Haitian federation, all Edson Tavares's fault. 'The coach really killed the dream of a nation,' an angry Henry Robert Dominique, the Haitian Football Federation spokesperson, told the *Antigua Observer* after the game. 'He really killed the dreams of fourteen million people and maybe because he is a foreigner, he is from Brazil and he doesn't understand what it means to wear the Haitian flag that we fought for along with independence way back in 1804 ... and this is the dream of the Haitians, to go to the World Cup.'

Not content with that, Dominique went further. 'He wanted to make his own move to be a hero. Now he is a zero. For the Haitian nation, the coach Tavares is a zero … Any soccer player in the world could have seen that Haiti was the better team tonight. But that wasn't enough. We need management. We need soccer fields. We need soccer balls. We need to send the kids to school and we want to say thank you to the president of Haiti, Michel Martelly, who is going to help the country with a new generation looking for change.' Unsurprisingly, Tavares was fired.

'Haiti were the obvious favourites in the group,' recalls Curtis of that historic game. 'They'd been to the '74 World Cup, they give top teams great games and they have players at Lens and PSG.' Curtis had agreed with Tavares that the atmosphere in Port au Prince would give Haiti a huge advantage and wanted to avoid going there needing a result to make it to the next round. 'Everyone told me Haiti was a difficult place to go to, both to get a result and because the crowd was so … hostile.' For the first time in a year I thought of the riots outside the stadium in Port au Prince before Haiti's first World Cup qualifier, and of the US Virgin Islands' coach passing by, players opened-mouthed and wide-eyed with terror as the violence unfolded before them. 'We rode our luck,' he admits. 'We hung on. The celebrations were fantastic, everyone was on the pitch. Everyone was ecstatic.' It was the greatest moment in Curtis's short coaching career. 'When we won the Haiti game I thought, oh my word, we'll have to play against USA and Jamaica,' he says. 'A friend said: "Don't worry, it's a long way off." It seemed a long way off. All of a sudden we are here.'

During that time Curtis has found it almost impossible to arrange any friendly matches with anyone, partly due to the fact it's so expensive to play another national team and partly because they are historically considered one of the worst teams in the world. Nobody wanted to play Antigua and Barbuda unless a lot of money changed hands. While the US had prepared for the Antigua match playing marquee friendlies against top teams,

Antigua and Barbuda hasn't played anyone. Well, hardly anyone. 'We've had to play local sides and amongst ourselves, which isn't ideal, but it's something we have to deal with as a small nation,' he says, with no little understatement. The problem is money. Organising international friendlies is an expensive business. 'There's stadium rental, appearance fees for foreign teams and these are things that we just cannot afford,' he says, before pointing to the fixtures in his plush apartment: a flat-screen TV on the wall, expensive carpets, ice cold, silent air conditioning. 'We're staying here but it's taken a bit of wheeling and dealing. We're not like US soccer, we don't have the same infrastructure or the financial backing. They've played Scotland, Brazil, Canada.'

Soccer is one of the rare arenas in almost any aspect of global culture in which the United States might be considered a minnow. At least for now. Even in a regional context, Mexico has prided itself on being CONCACAF's true futbol heir. Yet, if they made it, this would the United States' seventh World Cup. It is also an emerging football superpower, with a booming domestic league, impressive resources, a huge talent pool and a top coach. The United States could very well one day produce a team capable of winning the World Cup. For Antigua and Barbuda the US game was a very different proposition from thrashing their cousins in the Virgin Islands, or plotting the downfall of a country crippled by natural disaster. How do you even begin to prepare to play a team when the odds are so stacked against you? 'It's the players against the players not me versus Jürgen,' says Curtis, almost a little hurt by the question. 'We watched all the recent games the States have played. They played well in some,' he says as if about to deliver a back-handed compliment. 'But we've looked at their side and come up with a little plan that might upset them.' Part of that plan has involved taking the US on at their own game: sports psychology, visualisation techniques, cutting edge training methods cross-pollinated from other high-performance sports like rowing and rugby. 'We've been having sessions with a team psychologist who worked with [200-metres Olympic gold

satisfied there's enough of a connection to meet FIFA's nationality rules, he approaches them with an offer of international football that they will probably never get from the England team. 'The management are constantly asking: "Is he Antiguan? His surname's Antiguan ..."' he says of his unofficial role. 'I knew a lot of guys from playing professional football in England and I only have to ask a couple of questions to find out if they had any Antiguan heritage. So I've titled myself as Head of Recruitment.' His work has so far uncovered some impressive names, the likes of midfielder Mikele Leigertwood, who is playing in England for Championship side Reading, as well as Nottingham Forest striker Dexter Blackstock, who was once considered a potential international for the country of his birth after playing for the England Under 18, 19 and 21 teams. In the five years since Cochrane arrived he has been responsible, in part, for building a completely different type of national team. 'I'll get an email from the head of the Antiguan FA: "Can you find out if he's Antiguan?"' he explains when I ask about the process for recruiting potential new players. The biggest recruiting tool, though, isn't his sleuthing ability. It is matches against the likes of the US. 'The stature of this type of game will mean more and more will come.'

Virtually every national team I had met so far had employed the same tactics as Cochrane and the Antigua and Barbuda federation. And the same problems had arisen in every team. Resentment by and division among the local players. The new players might look like them, and might even speak their language, but they weren't their kin, not at first anyway. They were usurpers, outsiders, 'invaders', as the Haitian president Michel Martelly had called the foreign-born and raised players of Les Grenadiers after they had been eliminated from World Cup qualification. The import of these professional players from afar usually came with a subtext besmirching the abilities of the local players, even if that was unintentional. In many cases it wasn't even talent that was the issue. Local players with many of the teams I had seen were better, more technical. But the foreign players were fitter and could last the full ninety minutes. Every team, from Palestine to the Cook Islands, had somehow to heal the rift that inevitably emerged between the two sets of players. Antigua and Barbuda was no different. 'Initially there was a bit of friction, yeah,' Cochrane agrees. 'At first the guys weren't too welcoming. The Antiguan-born guys are different. They are not all high fives and hugs. They are a lot more quiet. But now we are together.' Victory, as ever, is always the best answer to division. 'Now there's a belief we can actually do something in this group,' he says with genuine optimism. 'The top two qualify [for the final round]. And why not? Why not have the belief? There have been bigger giant-killing results in football in the last hundred years. It's not just this one game, we have six games to get the points.'

Nearby several of the English players are scrubbing their boots clean around a single tap. 'Justine played a big role in the recruitment of the overseas player, so thanks to him more than anyone,' says Mikele Leigertwood after he's removed the mud from his cleats. 'Beating Haiti was a massive achievement and that shows how far we've come.' Leigertwood had played football at the highest level and really believed that qualification was a possibility. 'We've come this far against the odds so there's no point turning up and just being out there. Yeah, they have some big names. But they are just eleven men. A lot of the players haven't played in big stadiums, in big crowds. We've got nothing to fear.'

As the English players cleaned their boots, the Antiguans walked off the training pitch separately from each other. The professionalism and fitness of the English players might have helped the country's cause, but it had needed Antiguan goals to progress. Those had been scored by Peter Byers, the fisherman at the lake. He is currently one of the highest scorers in 2014 World Cup qualification with eight goals. 'It's a big, big, big challenge for all of us,' Byers says on the sidelines after training comes to an end, speaking with a soft Antiguan lilt. 'It doesn't matter how big the United States is. Antigua is a hundred and seven square miles, but it's eleven players versus eleven. So whoever puts the hard work out will be victorious.'

Back home, Antiguans had begun to expect victory, something that Tom Curtis had tried to damp down. That didn't deter the country's prime minister, Baldwin Spencer. He was so excited about the match that he turned up at St John's airport to pray with the team before sending them off. It is a deeply Christian country and the players pray before and after every training session. 'We won't let the people down. I know the prime minister will be watching live so we'll give them something to cheer about. We get our prayer done because you can't do anything in this world without the father above,' Byers says, pointing to the sky. 'It is good to thank Him every day even for the meal you get, even the time to play this lovely sport.'

Sure enough, at the end of training the IMG academy's very own lay preacher arrives to lead the group in prayer before the players leave for their afternoon siestas 'We need all the help and inspiration we can get,' explains Mark Bowers, Antigua's team manager. The team form a circle around the chaplain. 'This is a divine appointment. God's divine appointment,' he begins.

'I never bring my bible when I come to IMG, but something said I should bring it today. I believe God has given me the word for you guys. Philippians 4 verse 6: Do not fret or have any anxiety about anything but in every circumstance and in everything, by prayer and petition, with thanksgiving continue to make your request known to God. And God's peace will be with you.

'Let's pray together.

'Lord, I pray as they prepare for Friday night and for the qualifications that lie ahead of them and they continue to pursue the dreams that you have before them, that you bless them, encourage them and strengthen them knowing that peace ultimately only comes from you our God our creator. Lord pray a blessing, a special blessing, upon this team, that … they leave it all on the field and give you all the glory.

'And Lord, I pray your protection. There's one young gentleman who had an injury this morning. I pray you heal that quickly. I commit them to you in the name of the Father and Son and the Holy Spirit. Amen.'

'Do you think you will score?' I ask Byers as he leaves the pitch after the prayers.

'I don't think I am going to score,' he replies. 'I *know* I'm going to score.'

That evening Curtis holds a team meeting in his room. The national team's new jerseys have finally arrived from the manufacturers, but the team are not happy. There's only enough for one each and the workmanship is poor. The federation managed to negotiate a good deal with the manufacturers. If they want more, the man from the federation says, you'll have to buy them yourselves. For just $40. The room grumbles and complains. Why should we buy our own shirts? Shouldn't we have more than one? What about shirts for the family back home? But the players realise it is futile and hand over their greenbacks for the extra jerseys. 'Man, it's a business, I guess,' shrugs Keiran Murtagh, one of the English-born players, looking down at the single shirt in his hands. 'If you're not making, you're losing.'

**

Tampa, Florida, USA

The rain falls like a sheet of white metal across the causeway that links the disparate islands and marshes of the Florida Keys. The Antigua and Barbuda team sit in silence as their bus slices through the rain towards the Raymond James Stadium for their final training session. The huge angular stadium juts violently into the dark clouds above, the steep terracing open to the heavens. This is the home of the Tampa Bay Buccaneers who play in the warmth and the dry of the autumn through to the spring. Soccer is trespassing here and has to make do with being unprotected from the rainy season. As the bus arrives twenty-four hours before kick-off, it becomes clear that the pitch – waterlogged and presently unplayable – is in no fit state for a World Cup qualifier. The rain falls like clockwork at the same time every day. If it rains like this tomorrow, the match will be in jeopardy. Curtis directs his players into the biggest dressing room any of them has ever seen. 'I've been in some pretty nice dressing rooms,' says Dexter Blackstock, who has seen his fair share of Premier League grounds. 'But this...' The locker room is vast, with thirty semi-walk-in pods made for giants. Without the padding and para-phernalia of American football to fill each pod up, the Antigua and Barbuda squad look like children sitting there. A desk has been set up in the corner of the room; it is manned by a FIFA official. Each player approaches one by one, passport in hand, to prove that he is eligible to play.

Tom Curtis paces the centre of the room as the team admire their surroundings in silence before calling them to join him. The players link arms in a circle, pray, and shout: 'ANTIGUA, BARBUDA, UNITY!' The belly of the Raymond James Stadium is so vast that no one knows the way to the pitch. 'Which way do we go?' a confused Marvin McCoy asks. 'You go out and turn right, and then out of the tunnel,' Curtis says softly, as if directing a schoolboy to the toilet. 'Remember because that's the way you go out tomorrow.' But a few minutes after the start of training there is a downpour. It is impossible even to see the players on the other side of the pitch. After a few minutes Curtis realises that the exercise is fruitless and calls off the session. The team sprint for cover. They stand by the concrete-lined tunnel, out of the rain, squeezing the water out of their shirts and watching as the pitch slowly floods. The Americans have already cancelled their training session and moved it to an indoor pitch on the other side of town. Curtis has to troop his soaking wet team back to the changing room and back on to the bus for the long journey over the causeway. There are just two last pieces of the jigsaw for Curtis before Friday's big game. The first is a team session with Michael Jordan's former sports psychologist who imparts his wisdom on how to approach tomorrow's game mentally. Phrases like 'edu-trainer' and 'mental training' are used. The players snigger behind their hands, laughing at the seriousness of it all.

Much more effective is Curtis's final appointment. He has arranged for the team to watch a motivational film: the 2010 documentary *Fire in Babylon*. The film follows the great West Indies international cricket team of the 1970s and 1980s. That team contained Antigua's greatest ever sportsman, Sir Viv Richards, who dominated and terrified cricket in equal measure, remaining unbeaten for fifteen years. It is a feat unparalleled in a team sport anywhere in the world. But more than that, the film was also about colonialism and freedom, and how the rise of the West Indies cricket team mirrored the rise to independence. 'The film is about national identity,' Curtis says in his room as he searches for the film on his laptop. 'If the players can glean a little bit of confidence and a little bit of swagger then it can only be beneficial for them.'

The players cram into the auditorium at the academy to watch the film about how their national heroes strutted on the world stage, destroying their former colonial masters at the game they had invented. The film opens with a burst of speed and violence as one fast bowler after another powers his deliveries into the ribs, or the chins, or the arms of the batsmen before them. They cheer louder when the batsman on the receiving end is white. But they cheer loudest when Viv Richards, a man credited in the Caribbean with as much cultural and political importance as Bob Marley, appears on the screen to deliver his opening line. 'We had a mission, and a mission to prove we were as good as anyone,' he says to the camera. 'Equal, for that matter.'

**

The next day the bus back to the Raymond James Stadium is silent again. A storm is threatening the stadium just as it did the day before but the rain has held off for now. 'Everyone's positive and calm, they've got their headphones on,' says Curtis when we arrive at the stadium car park. 'Yesterday was the first time we saw the stadium. All our preparations are done now. On paper we're a tiny little island up against a superpower. It's not a bad thing they [the US] take us lightly.'

The Stars and Stripes were flying in their thousands in the soaking wet parking lot of the Raymond James Stadium. The pre-match entertainment is taking place out of the back of hundreds of pick-up trucks. Several thousand US fans sing the national anthem, drink beer and smoke cigars despite the sudden deluge of rain. It is their first 2014 World Cup qualifying match but also a rare chance to be in the majority during a home international. 'We're here and it's going to be a pro-American crowd, which is abnormal for the States,' explains one fan, Matt, a twenty-one-year-old student wearing a Stars and Stripes bandanna, smoking a thick cigar and drinking a beer. 'We're a country that has people coming from all over. Case in point: the Gold Cup match here last year, lot of Panamanian fans. In another, a lot of Guatemalan. It's an immigrant country. Makes it difficult, soccer is not the most important sport here. It's building, it's getting there.'

Sure enough, the away team is in the minority. Only a few Antiguan flags fly during the national anthems as close to 30,000 fans brave the awful conditions. The US team can call on any number of international stars. In the starting line-up is former Bradenton academy player Michael Bradley, who would soon sign for Roma in Italy's Serie A; Fulham midfielder Clint Dempsey, who was one of the best players in Europe last season; Everton goalkeeper Tim Howard, who was a regular in the English Premier League. Antigua and Barbuda, on the other hand, have thirty-five-year-old Marc Joseph marshalling the defence: he plays for semi-professional Kendal Town in the Northern Premier League, the seventh tier of English football. Curtis has made an important decision for the match, dropping top-scorer Peter Byers and replacing him with Dexter Blackstock, the English-born striker who has only just been recruited. But Byers will get his chance.

The match begins badly for Antigua. The crowd are singing and beating drums, the pitch of the chants higher than anywhere else I'd heard in the world. The US attack from the start. Landon Donovan is terrorising Marc Joseph. Within a few minutes they are 1-0 up. Molvin James (or Molvin Jones according to the ESPN commentator) makes a point-blank save from Herculez Gomez before Carlos Bocanegra fires home from close range. They are in complete control before Antigua and Barbuda give away a penalty, making it 2-0. Antigua only manage one attack, a glorious opening when Dexter Blackstock (or Darren Blackstock, as the ESPN commentator calls him) dawdles on the ball for too long in front of goal. Half-time comes but it could have been far worse: wave after wave of attacks have threatened to deluge the Antiguans. For a brief period it looks as if Antigua and Barbuda will be overwhelmed. But as the second half goes on Antigua grow, taking the game to the Americans. And then the moment Curtis had hoped for. He finally throws on Peter Byers. Byers harries the US back four, slaloming through them and generally being disruptive, looking for an opening. When Mikele Leigertwood gets loose down the left, he manages to loop a ball over the top. Byers cleverly spins the last defender, Oguchi Onyewu, sprints clear and passes the ball under Howard's falling body: 2-1. The stadium is a low hum of disbelief mixed with the shrieking of excitable kids not prepared for the possibility of defeat. Antigua continue to press, looking for the equaliser that will make headlines worldwide. They have their chances, too, but they leave space at the back and the Americans score a late third when Herculez Gomez barges through everyone and scores at close range. The match finishes 3-1 but Antigua have not been embarrassed. Later, at the post-match press conference, Klinsmann expresses shock that he has been run so close.

'I just said in the dressing room, everyone is a little disappointed we lost, which I think is testament to how far we have come,' says Curtis in the emptying press room after he's been grilled by US soccer journalists. Outside his players pile onto the bus back to Bradenton. On the road home the coach will stop at a nightclub run by an Antiguan who has invited everyone in for free to celebrate the result. The players sneak to the bar to buy beer without Curtis seeing. But it's not yet 9 p.m. and the nightclub is dead, a tiki bar with an open dance floor decorated to look like a jungle. Around the perimeter of the dance floor are doors to motel rooms where women wait inside. It takes a few moments before we realise that all is not what it should be. We stand around a little awkwardly, aware that we are not perhaps in a nightclub after all.

A few days later Antigua will win their first point of qualification, a 0-0 draw with Jamaica at the Sir Viv Richards Stadium. Matches against Honduras, Jamaica and, finally, the US again will decide their fate over the next year. The dream is still alive. But Curtis cannot shake the feeling that he could, he should, have won against the US on their own doorstep. 'At one point in the second half we were close,' he shrugs regretfully. 'And they were worried.'

8

SWITZERLAND, ALBANIA, KOSOVO

Zurich, Switzerland. September 2012.

Fadil Vokrri and Eroll Salihu are sitting side by side in a booth in a roadside diner on the outskirts of Zurich. They look out of place, slightly suspicious, crammed together on a red leatherette banquette that is too small for two grown men. They look as if they are about to negotiate an arms deal or arrange a gangland hit. Eroll looks nervous; Fadil not at all. Both men are middle-aged and, from a distance, appear smartly dressed. Fadil has dark hair and is heavy-set, wearing his suit in a dismissive, careless manner that suggests he would rather be wearing something else. He constantly pulls at the collar of his shirt, whose top two buttons are permanently undone. It is clear that Fadil is the boss. Eroll is taller, thinner, with blond hair and white shirtsleeves and tie. He looks like a sensible lab technician, the good cop to Fadil's brooding bad cop. Eroll explains their predicament because only he speaks English. It is true. They are not from round here. And they *do* have an important mission to undertake in Switzerland. They have to be careful, though, Eroll goes on. What they are doing is highly sensitive with the potential to upset a lot of people. The Serbs for one. The Russians for another. And let's not even begin with the Swiss, in whose country Fadil and Eroll's action is about to be played out. 'It is politically sensitive,' Eroll agrees. 'It is right, also.' He stops talking when the waitress brings Fadil's Coke (Diet) and our coffees (black).

Fadil and Eroll are not drug dealers or people smugglers or on the run from the Albanian mafia, as far as I am aware. They are both ex-footballers from the former Yugoslavia. Both had played in the country before the Yugoslav civil war, and later in Turkey after it. Fadil had a brief spell in France, too, and had also played for the Yugoslav national team before its demise. He was considered the finest player ever to represent Yugoslavia from Kosovo. Because he was the only player from Kosovo ever to represent Yugoslavia, which is why the two men are here, in Zurich. Fadil Vokrri is president of the Football Federation of Kosovo, the FFK. Eroll is his loyal general-secretary. The opening shots of European qualification for the World Cup finals in Brazil have been fired, but Kosovo is not among the fifty-three teams in the draw. They are an unrecognised nation, with an unrecognised national football team. Yet, like every territory from the former Yugoslavia, Kosovo has produced an inordinate amount of talent. The problem is that, with no recognition by UEFA and FIFA, that talent has ended up elsewhere.

Fadil and Eroll are here because they have had enough of seeing their players turn up in other national teams. In a few days' time Switzerland will play Albania in Lucerne. Kosovars see themselves as ethnically Albanian and Switzerland has a huge Kosovar population who fled there after the final battle in Yugoslavia's long, bloody disintegration, the Kosovo War, which took place between 1998 and 1999. Of the probable twenty-two players who will start in Lucerne, nine had either been born in Kosovo or had Kosovar parents who had fled the war, players like Bayern Munich's Xherdan Shaqiri and Napoli's Valon Behrami, who play for Switzerland, and Albania's captain Lorik Cana, who plays for Lazio. 'It's very special for me to see two different national teams with players born in Kosovo; in fact, it's like watching Kosovo A team play Kosovo B,' laughs Fadil. 'The real national team cannot be presented internationally.' Kosovo's quest for recognition has been thwarted at every step thanks to wider geopolitical issues, especially at the UN, and also thanks to the European Union, where five member states stubbornly refuse to recognise it. Kosovo's attempted membership of UEFA and FIFA has met the same fate for the same reasons.

The Kosovo War failed to achieve full independence from Yugoslavia. It remains unrecognised by the United Nations as Russia, a staunch ally of Serbia, has a veto on the Security Council. Within UEFA thirty-seven of its fifty-three members recognise Kosovo, but it is not enough. UEFA changed its statutes so that, to become a member, you have first to be a member of the United Nations. Now the Kosovo team has been stuck in limbo, partially recognised but not enough. As a result the territory has been haemorrhaging players to other leagues and to other national teams. There has been some movement, though. A few months ago Sepp Blatter announced that Kosovo will be allowed to play friendly internationals against other FIFA members, a move which has caused a huge row in Serbia. Serbia has always maintained that Kosovo is, historically, an inviolable part of its territory, essentially colonised by the Kosovars. An enclave of Serbs, making up 5 per cent of its population, still live in Kosovo. Later this month FIFA's executive committee in Zurich will sit down and discuss the practicalities of Kosovo playing friendly matches against other members. So Fadil and Eroll are here with a petition they have drawn up, demanding that Kosovo be allowed to play. When Switzerland and Albania were drawn in the same group for 2014 World Cup qualification, the two men hatched a plan. They would pull all the strings they could to get the big-name Kosovar players on both sides to sign it and present it to FIFA. Unsurprisingly, this has become a hugely sensitive topic, so much so that Blatter postponed a decision on Kosovo's friendlies for six months. Parliamentary elections were taking place in Serbia and there was a fear that increasing Kosovo's visibility might inflame an already fervently nationalistic atmosphere.

The issue of Switzerland's Kosovar players has become hugely controversial here, too. Many of the players have been raised in Switzerland from birth, have been given a quality of life they would have been unlikely to experience in Kosovo and brought up through Switzerland's first-class training academies. Switzerland has given these talented players every opportunity to make the most of their gifts. The fear is that they may turn their backs on it. That morning *SonntagsBlick* published a front-page story on the issue with the headline 'The Fear of Kosovo'. Next to it was a photograph of Xherdan Shaqiri, one of Europe's most talented young players and the one the Swiss fear losing above all others. But the subtext was clear. The players' allegiances were also being questioned.

Fadil understood the idea of divided loyalties. He was part of Kosovo's best football side, FC Prishtina, from the capital. Back in the mid-1980s Kosovo wasn't one of the six socialist republics that officially made up Yugoslavia, but it was an autonomous province. In 1974 Tito had given Kosovo virtually the same rights as the Bosnians, Croats, Serbs, Slovenians, Macedonians and Montenegrans. Eroll played for FC Prishtina, too, a little later, but Fadil was the undisputed star. As we talk, nervous middle-aged men in suits approach every few minutes, bowing and scraping in the hope of getting an autograph. Even the twenty-one-year-old waiter asks for Fadil's autograph, midway through serving him. At first FC Prishtina was just another team from another part of Yugoslavia, whose identity had been moulded by its host region, such as Dinamo Zagreb from Croatia, Red Star Belgrade from Serbia, Željezničar Sarajevo from Bosnia. Between 1983 and 1988, FC Prishtina survived in the top division of Yugoslav football. They even beat the mighty Red Star Belgrade in Belgrade in their first season.

'Then it began, repression against all Yugoslavs by the Serbs,' says Fadil of life after 1989, when Slobodan Milošević became president of Serbia and rolled back all of the autonomous gains that Kosovo had made under Tito. 'But football was a beautiful story. Everybody in Kosovo was behind the club and it was a symbol of resistance. It was the only sphere in life where Albanians could express their love for football and other things.'

The team also featured the father of the current Albanian captain, Lorik Cana. The club made them the most famous men in Kosovo. 'FC Prishtina was not only a football club; it means something more. Resistance,' Fadil explains. 'It was a great time, a great generation. We were really a symbol of all the things they could not express in other ways.' The authorities were always on the lookout for any signs of overt Kosovar nationalism that spilt over the boundaries of what was acceptable. 'The most significant [sign of this] was against Red Star Belgrade,' recalls Eroll. Red Star was seen as a bastion of Yugoslav and, later, of Serbian nationalism. 'There was one game where sixty people were jailed because they were singing.' Eroll clears his throat and sings. 'Eh, Oh. Eh, Oh.' He is singing to the tune of 'Day-O' (The Banana Boat Song). It didn't sound like something that would land sixty people in jail. 'They said it was similar to Enver Hoxha [pronounced Hodger]', the former Albanian dictator, Eroll replies.

Fadil's performances got him noticed by the bigger sides in the Yugoslav league and he signed for Partizan Belgrade. But unlike at Red Star (a team that would later become such an overt channel of Serb nationalism that many of its ultras would end up fighting for Arkan's Tigers, one of the most feared and brutal of all Serbian paramilitary groups during the civil war), Partizan had a history of tolerance and of signing players regardless of their ethnicity. 'I was very well accepted,' Fadil recalls of his time there. He was voted players' player of the year in 1987 and made most of his thirteen appearances for Yugoslavia while at the club. 'Partizan had a tradition of playing all nationalities,' he says. 'Even now I am very accepted by all Partizan fans. Partizan played a lot of Albanian players. They recruited the player because of the talent not because of the political reasons.' It was because of this that he saw playing for the national team as a moment of pride rather than betrayal. By playing for Yugoslavia he was representing Kosovo on the world stage. 'I was proud to represent Kosovo and play for Yugoslavia,' he says. But he believes that the Yugoslav system was still prejudiced. 'I am sure that if I was not Albanian, with my quality, I would have played a lot, a lot of games,' he says a little regretfully. 'I played just thirteen times. As a player I never thought about it. As a sportsman you don't want to think that could happen. But it is related.'

By the time the Kosovo War broke out Fadil was a French citizen, starring for Nîmes in the French league. 'It was the most difficult time in my life,' he recalls. 'My entire family, my brothers, sisters, were all there. And we couldn't help anything. It was the worst time I've ever had.' Eroll, though, saw how it all played out. Kosovo remained welded to the shrinking rump of a Serbian-dominated Yugoslavia. 'Until Slobodan Milošević we were equal,' says Eroll. 'In 1991 we quit the league and formed our own.' This wasn't as easy as it sounds. 'Five per cent of Kosovo are Serbs, and took over all the stadiums. Milošević suspended everything. You must understand what the destruction was like.' Yet, according to Eroll, the illegal Kosovo league continued. Under threat of beatings and arrest the teams would meet every week to play. 'We play on our improvised fields and then washed in rivers afterwards,' Eroll recalls. 'We just survived,' he says of those bleak years between 1991 and 1999. 'After games the police would beat, arrest, put pressure. We were put in jail. They would always ask us: "Why are you playing in illegal games?" It was difficult times.'

Then came the American and British bombing of Belgrade. The Kosovo War left an imperfect peace behind; a state of limbo between recognition and full independence. Kosovo now enjoyed a degree of autonomy, that was true. The UN, which had held the reins in Kosovo since the conflict, had, only a few days before, handed over control of all governmental affairs to the Kosovars. A statue of Bill Clinton stands in Pristina. Both he and Tony Blair, Eroll says, remain hugely popular, regarded as saviours of the nation. 'We have had one problem,' Fadil deadpans. 'The United States is not strong enough in football! It is not strong like in politics.'

Now a twelve-team Super League exists in Kosovo, with clubs that have Serbian, Bosnian and Roma identities as well as Kosovar. But being outside UEFA means there is little money to develop the league, the clubs or the players. The stadiums, Eroll explains, have not been updated in four decades and are crumbling. Kosovar players are easily, and cheaply, taken, too. 'Presidents from

Albanian clubs come here to take our players,' says Eroll. 'They say: "How can you produce so many players? We can't do this."'

When Fadil was elected as president of the FFK in 2008, his mandate was clear. 'The first task was international recognition,' he says. 'Admittance to UEFA and FIFA. This is the first goal. And then work with the youth because twenty years of isolation is a unique case in the heart of Europe.' Kosovo's quest for membership became even harder after a battle that was not of their making. Since 1997 Gibraltar has been trying to join UEFA, much to the displeasure of the Spanish who still view the territory as theirs. Gibraltar is the last colony in Europe. When Gibraltar overcame every hurdle to join UEFA, the Spanish federation threatened to pull all of its teams from international competition. They feared that a successful bid by Gibraltar would give Spain's restive regions, namely Catalonia and the Basque Country, ideas about having their own national teams. UEFA changed its statutes. While FIFA requires that an association only be 'internationally recognised', a term that is open to interpretation, UEFA now states that an association's country must be recognised by the United Nations. It didn't stop Gibraltar. They successfully appealed to the Court of Arbitration for Sport, arguing that they had made their original application before the rule change. In May 2013, UEFA had no choice but to accept Gibraltar as its fifty-fourth member. But the UN requirement remains, and Kosovo can do little about it even if Sepp Blatter had announced that Kosovo should be allowed to play international friendlies against FIFA members. UEFA president Michel Platini was vehemently against the move. 'Blatter knows the situation very well and knows it is an injustice,' Fadil says. 'He has goodwill and is very positive. He says: "sports for all". But Platini?' he adds mockingly. 'I can't understand him. He doesn't want the risk, even though twenty-two out of the twenty-seven countries in the European Union recognise us.' The talk now was of trying to win Platini over, to make him see what the lack of UEFA membership was doing to young footballers in Kosovo, how it was pushing players away from what should be their natural homes into other national teams, into Switzerland, Albania, Finland and Belgium. 'Who is stopping us? The big issue is the five EU states that did not recognise Kosovo. That is a huge problem,' says Fadil. 'We are talking [about] Spain, Cyprus, Greece, Slovakia and Romania.' Eroll, in particular, is incredulous. 'We are recognised by half of the world,' he says, getting a little angrier now. 'After a request to Serbia and Russia we are recognised by the International Criminal Court. Recognised by most of the states from Europe, from all the continents.'

It is this perceived injustice that has brought the two men, dressed as smartly as they can muster, into the diner in Zurich. With the discussions on how and when and against whom Kosovo might be allowed to play friendly matches dragging on, they have come prepared to embark on a more direct campaign: guerrilla action to secure their interests. Eroll slides a piece of paper on to the table in front of me. The headline reads:

DECLARATION FOR THE RIGHT
TO KOSOVO
TO PLAY INTERNATIONAL FOOTBALL.

The petition sets out several points for those who sign it to agree with, namely that they support Kosovo's right to play international football, that they applaud Blatter and FIFA's declaration of support for Kosovo to play international friendlies and agree that Kosovo – recognised by ninety-one countries, the IMF, the World Bank and six other sports federations – is a unique case that needs a unique, one-off solution that would not, as the Spanish fear, set a precedent for other breakaway regions with designs on their own national team. The final two points, however, are the most illuminating.

We confirm our loyalty to the national team of the countries
for which we have the honour and privilege to play but we

regret that our passion for football cannot be expressed for the national team of the country where our roots and ancestry come from.

We finally commit our support to the Football Federation of Kosovo in this common fight for the implementation of the principles contained in the FIFA statutes: justice, respect, non-discrimination, refusal of political interference and universality of football.

Fadil and Eroll will fill the blank spaces at the bottom of the paper with the names and signatures of some of Europe's most talented players. Starting with the Swiss team. They are just waiting for the right moment to meet them all. Eroll's phone rings. It is someone close to the Swiss camp, staying in a hotel a few miles drive from here. 'We have to be ... sensitive with the Switzerland Football Association,' Eroll says when he puts the phone down. 'We do not want to be exposed.' We are to leave straightaway and drive into the hills and wait for instructions. The meeting is on.

**

FIFA's headquarters in Zurich can be found at the end of a tram line next to the city's zoo. It is peaceful and quiet, in rolling green countryside. Approaching the main building, you follow steps down towards the entrance, one stone for each of FIFA's 209 members, in alphabetical order, starting with Afghanistan and ending with Zimbabwe. One step is darker than the others. South Sudan has just been accepted as FIFA's newest member and workmen have only just set a new stone into the walkway. The concrete is still wet. The building itself is an expensive, modern glass and stone construction; both light and dark. It is from here that world football is run. To many it is the United Nations of world sport, a Tower of Babel united by the common language of football, spreading the gospel of the game to all four corners of the earth.

To others, though, FIFA's headquarters is a modern-day Death Star, representative of nothing more than villainy, theft and corruption. Global soccer's governing body has been beset by allegations of corruption and vice. It was here, two years previously, that FIFA's powerful executive committee – FIFA's decision-making body – gathered to vote on who should host the 2018 and 2022 World Cup finals. Even before the vote had taken place two of the executive committee's members had been suspended after the *Sunday Times* caught both of them in an undercover sting agreeing to vote for a bid in return for cash. Russia and Qatar won the votes, but the vote, and the success of Qatar's bid in particular, had opened the lid on a world of influence, power, money and conflicts of interest that had seriously damaged football's standing in the world. But it was the president of FIFA who divided opinion the most. Sepp Blatter had spent most his time as president of FIFA operating largely under the radar of intense media scrutiny. There had been some scandals and allegations made but they had largely been ignored by the wider world.

He was elected in 1998, on a globalist platform of encouraging the growth of football away from Europe. Blatter commanded a lot of support in Asia and Africa, where he oversaw the first World Cups on both continents and was a hugely popular figure in the Middle East. One of his first acts in power was to recognise the Palestinian national football team. He flew in to Gaza, to the Rafah airstrip, to be greeted as a hero. No one, not even the United Nations, had given parity to the Palestinians before. Their national team would be able to play in World Cup qualification matches and, as part of the Asian Football Confederation, access development funds. More importantly, there was now a mechanism through which the Palestinians could try and stop what they viewed as the manifestly unfair practice of border restrictions and arrests levelled at its players every time they tried to leave Gaza or the West Bank to play a match overseas. In the West, though, he was viewed with disdain, mocked as a hapless relic of a bygone age. That perception wasn't helped when the FIFA presidential elections took place in 2011. His opponent, Qatar's Mohamed Bin Hammam, looked to capitalise on Blatter's unpopularity in the West to unseat him. Instead, Bin Hammam's name was taken off the ballot after it was alleged that he offered cash for votes in the Caribbean. Blatter was re-elected unopposed and Bin Hammam was banned from football for life. The whole saga may have been a masterclass in bureaucratic management but, to the outside world, it looked unseemly. The morning after Blatter's election, the *Sun* newspaper ran a front page with a picture of Blatter next to that of Colonel Gaddafi. The headline ran: 'Despot the Difference'.

I am waiting for Blatter in a special room designed to receive representatives from all around the globe, from statesmen and presidents to royalty and dictators. It is a glass corner office with views out over Zurich's green and pleasant landscape. Blatter is short, charismatic and friendly. He speaks in an expansive, rather loose English. It is one of five languages he speaks fluently. We talk a little about his native Switzerland, how the national team has one of its finest crop of players in years and how immigration has allowed the Swiss to tap into the global movements of people across boundaries. 'We tried for a long time to maintain the so-called national team with nationals of the countries but in the last years there has been such a development in history,' he says as we sit down. It is early in the morning, his first meeting of the day, so early he's not wearing a tie. 'It started with the collapse of the Soviet Union then at the same time also the collapse or disintegration of the Balkans. So all of a sudden FIFA has twenty or twenty-five more associations, all these satellite states ... and this has produced a lot of migrations inside Europe.'

FIFA's membership grew as the United Nations' membership did the same. The collapse of the former Yugoslavia alone created six new countries, each with a national football team that would become a vitally important tool in building a new national identity and projecting that out on to the world. Kosovo, though, was a unique case. A Swiss passport is one of the toughest, and the most sought after, in the world to obtain. Yet the war had seen Switzerland accept more than 300,000 Kosovars. 'You have to make a choice: play for the national team of your origin or the country of your birth,' Blatter says. 'For Kosovo it was easy as they had no national team. They have no independence. Therefore the Kosovo players in Switzerland agreed to be Swiss.' He was clear that Swiss concerns about losing their best players to a new Kosovo nation team – as that *SonnstagsBlick* front page had suggested – were unfounded. Fadil and Eroll had earlier told me that Kosovo was such a unique case that they hoped FIFA would allow a one-off nationality switch for Kosovar players if they chose to represent their new team. That seemed unlikely. 'Even the day Kosovo becomes a full member of FIFA,' Blatter says with certainty, as if it is a matter of when, not if, Kosovo will join. 'If the players can recover their other nationality, this will not be possible [for them to play for Kosovo] as they have to protect the other national teams.'

Yet Blatter had taken on the issue of Kosovo's limbo status, despite the fact that there was powerful political opposition to the move, in Russia and Serbia. 'I'm a footballer and I've been working for thirty-seven years serving in football,' he says. 'I took the initiative to say let them play. At least let them play on the level of clubs and the level of youth teams. Here we are at the end of the first step. I said we have to do something. It's not fair. It's not fair.' He sounds genuinely upset by the restrictions imposed on the Kosovars, especially the youth players whose careers have been hampered by the political bickering. I begin to believe him. 'We had the political opposition from Serbia before their [parliamentary] elections. But the elections are over now. There aren't any hurdles,' he continues. 'They still think in Serbia there will be some security problems as there is a Serb minority in Kosovo,' he explains, pointing out that by FIFA's threshold, there was sufficient international recognition already for Kosovo to become a full member, as Palestine had. 'But yesterday there was a decision at the UN that there will be no more supervision [of Kosovo's government]. So we can play now.'

The biggest hurdle for Kosovo's quest for footballing recognition, though, wasn't FIFA. It was UEFA, and in particular Michel Platini. Ever since the legendary French former player was elected president of European football's governing body, he had been lauded as Blatter's eventual successor as FIFA president. He was a football man, his supporters insisted, a man who had played the game at the highest level and knew football in a way that Blatter could only dream of. As head of UEFA he was also in charge of the Champions League, the world's most lucrative club competition. The friction in recent years between clubs and national teams had become open warfare. The wealthy clubs from Spain, Germany, France and especially England resented the fact that their property, their investments (the players) were being used to feather FIFA's nest through the World Cup. Platini was a man, they reasoned, who would fight for their interests. Blatter, they said disparagingly, seemed more interested in football in China or Saudi Arabia than in the region that was still the economic and cultural driver of the global game.

The two had clashed repeatedly and were now playing cat and mouse, a game of veiled criticisms and back-handed compliments. The FIFA presidential elections were due to be held in 2015 and unofficial campaigning had begun. 'I have just seen this morning, that the opposition [to Kosovo's recognition] has always come from UEFA but I just had this ...' Blatter passes me a printout of an article from *Inside World Football* by sports journalist Andrew Warshaw: 'Platini Gives Kosovo Fresh Hope' reads the headline. In it Platini seems to suggest that Kosovo might be able to play friendly games in the future after all, while reiterating his belief that Kosovo can't join without UN membership. Blatter gives a satisfied, almost condescending smile. 'I am happy that my colleague Michel Platini has now abandoned his very strong position,' he says, insisting I keep the article. 'That's for you. I talked with him, and he is a footballer. It is wrong, I told him, to hinder footballers playing football. He said: "No, I am fully with you. I am a footballer but these are the sacrosanct [UEFA] statutes I have [to work with]".'

Blatter is now warming to the theme of chiding his proxy opponent. The issue of Qatar's 2022 World Cup finals is another that Platini had been troubled by. The fallout from the vote had seen a level of scrutiny over the process that was unique for FIFA. Issues of alleged vote buying, vote swapping and political pressure had been raised. *France Football* ran an investigation into the vote and the strong links between Qatari money and the French government. Qatar's sovereign wealth fund had bought Paris Saint-Germain, turning it overnight into one of the richest clubs in the world. On the eve of the World Cup vote, in November 2010, Platini was invited to the Elysée Palace for a meeting with then French President Nicolas Sarkozy, a PSG fan. The Crown Prince of Qatar, who was later to become Emir, was also there. Platini denied that any pressure had been put on him to vote for Qatar, but he admitted that he had voted for the bid even if he later said he wanted the finals to be played in winter rather than in summer, as planned, where a Persian Gulf summer regularly hits 50 degrees Celsius. 'This is his approach and, first of all, it was a secret ballot and if it's a secret ballot you should not disclose who you are voting for. This is a democratic principle,' Blatter says in perfectly judged mock annoyance. 'Secondly, the location of the World Cup in Qatar is still clear in our books: Qatar in June, July 2022. That is it.'

Blatter is a man of perpetual movement. One former wife described how the marriage foundered because he was 'married to football'. Insiders had told me how he works fourteen hours a day. His energy, at the age of seventy-six is remarkable. By the time the 2015 FIFA presidential election takes place he'll be seventy-nine. If he stands, and wins again, he'll be eighty-three when his term ends. But those discussions are for another day. He has another appointment to go to and shakes my hand before leaving on his never-ending conveyor belt of handshakes and platitudes. In a few weeks the issue of Kosovo being allowed to play international friendlies will again go before FIFA's executive committee. Blatter is upbeat. Platini has come around to his way of thinking, he says, and he believes that his executive committee could even go further than merely approving friendlies. He hints at something far bigger on the horizon. 'There is a fascination of the game which we can't explain,' he says before he leaves. 'Football gives you balance when you have no balance in your life.' It wasn't clear whether he was talking about Kosovo or himself.

**

Eroll is driving a little too fast around the winding roads of the Swiss countryside. The single-lane track meanders uphill, through fields that look so Swiss they are almost a pastiche: a chocolate-box view of wooden chalets with white smoke rising from their chimneys and cows with bells around their necks chewing in the pastures. We arrive at what looks like one of the most expensive hotels in the world. The Swiss national team are staying here to prepare for their World Cup match against Albania. Fadil, Eroll and I get out of the car, straighten our jackets and walk with a false confidence in the hope that the doorman won't realise that we don't really belong here. Fadil is the most confident, and strides through the open door first, Eroll less so. The doorman eyes me suspiciously as I walk past him last. Perhaps he suspects we are arm dealers, too. Or perhaps he has seen the hole in the sole of my right shoe. It is getting late and the sun is setting on a terrace with an incredible panorama: a lake spread out in a valley below. The last of the Indian summer sun is still warm, but the wind is cool, an early harbinger of winter. We order the cheapest things on the menu, Diet Coke and coffee, and we wait until nightfall. Fadil's phone rings. The players are ready to receive us.

We walk through the hotel's maze of corridors, past the waiters in immaculately starched aprons, to the end of the building: an

Arab-style shisha lounge. Half the Swiss team is waiting for us. Sitting on the Moroccan-style sofa is Bayern Munich's Xherdan Shaqiri, Borussia Mönchengladbach's Granit Xhaka, Napoli's Valon Behrami and Dynamo Kiev's Admir Mehmedi. Fadil greets each of them warmly in Albanian. Eroll is behind, shaking hands and laying out his declaration on the table in front of them. Each of the players signs it without hesitation. Xherdan Shaqiri is the first. It has been a tough day for the Bayern Munich winger in the papers. It was his face on the front page of *SonntagsBlick*, the newspaper that had outlined the damage a Kosovo team could do to Switzerland. And it was his face on almost every one of the thirteen pages that followed it. 'Yeah, the Swiss papers are always like this,' Shaqiri says. 'The big paper was on me. "Maybe we'll lose Shaqiri." But now we don't have a team. Kosovo doesn't have a team in FIFA. And for the time being I play for Switzerland.' Shaqiri, like almost all the Swiss players of Kosovar descent of the same age, was born there, in the town of Gjilan in eastern Kosovo. Shaqiri's allegiance, like that of all of Switzerland's foreign-born players, had been questioned both directly and indirectly. But the issue was far more complex than that for Shaqiri. 'My mother and father are 100 per cent from Kosovo, my name says to all that my name is not from Switzerland and is from Kosovo and I was born in Kosovo,' he says when I ask how he would describe his identity. 'But after I was born I came here with my parents. I made my school here, played my first football here. For me it was always that I play for Switzerland. If I play, I play for Switzerland.'

It is a sentiment shared by all the players: pride in their homeland and their heritage, but also pride in the country that raised them and gave them opportunities they would never have dreamt of back in Kosovo. Valon Behrami left Kosovo when he was four years old and barely remembers anything except certain family comforts and a feeling of great loss. 'I remember I used to go to my grandma and play with a cat and a dog,' he recalls of his early days. He wears a tattoo of the flag of Kosovo on his forearm. 'These are the only things I remember. Coming to Switzerland I

equally talented young winger for FC Basel, were born in Switzerland after his parents fled Yugoslavia. 'Yes, of course,' he says when I asked whether he would consider playing for Kosovo. 'I don't know when Kosovo will have a national team. Two, three or five years' time. We have three players here who could play. For now we play for Switzerland, but later we will see what will happen.' First comes the Albania game. Switzerland have already won their first match in European qualification a few days before, a 2-0 victory against Slovenia. Granit Xhaka scored Switzerland's first goal but the star of the team was Xherdan Shaqiri. 'We are waiting for this match for six months,' he says of the Albania game before we leave, Eroll gathering the petition and holding it as if it is a winning lottery ticket. 'There will be more problems when we go to Tirana. The fans are little crazy. They are very loud.' He would hear in a few days' time exactly how loud the Albanian fans would be.

**

Lucerne, Switzerland

The Albanian's team hotel couldn't be more different from their Swiss opponents'. It is situated in the heart of the city of Lucerne and is being swamped by Albanians in red and black jerseys. The lobby is a chaotic mix of film crews, fans, players, models, ex-models, families, lovers, bemused Taiwanese tourists and Swiss businessmen. An Albanian sports TV station has even constructed its studio in the lobby, broadcasting live from amidst the turmoil. Fadil Vokrri is greeted warmly by the president of the Albanian federation, as well he might be, given how many Kosovar players will turn out for Albania tomorrow. But he reserves the warmest greeting for Agim Cana, the father of current Albanian captain Lorik Cana. Agim and Fadil had played in that great FC Prishtina side of the mid-1980s.

While Fadil meets old acquaintances, Eroll works the room. He is sitting next to Lorik Cana passing him the petition that

Shaqiri, Behrami and Xhaka signed the previous day. Like them, Cana also fled to Switzerland as a young boy when the civil war broke out. 'I lived in Switzerland for ten years,' he says after he signs the form and hands it back. Eroll disappears quickly, off to farm as many signatures as he can before tomorrow's match. It might have been a homecoming of sorts for Cana, but he had none of the split loyalties that the Swiss players had. 'From the start it was clear I would play for the Albanian national team,' he says, definitely. 'I would not play for another nation.' Perhaps it was the Cana family's earlier experiences in Switzerland that shaped Lorik's views. As political refugees they had to renew their visa every six months, never knowing if this one was to be their last. Perhaps it was the fact that he was signed by PSG as a sixteen-year-old and moved to France not long after getting to Switzerland. Either way, Cana's view of his heritage was one of a wider Albanian identity. Many Albanians still believed in a 'Greater Albania', claiming much of the territory surrounding the country, including parts of Serbia proper, Montenegro, Macedonia, Kosovo and even Greece. Kosovo was the only ethnically Albanian territory that had any real claim to independence. But Cana saw the Albanian national team as an alternative to an unlikely dream of a Greater Albania. 'When we are part of the Albanian national team, we represent all the Albanians around the world not just those in Albania,' he explains. 'More than half of the nation live around the state. When we are part of this national team we make something unique and amazing. We make a union between all our people and the national team is the only thing that does that.' The injustice of his homeland not being acknowledged, despite close to one hundred countries recognising it, was of immediate concern. Which was why he agreed to sign the pledge. 'It is difficult if you are not recognised by the world,' he says. 'The United Nations and football is the same thing. The country deserves to be recognised as a country, as a state and to be recognised in football as well. They deserve to play football.'

Would you play for Kosovo, if Fadil, Eroll and the Football Federation of Kosovo requested it, I ask.

'They already asked me,' he replies, although he turned down the request. 'When you say the national team, I already represent and play for my nation. Sure, I was born in Kosovo. One day we want to have all the Albanian players in the world play for one team.' I'm not sure this is what Fadil and Eroll had in mind when they approached the Albanian team for their support. But Cana makes one final point that everyone can agree on. Switzerland are the favourites and Albania are massive underdogs who have never qualified for the finals of any major tournament. 'We would be a great team,' he says of his dream for a Greater Albania national team. 'We would qualify for the World Cup.'

Eroll has everything he needs for the time being. His petition is full of names, as he had planned. We wait to leave, but Fadil is still occupied. Groups of Albanian fans are taking it in turn to have their pictures taken with him. We wait an hour until he is finished.

**

The Swissporarena does not look or feel like a home crowd. In one hour's time the 2014 World Cup qualifier between Switzerland and Albania will begin but there are few Swiss flags being flown. Rather, it is the red flag with black eagle of Albania that is on display. But among the red and black is the blue and gold of the Kosovo flag. Many have come with the two sides fused together – one half Albanian, one half Kosovar: flags, scarves, T-shirts, painted faces. T-shirts proudly declare the desire to form a Greater Albania, showing a future superstate stretching from Greece into Serbia. The match has been declared as 'High Risk' by the Swiss authorities given that the Swiss fans will be in the minority. But the crowd is not aggressively anti-Swiss. Almost no one has travelled from Albania or Kosovo to be here. Everyone, it appears, already lives in Switzerland.

In the stadium more than two-thirds of the crowd are pro-Albanian. In one stand, behind the goal where some of the Albanian fans sit, they unfurl a banner that reads in English: 'Proud to be

Albanian'. The referee's whistle could barely be heard over the roar of the crowd. As predicted, of the twenty-two players on the pitch, nine had either been born in Kosovo or raised by Kosovar parents, three for Switzerland and six for Albania, over half of their team. As Shaqiri had feared, he was in for a ferocious night, but not from the Swiss. Every time he, or Behrami, or Xhaka, touched the ball they were met with a wall of boos and screams. 'Traitor!' the 'away' fans chanted in Albanian. Shaqiri was unaffected by the hostility. He had walked out on to the pitch with the Swiss, Albanian and Kosovo flags stitched on to his boots for the occasion. When they played the national anthems he stayed silent through both of them. When the first goal came, it was scored by Shaqiri for Switzerland. He dummied, sent Albania's Kosovo-born goalkeeper Samir Ujkani the wrong way and scored in the left-hand corner. He did not celebrate either.

Granit Xhaka – the youngest of the players to sign Fadil and Eroll's pledge who had also appeared to be the most likely to want to switch his allegiance to a Kosovo national team – seems to be struggling with the vitriol that is raining down on him. He is having a bad game. The boos and the chants only get worse when Gorkan Inler scores a second from the penalty spot. The biggest noise of the night comes from the Albanian fans when Xhaka is substituted. He had missed an open goal which would have made it 3-0 shortly before, but Switzerland have done their job and won the game, making it two World Cup qualification victories out of two. They are top of their group. The Swiss-Kosovar players meet with their Albanian opponents in the centre circle and embrace. Shaqiri swaps his jersey and leaves the field with an Albanian shirt on his chest.

Fadil and Eroll watched the match from the stands with a mixture of pride and uneasiness at the negative chanting from the Albanian section. Shaqiri, though, had led by example. 'We are proud,' Eroll says, still sitting in his seat, as Fadil is again mobbed by fans. 'We must learn that Albanians can play for other national teams.' The big decision, though, takes place a few hours' drive down the road, in Zurich, at FIFA's HQ. 'We are waiting for the decision of the executive committee,' Eroll says. It is surely only a matter of time, he believes, given Sepp Blatter's staunch support for the campaign. He sounds excited rather than nervous. It will be, he reasons, another important move towards recognition. 'After that, step by step, more countries will recognise us. Maybe we could play with a symbol, under a UN or UEFA flag? It is unbelievable how we can have such talented players without a national team.'

The controversy that surrounded the match doesn't end at the final whistle. A Swiss TV commentator has to apologise after accusing Granit Xhaka of missing his chance on purpose because he felt more Albanian than Swiss. A few hours after the game it is also reported that Xhaka has taken to Facebook to apologise to the Albanian nation, insisting that he isn't a traitor as had been suggested because he had, in fact, missed the chance on purpose. The post ended: 'Proud to be ALBANIAN'. The comments were picked up by the Swiss press and went around the world. None of it was true. It was a fake account. Xhaka had written no such words, but the speed with which it was believed and spread across the world told its own story.

Fadil and Eroll took their petition and handed it to Sepp Blatter before the FIFA executive committee meeting a few weeks later. They were hopeful. And why not? They had a unique, high-profile collection of signatures and the support of the most powerful man in football. True, the issue of Kosovo had been taken off the meeting's actual agenda, and replaced by an 'XXX'. But they had been made promises. What could go wrong?

The executive committee held their meeting and Kosovo was not discussed. The next day Sepp Blatter flew to Russia, to announce the host cities for the 2018 World Cup finals. There Blatter embraced the man who was, more than any other, preventing Kosovo's recognition as a sovereign state: Russian president Vladimir Putin. The issue of Kosovo's national football team had been postponed for another, less embarrassing day.

9

CROATIA, SERBIA

Belgrade, Socialist Federal Republic of Yugoslavia. May 1991.

It was 8 May 1991 and 7,000 people had gathered at the Partizan Stadium in Belgrade for the final of the Marshal Tito Cup. The match was between Hajduk Split, a team from the Croatian city on the Adriatic Sea, and Red Star Belgrade, a team that had once embodied the Yugoslav ideal by featuring players from each of its constituent socialist republics, but which would later become steeped in Serbian ultra-nationalism.

The cup was named after the communist dictator who had held together Yugoslavia's ethnically and religiously diverse republics after the Second World War. It had been something of a success, too. Compared to the communist repression in, say, Hungary or Czechoslovakia, Yugoslavs had enjoyed greater personal and economic freedom. Tito had been revered by many Yugoslavs, too, something that couldn't be said of General Jaruzelski in Poland, or the egregious Ceauşescu in Romania. But after Tito's death in 1980, the ancient enmities that had been buried under his banner of state federalism began to rise to the surface. In 1991 those enmities were about to explode into a vicious conflict, the like of which hadn't been seen in Europe for nearly five decades. Civil war was breathing down their necks.

The two teams lined up for the national anthem. The Hajduk Split players didn't sing it. They wore black armbands in that game, to honour twelve Croatian policemen killed in Borovo Selo, a suburb of Vukovar, itself on the Croatian/Serbian border.

It was a Croatian city, but with a large Serbian minority. The two communities had co-existed under Tito, living next to each other, working together, inter-marrying, as always happens with proximity in times of peace. But Vukovar was a city where the opening fault lines of the coming civil war were to swallow it whole. The Serb and Croat communities had turned on each other. The Borovo Selo incident was sparked when the local Croatian police force tried to replace a Yugoslav flag with a Croatian one. A local Serb militia intervened and arrested them. When more Croatian police were sent to free them, fighting broke out and the twelve were killed, alongside three Serbs. Temporary calm was only restored when the army intervened. It was just the start, and more was to follow: tit-for-tat murders, provocations and massacres. In Vukovar in 1991 you were either a Serb or a Croat, and nothing in between.

Yet Siniša Mihajlović did stand between both, even as he stood with his Red Star Belgrade team-mates. His perm was fashioned short at the sides and long at the back. It bounced as he walked as if attached by springs. Even the miserable downpour that had doused the Partizan Stadium couldn't dampen its enthusiasm. Mihajlović was one of the most promising players to emerge from Yugoslavia's impressive conveyor belt of talent. He'd starred for FK Vojvodina, a small, unfancied team from the northern Serbian city of Novi Sad which had broken the monopoly of the 'big four' clubs in Yugoslav football and managed to win the league title two seasons before. To put it into some kind of comparison it would be similar to Norwich City building a team that beat Manchester City, Manchester United, Arsenal and Chelsea before clinching the league title. That success had brought Mihajlović to the notice of a team that was rightly heralded as one of the finest in Europe. In a few weeks' time Red Star Belgrade would play in the final of the European Cup against Marseille. Hajduk Split hadn't won the Yugoslav league since the 1970s, but it, too, had a young team of talented players who would emerge to achieve greater things, players like Slaven Bilić, Robert Jarni, Alen Bokšić and their young captain Igor Štimac. Still, the Marshal Tito Cup final was against a Hajduk Split side that was a shadow of the great team of the 1970s and would clearly be a whitewash.

Mihajlović already had a reputation as a hothead who had thrown himself into Red Star Belgrade's Serb nationalist identity. But he wasn't fully accepted at first. He was was born in Vukovar to a Croatian mother and a Serbian father. Much like a born-again Christian, he was eager to prove beyond doubt his dedication to the cause. He knew many of the Croatian players on the pitch that day, having played with them in local clubs in and around Vukovar. They had all once even considered each other friends. But not any more.

That cup final was a remarkable match for several reasons. For one, Hajduk won the game 1-0 thanks to a solitary goal from Bokšić, the future Croatia international striker who would go on to star for Marseille and win the Champions League with them. Exactly three weeks later, Red Star Belgrade would win the European Cup, after beating Marseille in the final. Red Star had been a revelation in the competition, defeating Bayern Munich in the semi-finals. Mihajlović scored in a sensational second leg in Belgrade. A comical injury-time own goal saw Red Star qualify for the final. A pitch invasion followed and the turf was torn to pieces for souvenirs. The final itself, though, would turn out to be one of the worst in living memory, something that even Mihajlović would later admit. After playing expansive football en route to the final, Red Star seemed content to wait for penalties, grinding out a 0-0 draw. They won the shoot-out 5-3 and Mihajlović was one of the five trusted to take a spot-kick.

Yet the Hajduk–Red Star match is remembered for other reasons: a battle on the pitch between Mihajlović and Štimac that is today still wrapped in the myths and half-truths of war propaganda. While Mihajlović had embraced Red Star and everything that it stood for, Štimac was an avowed Croatian nationalist who would later lament that he didn't get the chance to fight in the civil war. Mihajlović careered around the pitch on that dreadful wet May afternoon like a man possessed, launching into tackles that today would almost certainly have resulted in red cards. Štimac was on the receiving end of almost all of them, but he gave as good as he got. One Hajduk Split player had to be substituted as a result of a Mihajlović tackle and a brawl broke out between the players as he lay on the turf. Štimac was in the middle of it and the referee eventually sent off both men. Words were spoken between the two, words that to this day still engender speculation in the Serbian and Croatian press. Some say death threats were exchanged. Others, promises that home towns would be destroyed in the coming war. Either way, it was the start of a two-decade feud between the two men, a feud that embodied something of Yugoslavia's own bloody demise.

The Marshal Tito Cup final would also be one of the last matches that any Croatian or Slovenian team would play in Yugoslav football. Full, open war descended and Croatian and Slovenian independence was declared soon after, although the league limped on for one more season without them. Vukovar was destroyed. The 7,000 fans watching in the Partizan Stadium didn't know it yet but they were witnessing the beginning of the end of Yugoslavia.

**

Zagreb, Croatia. March 2013.

Igor Štimac is in a private, sound-proof dining room. He closes the door behind him, sits down and leans forward, talking in a low and powerful growl. 'It doesn't need lots of explanation,' he says with an intense, quiet violence. 'Everyone in the world knows what was going on twenty years ago.' Štimac looks disarmingly similar to the young man who had captained Hajduk Split on that afternoon in 1991. His hair is a little thinner, but he has always looked like a heavyweight boxer one fight away from his last, even in his twenties when he was captain of the newly independent Croatia national team. He is now its coach and is preparing for a World Cup qualification match that needs little introduction. Croatia have been drawn against Serbia and will play in Zagreb in a few days' time.

On paper Croatia are the favourites. Outside the door the Croatian national team is having lunch. I spotted Real Madrid's Luka Modrić perusing the buffet alongside Bayern Munich striker Mario Mandžukić. Croatia are currently ranked ninth by FIFA and can lay claim to being one of the best teams in the world. Serbia, however, isn't an opponent to be judged by form or rank. Instead, a clash between the two revives memories of the recent past. It brings the war and everything that was won, as well as everything that was lost, into sharp focus. 'We are trying to isolate my team from the surrounding euphoria,' Štimac says of the intense media pressure his players have been put under since the draw was made. No one wants to be part of the team that lost to Serbia and it's not just the unrealistic expectations of Croatia's tabloid journalists. It is also, as Štimac points out, the expectations of 'the supporters and all those people that lost their families and homes in the war'. It is just eighteen years since the end of the Yugoslav civil war, recent enough in the collective memory to remember a time before, during and after. Štimac lived through all three and had his own demons of that time to take care of in the lead-up to this match. While he takes charge of Croatia, Serbia is being coached by Siniša Mihajlović, Štimac's old enemy, a man he hasn't spoken to for twenty years, since that day in Belgrade in May 1991 when they were both sent off in the Marshal Tito Cup final.

Štimac grimaces when I ask about that match. Of course, his memories of that game in 1991 are happier. He was sent off, but, as captain, he lifted the cup after the final whistle. He still feels injustice for being sent off and especially for being accused, falsely he claims, of pulling Mihajlović's hair. 'You have to take the game and watch it,' he urges me. I have done, and it appears that, on this point at least, Štimac is telling the truth: he did not indecently assault Mihajlović's magnificent mullet. 'That was one of the best leagues in Europe,' Štimac recalls. 'We had the European champions, and we beat them in the final.' The reason for its strength, according to Štimac, was a rule that prevented any player from leaving to play abroad until he was twenty-eight. 'You can imagine how big the quality was. Compare to now, six countries out of that one. Now we have to work with young talented players for ten years, they play one season and go to a big club,' he says, sounding almost rueful for the league that was lost. 'Now it is corporate football.' Yet, in 1991, the spectre of war was there and everyone knew life would change for ever. 'It was at the door,' Štimac remembers. 'It was knocking on the door.'

The Marshal Tito Cup final was Hajduk Split's only chance of silverware that season. They were lagging behind Red Star in the league, but Red Star had one eye on the European Cup final. Yet the match attained much more importance for both sides because of the rising tensions. It was decided by a single Alen Bokšić goal. Bokšić is here in Zagreb, too, as Štimac's assistant. But Štimac still maintains he did little to deserve his sending off. 'We had a few tackles on each other and then the second tackle he got sent off,' Štimac recalls. 'In the mess caused by his tackle I was staying in the middle keeping the players aside. The referee decided to send me off!' The red card wasn't controversial. But what was said between the two that sparked such a violent confrontation was. 'There are lots and lots of false stores that were created,' he says. 'That I was fighting him, that I said something to him, he said something to me, that I pulled his hair.' A few years after the incident Mihajlović remembered it differently. 'In one moment we were face to face,' he said in an interview. 'He leaned to me and said, his voice full of hatred: "I pray to God your whole family in Borovo gets murdered!" At that moment I could have killed him with my teeth.'

Štimac denies he said anything at all. 'Siniša was very young then,' he says of his memories of Mihajlović at that time. 'But Siniša's problem was that he obviously had to prove something to others because his mother was, and still is, Croatian. His father

Serb. So you have to put that question to him. What was there to prove? To whom? And why?' Mihajlović's mixed parentage had certainly been a problem at his new club, where Red Star's officials and the club's notorious ultras, the Delije, had been uncomfortable with his Croatian heritage. The Delije were led by Željko Ražnatović, better known as Arkan. Arkan would rise to become a powerful Serb warlord and his bloodthirsty paramilitary group – Arkan's Tigers – was, in an early incarnation at least, drawn from the ranks of the Delije. They would become one of the most feared fighting forces during the civil war. Mihajlović was a close friend of Arkan, who had taken him under his wing and offered him protection while he was in Belgrade. Arkan even informed Mihajlović when Serb forces had captured his uncle, an officer in the Croatian army. The tip-off allowed Mihajlović to arrange his release before he was executed.

When the Yugoslavia that Tito built was breathing its last in 1992, both players moved to Europe. Štimac would end up in England playing for Derby County and West Ham United. Mihajlović thrived in Italy and became one of the most feared midfielders in the world. The Yugoslavia team continued on in various guises – from the Federal Republic of Yugoslavia to Serbia and Montenegro to, finally, just Serbia. As that team was morphing to fit the changing political world, the Croatia team had taken a leading role in moulding its fledgling nation, which declared independence in 1991. 'We were lucky to be promoters of a young country. It was a special pride,' says Štimac of those early years. 'We were singing the Croatian national anthem and flying our flag around the world.' Praise came from higher quarters, too. 'Our first president Franjo Tudjman said that the Croatian football team had done much more than all politicians together will ever do for Croatia.'

Before they were drawn in the same group for 2014 World Cup qualification, Croatia and Serbia had never played each other before, at least not in Serbia's current form. In 1999, with Croatia flush from finishing third at the 1998 World Cup, Štimac and

Mihajlović faced each other when Croatia and what was then called the Federal Republic of Yugoslavia – essentially Serbia and Montenegro – were drawn in the same qualification group for the 2000 European Championships in Holland and Belgium. It was only four years since the end of the fighting and a few months after Belgrade had been under NATO attack to punish Slobodan Milošović's new war against the Kosovars in the south of the country. 'The wounds were still fresh then,' Štimac remembers of the atmosphere that surrounded that game. The Croatia team travelled to Belgrade under army escort. 'There was lots of pressure, the NATO attacks on Belgrade, it was difficult to go there and play that game.'

Both men starred in their respective away matches. Štimac was the rock at the heart of the defence in Belgrade, if he does say so himself, where Croatia secured a 0-0 draw. 'I remember the first game in Belgrade. I played it. I was one of the best players on the pitch.' His other big memory from that game was a floodlight failure that plunged the stadium into darkness. Štimac still suspects it was a deliberate attempt to intimidate the team. 'The lights went off, just like that,' he smiles. 'You didn't know what is going to happen next. It was kind of intentional to bring us into shock.' The return fixture saw Mihajlović arrive back in Zagreb. When the home fans hung a flag with 'Vukovar' on it, Mihajlović fell to his knees in front of it. He maintained it was to show respect to all those who had died, but it incensed the crowd, who were further infuriated when the game ended 2-2, despite the Yugoslav team having played with ten men for the entire second half. The Federal Republic of Yugoslavia finished top of the group and qualified for the European Championships. Croatia was eliminated. 'I didn't play because I had two yellow cards but we had five players out injured, Prosinečki, Boban, Bilić …' Štimac says by way of explanation for the failure, but clearly still smarting from the humiliation. Especially the fact that, in his opinion, a perfectly good goal had been disallowed. 'One of the balls was put behind their goalkeeper. It was behind the line by thirty-nine centimetres.'

Today's game has been singled out as a potential flashpoint ever since the 2014 qualification draw was made. It was agreed that away fans from both teams would be banned, for both matches. It was also, arguably, the toughest group of all in European World Cup qualification. Belgium was in the group, as well as a third former republic of Yugoslavia: Macedonia. Scotland and Wales would have their say on the outcome, too. 'We are favourites,' says Štimac before he leaves to get back to his players. He talks about protecting them from the storm that is about to hit them. Many of them were born after the war and have no memory of it. To them the war stories are largely second-hand tales. For some, like Australian-born defender Josep Šimunić, the war was filtered through the enlarged lens of a refugee family's experience many miles from home. Others now played with Serbs in their club teams with no problems. 'I will take this on to my chest,' Štimac says of the expectation that will bear down on his team at kick-off. 'We are grateful to God that we are the generation that has the opportunity to win the game on Friday and give our nation happiness and joy. But that does not mean,' he says, correcting himself so as not to sound overly nationalistic or triumphalist, 'that we need revenge against someone.'

**

Novi Sad, Serbia

The Football Association of Serbia's brand new training complex can be found thirty kilometres north of the capital, Belgrade, near the city of Novi Sad. Stickers on the glass of the automatic sliding doors at the complex entrance warn visitors of articles that may not be brought in: cigarettes, guns and, most importantly, ice cream. Inside, frightening looking security guards prowl the lobby, ready to pounce on any forbidden frozen dairy products. Siniša Mihajlović is giving his daily press conference before Belgrade's sports journalists. Serbia hasn't enjoyed the same success as Croatia in recent years, but that hasn't stopped them producing players who star at top European clubs. Nemanja Vidić is one Serbian player, at Manchester United; Branislav Ivanović, at Chelsea, is another. Still, Mihajlović is now trusting in youth and has constructed, as he will say on numerous occasions over the course of the next week, the youngest squad in Europe for Serbia's World Cup qualification campaign. Perhaps he has learned from his time at Red Star Belgrade, when a team of players barely out of their teens managed somehow to win the 1991 European Cup. But those players were old before their time and had thrived in a poisonous atmosphere. Like Štimac's team, almost all of Mihajlović's current side of youngsters were born around or after the war. Either way, they are too young to remember. While Mihajlović, Štimac, even the Kosovar midfielder Fadil Vokrri, who played for Partizan Belgrade, had been raised on inter-republic rivalries, none of this generation of players would have played in a match steeped in the kind of hatred that engulfed Croatia v Serbia. Most of them had probably never even set foot in Croatia before. Yet in a few days they will travel to the Maksimir Stadium in Zagreb.

The Maksimir has a special place in both Croatian and Serbian lore. It is often referred to as the site of the first battle of Croatian independence. It was here that, in 1990, a match between Dinamo Zagreb and Red Star descended into a riot between Red Star's Delije ultras, led by Arkan, and Dinamo's Bad Blue Boys. Famously, Dinamo's star striker Zvonimir Boban launched a kick at a policeman who was allegedly attacking a Dinamo Zagreb fan, cementing his legend for ever with Croatian nationalists; Boban's was the first kick of the Croatian War of Independence. Never mind that Dinamo Zagreb played the whole of the next season in the Yugoslav league, nor the fact that the 'Serbian' police officer Boban attacked was in fact a Bosnian Muslim. But the stadium was still a sacred space. Outside the Maksimir a shrine has been built to commemorate the members of the Bad Blue Boys who died fighting in the civil war. Serbia's current crop of young players will be walking into a time machine. They will be on their own, too, because of that ban on travelling fans. The only Serbians allowed into the ground, other than the players and the officials, will be a busload of journalists. Special precautions are being taken in case a 'welcoming party' of Croatian fans is waiting for them at the Serbia/Croatia border. The Serbs even have their own armed security guards.

It has taken me far longer than it should to get to Serbia. The two countries may be neighbours, but links between the two are kept to a bare minimum. A handful of half-empty buses set off on the seven-hour drive from Zagreb to Belgrade. On arrival in the middle of the night, a Serbian taxi driver in his fifties vents his fury at me about the US, England, Tony Blair and NATO. He only stops when I convince him with the few phrases I know that I am in fact Polish. His face turns from hateful scowl to beaming happiness in a heartbeat. The Poles are acceptable. He believes we are in fact now brothers. On the drive from Belgrade to Novi Sad it is clear that Serbia is visibly poorer than Croatia. While Croatia is preparing to join the European Union in a few months' time, Serbia's sense of injustice has festered in isolation. It is partially understandable. Serbia has endured two wars, a period of UN sanctions and seen its territory shrink with every successful secessionist claim. The next in line is Kosovo. I thought of Fadil and the Kosovar FA. He had played here, in Belgrade, just as Slobodan Milošović was rolling back the autonomy Tito had granted Kosovo in the 1970s. He would play his home games at the Partizan Stadium, the same stadium at which that famous Marshal Tito Cup final had taken place in 1991. By then he had long gone, and was playing for Fenerbahçe in the Turkish league.

Siniša Mihajlović is now sitting in a back office after finishing his press conference. He looks older, wiser and greyer. His mop of long hair that opposition players would frequently tug has long gone. Also absent is the rage. He is calm and friendly. 'I don't want to open old stories,' he says when I ask him about that match in 1991. 'I know what I said and he [Štimac] knows what he said.

And only the two of us know what was really said in that moment.' Over the years both Mihajlović and Štimac had made various claims as to what *was* said, and Štimac also made his views known. 'Here is a man who spread lies about me such as that I was gay, he also said he could strangle me with his bare hands,' Štimac had explained in an interview long before he became Croatia coach. But now both men were national team coaches. They had responsibilities and their actions could have far greater and far more inflammatory repercussions than a single player's indiscretion ever could.

As a player Mihajlović had been blessed with a sublime left foot. He still holds the record for the most number of goals scored from free-kicks in Serie A, where he played for Lazio and Sampdoria. But in 1991 he was an angry, talented young man conflicted by the world around him. Yet his early life in Vukovar was happy; idyllic even. 'I had a great childhood, we never asked someone if they were Serbian or Croatian,' he recalls when I ask him about those early days growing up in Croatia. 'You only recognised that by their name or which club they supported. Hajduk and Dinamo, you are Croatian. Red Star, Partizan, Serbian. Nobody asked which country you are from until one day. And then everything changed.' His talent was spotted in the smaller clubs around Vukovar that had produced a slew of incredible players. Many of the future Croatia national team, including Slaven Bilić, had been born from the same teams. Mihajlović also very nearly signed for Dinamo Zagreb in 1987, but his stubborn nature got the better of him. As the *Guardian*'s Jonathan Wilson wrote in a profile of Mihajlović, 'he was told by Mirko Jović, the Croatian coach of the Yugoslavia Under-20 side, that he would be selected for the youth World Cup only if he signed' for Dinamo Zagreb. Incensed by what he saw as blackmail, he instead chose to sign for FK Vojvodina. It was to prove a pivotal moment in his life. Rather than joining the other Croatian players who went on TO star at the 1998 World Cup – a moment every bit as important to Croatians as independence itself

– Mihajlović eventually moved to Red Star and embraced the growing Serbian nationalism at the club. It was here he met and befriended Arkan and watched from Belgrade as his home city was destroyed. 'My mother is Croatian, my father was Serbian, I was born in Vukovar and I remember one Vukovar,' he says when I ask him about his home city. He has only returned once, after the war, but the experience was so harrowing he has not been back since. 'Everything was crushed. I met some soldiers after the war. They had some instruments, to detect bombs, and showed me a way to my old house,' he recalls of his return. The bomb detection devices were necessary because his neighbourhood had been heavily mined. 'There was nothing. Mine was the first house in Vukovar that was crushed.' He toured the city but nothing existed of the old life he remembered. 'I tried to walk to my school and I could not recognise the way,' he says. 'I had lived there eighteen years. Someone had to show me the way. It was crushed. There were no houses, nothing. It's a totally different city now. For me it is too hard to be there.'

As the careers of Mihajlović and Štimac progressed, the war ended, new ones began and new countries were formed. Both retired and found their way back to their respective national teams. They remained the best of enemies, until a chance meeting a few months ago when the pair were at a UEFA conference that brought together the national team coaches of all fifty-three members. It was the first time in twenty-three years that they had spoken to each other, the first words since that match in May 1991. 'We had a coffee, sat down and discussed a few things,' Štimac had said, coolly, when we spoke back in Zagreb. 'As national team managers for our countries we have responsibilities to act responsibly. Not to bring tension. Not to put gasoline on the fire.' Did you get on, I asked Štimac. Did you like him? 'I didn't have a problem with him,' he replied non-committally. Mihajlović, though, was cautiously positive. 'We cleared something between us,' he said. 'I can say he has respect for my side and I feel some respect for his side. Now our relations are clear.

That old story stays history.' Mihajlović believed that now was the time for peace. He knew what the match meant to the Serbs and the Croats. The national team, he says, was very important for his country, especially after the wars and the sanctions and the current financial hardships that Serbia is currently experiencing. 'We have additional obligations to give something more, to give victory in Croatia so they may be happy with the win. But if we lose,' he says, 'it is like a knife.'

Both coaches believe that, if they could bury the hatchet, others can follow suit. 'I will be peaceful during the game and we must put aside what has happened between our nations, between our countries,' Mihajlović says. 'What I can guarantee is full respect from our side for our opponents. We will show the highest level of fair play. I suspect they will do the same and I suspect sport and fair play will win. I want to show that we are a civilised people.' For many of Serbia's players the old stories are indeed history. 'I asked the players: "Where were you born? Have any of you ever been in Croatia, in Zagreb or Split?" The answer was no,' he says. 'The players are so young they don't know what we had and what we lost. They live today in a new world with a new country. They do not have the impressions or memories that we have who were born in Yugoslavia.'

**

Zagreb, Croatia

Ban Jelačić Square in central Zagreb has been filled with fans drinking since the morning of the game. The white and red checked shirt of the Croatian national team can be seen on all sides, but the main throng of supporters are gathering around the statue of Josip Jelačić, a nineteenth-century Croatian nationalist leader who had fallen out of favour with Yugoslavia's rulers but who had been rehabilitated since independence and his statue restored to his position, on his horse, sword in hand, on the square. Around him a few dozen skinheads are singing nationalist songs while letting off smoke bombs. Several of them give Nazi salutes as they sing, a reminder of the nastier edge of Croatian ultra-nationalism.

During the Second World War, a prototype Croatian state was run by the puppet Ustaše regime, a fascist movement that butchered hundreds of thousands of Serbs, Jews and Roma until the Axis fell. Their chants and salutes can still be heard at the Maksimir, rehabilitated and repackaged as no more, many fans claim, than an expression of nationalist pride. The straight-arm salutes, though, are impossible to misconstrue. The riot police stationed nearby lean against a shop window, viewing their behaviour impassively. Every Croatian town and city seems to be represented here. Their names have been carefully written over the white strip in the middle of the Croatian flag. One place has been honoured more than any other: Vukovar. On the road towards the Maksimir Stadium thousands of fans can be seen all the way to the horizon. They have taken over a main junction near the stadium and have laid a Croatian flag with the word 'Vukovar' emblazoned across its centre. The crowd crouches low, shaking the huge flag as they chant the city's name before raising it up above the throng. A female blow-up doll decked out to look like a Serbian player, its front and back orifices prised open, is passed above the crowd, too. 'We will fuck them!' a fan screams with a smile on his face, holding the blonde, big-lipped rubber doll by the ankle as I take a picture. At the nearby shrine to the Bad Blue Boys who died in the fight for Croatian independence fresh flowers have been laid and candles lit.

The great and good of Croatian society are sitting in a VIP tent outside the stadium watching a traditional folk band play on stage. An obscenely large gourmet buffet has been laid out as beautiful girls, employed for the occasion ostensibly to give directions, stand in pairs looking moody. Davor Šuker is moving effortlessly between tables, cracking jokes and chatting up any woman who appears to be on her own. Šuker had played in the same Croatia team as Štimac. While two of the abiding memories of the 1998 World Cup were Croatia's incredible run to the semi-finals, and Slaven Bilić's hilariously faked facial injury, successfully engineered to get France defender Laurent Blanc sent off, it was Šuker who had scored the six goals that had taken them there in the first place, winning him the Golden Boot in the process. He has a reputation as a party animal and a ladies' man, but is now chairman of the Croatian Football Federation and appears to be on his best behaviour. 'We are old people in football and this match means more than football, of course. It means a lot in the Balkan regions,' he says of the game. For Šuker it is vital that the game goes ahead peacefully. The world is watching. Croatia will be joining the European Union in July and the match offers a chance for the outside world to see how the country is dealing with the intolerance that has blighted the terraces of Croatian football since independence. 'I am sure there will not be one problem in the crowd or on the pitch,' he says defiantly. 'I am the chairman and I need to be calm. We need to bring this game to an end. We want the three points but we don't need them. It is more crucial for Serbia.'

Croatia's success in recent years has obscured an important point about their improbable rise. The country's population is just five million yet they qualify regularly for the finals of major championships and their players can be found in Europe's best sides. 'We qualified for Euro '96 and France '98 and made a big pride to be a Croat,' Šuker says, revealing the importance of the national team in projecting his country's identity on to the world stage. 'We are just five million people. Everyone recognises us now, our small country. It is not easy to beat Italy, to beat England, to beat Germany. But Croatia always does this. I think we made a great introduction for Croatia in the world. And now we have a new generation of players like Modrić and Mandžukić.'

As the night draws in and kick-off approaches, the remnants of the old world that Štimac and Mihajlović both know, but hope to counter, are in the ground. The freezing Maksimir Stadium is packed on all sides. It is strange-looking: all four stands are uncovered thanks to a botched attempt at renovating it. Three tiers rise into the sky, yet only the top two are accessible. The bottom tier has been hidden behind thick blue material, no doubt a measure aimed at preventing a repeat of the pitch invasion and riots that took place here during the match between Dinamo and Red Star in 1991. The songs of the crowd move through the air like an electrical current. Every inch of space at the front of the stands is covered in flags and banners. As the teams walk out on to the pitch, and each Serbian player's name is announced, a roar rises from the stands in a frenzied crescendo, reaching a peak when that of Siniša Mihajlović is called out. Two sections of crowd chant 'Vukovar, Vukovar' when he appears. Later they will chant 'Kill the Serbs'. A huge banner, covering three stands, is brought out as the whistle is blown to start the match. It translates:

Through the Rough Times and Through the Battles
We Defended Honourably Our Homes.
The Ones Who Defended Our Land Didn't Die In Vain.
Our Flag Is Flying and We Don't Have To Hide it Any More.

Here, too, were the Serbian journalists who had made the trip from Belgrade. I had travelled with them as their coach had been stopped at the Serbia/Croatia border. They had been met by three Croatian riot vans, two police cars and motorcades of police motorcycles that travelled with them front and back. A Croatian police officer had boarded the coach and addressed the passengers over a loudspeaker: 'You should not,' he intoned gravely, 'respond to any provocation.' He ordered the journalists off the bus, who were then transferred to a waiting Croatian coach. The other coach's Serbian number plates were deemed too much of a risk. The motorcade flashed through the streets of the Croatian capital as confused onlookers wondered what the fuss was about, and then we arrived at the hotel. But there was no welcoming party of ultras, no provocation, just polite waiters handing out complimentary glasses of Croatian brandy. Soon, though, the Serbians would wish they had stayed at home.

The Serbian anthem was drowned out by screams and boos. Perhaps it was the pressure, or the occasion, but Croatia quickly took control of the match. After forty minutes Croatia are 2-0 up, both goals the result of mistakes by the two most experienced players on the Serbian team. Manchester City's Aleksandar Kolarov carelessly gives the ball away near his own penalty box, allowing striker Ivica Olić to feed Mario Mandžukić, who blasts Croatia ahead. Olić scores the second when a cross evades everybody, including Serbia's captain Branislav Ivanović, who, inexplicably, doesn't clear the ball into the stand. Instead, he dithers, lets the ball pass him by and allows Olić to steal in at the back post. Even he is surprised when the ball comes to him, and it bounces off his chest into the goal. The second goal has a miraculous effect on one man sitting in the disabled area in front of the press box. He leaps from his wheelchair and celebrates with the rest of the stadium. He spends the rest of the match sheepishly smoking and drinking beer, but paces back and forth alongside the pitch until the final whistle.

There would be no comeback for Serbia. Croatia had done enough in the first half and the match finished 2-0. There was no trouble either. The Serbian journalists could only hold their hands up and admit the better side won. One predicted that Mihajlović would be sacked in the morning. The players on both sides embraced, the barriers erected by their fathers' generation now a little smaller than they had been before the match. But, most poignantly of all, after the final whistle Mihajlović and Štimac approached each other. The peace between the two had held for four months. It had survived for the ninety minutes, even as the ultra-nationalistic chants from the Croatian fans rained down on Mihajlović. And it would survive the full-time whistle and a defeat that had surely condemned Serbia to elimination from World Cup qualification. The two men met each other again on the pitch. They embraced warmly.

For all the chants and the frenetic build-up to the game in both Zagreb and Belgrade, there was little triumphalism afterwards. Croatia had won, that was true, but the crowds went home quietly. There weren't big celebrations in the main square, like those that had met Croatia's qualification for the 1998 World Cup. And the anti-Serb chants, although ferocious at first, died down as the match petered out in the second half. Mihajlović and Štimac had achieved what they had set out to do. They had taken the sting out of the occasion and proved that if *they* could bury the hatchet, there was hope for even the most intractable of divisions. 'I think that we saw a very fair game tonight from both sets of players,' a clearly disappointed Mihajlović says after the game. 'The players gave a very good example for the people back home how they should be on the pitch. We must be satisfied with that.' The 'people back home' in Serbia, however, were not satisfied with that. Mihajlović would be castigated for his team's surprisingly limp performance. He may have acted with grace, but his team had frozen on the day. The calls for his resignation started almost immediately. Igor Štimac's reputation could not have been better. He had bested Serbia and kept pace with Belgium at the top of the group. It is easier to be magnanimous in victory than in defeat, but he was clear that something had changed that night in the Maksimir. 'It sends a very clear message,' he says when I ask him about his embrace with Mihajlović on the pitch after the final whistle. 'Let's forget the past, we have a great future. We cannot build a future on the past. We are neighbours. There is plenty to live for in front of us.' Peace had spilled over and beyond the allotted ninety minutes. Back in the VIP tent, the folk band had gone home, the cold cuts were being packed away and Davor Šuker was leaving, his job satisfactorily done for the evening, a model on each arm.

10

EGYPT, LEBANON, RWANDA AND ERITREA REPRISED

Cairo, Egypt. February 2013.

Bob Bradley is sitting in his stationary car on a highway out of Cairo listening to the first minute of the Egyptian league season on the radio. He is supposed to be at the match, in the stands, to watch Al Ahly take on Ghazel el Mahallah. But we haven't made it as planned. A herd of sheep has blocked the traffic in front of us. They casually mooch around the cars, moving slowly towards a pile of rotten vegetables by the roadside. 'Café, sheep, fruit, hubcap shop,' Bradley relays, listing the things he sees around him. Despite everything that he has seen over the past eighteen months – a faltering revolution amid the chaos of normal life – a rogue flock of hungry sheep blocking the highway is a new experience for him. 'If I showed people back home all this,' he says, now beyond exasperation, 'they still wouldn't believe me.' Around him other drivers soon realise there's a celebrity in their midst. Taxi drivers, delivery trucks, families, groups of young men on the way to the match, all wind down their windows and call out the same thing, 'Captain!', vying for Bradley's attention. He is famous now in Egypt: Captain Bob, the man who will finally end Egyptian football's World Cup heartache. He waves back to every request, forcing a smile for each even if he is clearly annoyed at missing the opening moments of the game he has waited a long time to see. 'There's been no football in Egypt,'

Bradley says, stoically staring at the jam of sheep and cars that has coagulated in front of him, 'and we are late for the first match in a year ...'

It is eight months since I last saw Bob Bradley, after his first competitive victory as coach of the Egyptian national team. As was the way in post-revolutionary Egypt, everything and not much at all had changed since then. A few days after that victory Egypt held the second round of its first free and (largely) fair presidential election. It was won by the Muslim Brotherhood's candidate Mohamed Morsi, an academic with a Ph.D. in engineering who had come from nowhere to become president. Although they were by far the biggest civil group in Egypt, the Brotherhood had been banned under Mubarak, who feared that they would further radicalise the country, moving it towards the Islamic fundamentalism of Hamas in neighbouring Gaza. Egypt's Christians, who make up close to 10 per cent of the country's population, were particularly fearful of the Brotherhood. Yet, despite the Brotherhood's support among the poor and in the countryside, there was still a thirst for a revolutionary candidate to take power. The rules of the election were set, based on the French 'two round' system: a first round of voting for multiple candidates with the top two going through to the final round run-off. Several leading candidates had been banned from standing for various rather tenuous reasons. But the revolutionary candidates could not agree on one figure to lead them. The vote was evenly split. Morsi or Ahmed Shafiq, the former regime figure, was the choice they were left with. Faced with holding their noses and voting for a former Mubarak era man, or Morsi, many chose Morsi. For those who had fought, been arrested and seen friends die in the revolution, it didn't taste like victory.

There was one revolutionary force, however, that remained strong: the Ahlawy, the ultras of Al Ahly. The last football league match Bradley had seen in Egypt was on 1 February 2012, almost exactly a year ago to the day. Since the tragedy of Port Said, the league had remained suspended, largely because of the Ahlawy.

Driven by the need for justice the Ahlawy prevented the league from restarting until they had secured exactly that. Seventy-three people, mainly Al Masry fans but also the head of security in Port Said, had been arrested and the trial meandered on without conclusion. Every time the Egyptian FA set a date for the league to restart, the Ahlawy would protest in huge numbers and the date would be postponed. New dates came, more protests followed and new dates went. Finally, a date for the verdict was set for 26 January 2013, a day after the second anniversary of the revolution and only six days before the first anniversary of the Port Said tragedy itself. If the Ahlawy were satisfied, the league could restart. If they weren't, Cairo would burn.

I had arrived in Cairo to what felt like a second revolution. Tahrir Square was again thick with tear gas. It had again been taken over by protesters but this time it felt different. Most seem to be angry, disaffected youth but the protests were much more violent than I had seen before. They were aimless, nihilistic even. By the Nile, near 6 October Bridge, I had accidentally walked into a running standoff between the police and hundreds of youths. The police would fire canister after canister of tear gas at the mob, while the youths would return with rocks and fire-works, throwing the canisters they could grab hold of into the Nile before they had expelled too much of their noxious contents. The dance had been repeated for days now. From a distance, on the other side of the Nile, it was beautiful to watch: trails of white smoke arcing in the air; green and red stars exploding in the sky in reply. But up close it was ugly. When I crossed the bridge for a closer look one of the American-manufactured canisters landed at my feet. It was the first time I had been so close to one and it didn't look too dangerous. I grabbed my camera out of my bag and took photos of the white smoke spinning crazily out. Then it hit me. Every inch of my face burned, the pain intensifying around my nose, mouth and eyes. I was blind, on my knees, unable to move as the fighting raged around me. A soft hand touched my face, arched my head back and poured liquid into my eyes. It was vinegar, and it stung, but it cleared the blindness. A young girl in a hijab had tended to me, nodded her head in acknowledgement when I thanked her and disappeared to help another person. A few days later, the large, blue riot van that the police were hiding behind when firing the tear gas was stolen by the protesters, driven to the centre of Tahrir Square and set on fire. There the burned-out shell stayed, a monument to the impotence of the police.

It was in this atmosphere that the verdict in the Port Said trial was to be heard. President Morsi knew that a postponement was not possible. An already volatile situation in and around Tahrir Square would be ignited further by the presence of thousands of well-organised and angry Al Ahly ultras. They had already helped bring down one president. A second would be a piece of cake. The league had provisionally been set to restart on 2 February, a day after the Port Said anniversay and five days after the verdict. On the morning of the verdict I arrived at Al Ahly's training complex on Zamalek. More than 15,000 Al Ahly fans gathered outside its doors. Many had come armed, in anticipation of a further postponement or, worse still, a not-guilty verdict. Some carried clubs, others home-made pistols and double-barrelled, sawn-off shotguns. On national television at 10 a.m. the judge rose to deliver his verdict. Twenty-one of the accused were sentenced to death. The news swept through the crowd, reducing those in its path to tears of joy. The father of one of the football fans killed was hoisted on to the shoulders of the Cairean crowd as he blasted birdshot into the air. But the crowd were satisfied

Conversely, the verdicts were greeted with astonishment, disbelief and anger by Al Masry's fans and the families of the seventy-three accused who had gathered outside the prison in Port Said where the suspects were being held. Like the Ahlawy supporters in Cairo, they, too, had come prepared. Two policemen were shot dead as the relatives tried to storm the prison. The police fired back. At least thirty people were killed in clashes over the next few days, among them a former Al Masry player. President Morsi addressed the nation and announced a thirty-day curfew, from 9 p.m. until 6 a.m., in the cities worst affected by the violence. I had travelled to Port Said, too, and seen the anger on the streets myself: protesters shot dead by police, broken curfews, the daily procession of bodies carried from mosque to grave on the shoulders of thousands, the effigies of President Morsi being burned, his pictures defaced with the horns of the devil. Everyone I spoke to had said the same thing. The verdict was a sham. Port Said had been sacrificed by Morsi to prevent Cairo from exploding.

Back in Cairo a few days later, on the same spot where the 15,000 Ahlawy celebrated the Al Masry death sentences with gunfire, flares, smoke bombs and fireworks, a very different mood covered the solemn crowd. A few thousand members of the Ahlawy had filed into the stadium, muted and reflective for a memorial service to mark exactly one year since the tragedy. Those who were there that day wept as they remembered. The name of each victim was sung in front of the families of the dead, who had gathered on the pitch. The first people on to the pitch to meet them and to greet the fans had been Bob Bradley and his wife. The crowd cheered him and sang Bradley's name. The Ahlawy have not been fans of the national team in recent years. In the previous regime Mubarak and his family had been closely associated with the Egyptian Football Association and had sought to harness the feelgood factor of the team when it was at its devastating best. Many in the Ahlawy saw it as blindly nationalistic, epitomising the regime at its 'bread and circuses' worst. But they appreciated Bradley for being there and for all that he and his family had done. 'We managed to spend some time with the families,' Bradley says, amongst the gridlock. He and his wife met almost all of those who had lost someone at the memorial and each family had given them photographs of their loved ones. Bradley's wife returned home with a heartbreaking stack of memories. 'They were young people who went to a football match and tragically never returned,' he recalls. 'To be there and provide a little bit of support was important.'

**

Once the sheep have finished eating and the traffic jam has eased, we race towards the Air Force Stadium on the outskirts of town. It is isolated, far from any of Cairo's suburbs, making it almost impossible to get here without driving. The Port Said verdict means that the league has returned but, as with all of Bradley's home matches with the national team, the fans remain banned. Hundreds of armed troops protect the stadium anyway, stopping Bradley's car and checking ID every few minutes before we arrive at the stadium's main entrance. By the time we take our seats among the empty, soulless stands for the first Egyptian league match in 366 days, Dominique Da Silva, Al Ahly's Mauritanian striker, has scored the first goal of the season. He removes his jersey to reveal a T-shirt underneath. On it is written: 'Will Never Forget You', a tribute to those that died in Post Said.

'I think it's important, after a year and a day, seeing football in the stadium,' Bradley says as we watch the match. 'We all recognise this tragedy will never, ever be out of our minds or out of our hearts, but there's also a point, without ever forgetting, that you try to move forward.' The match is awful. Al Ahly had been one of the few Egyptian clubs to be able to play any kind of competitive football after Port Said. Somehow the team had reached the African Championss League final, driven on by a desire to win the title and dedicate the victory to the fans who died. In November that is exactly what they did, by beating Tunisian side Esperenace. The victory saw them qualify for FIFA's Club World Cup in Japan. Mohamed Aboutrika starred in that tournament, scoring a goal in his first match to equal Lionel Messi as the Club World Cup's all-time joint top scorer. They narrowly lost and were knocked out by Brazil's Corinthians but Aboutrika was sublime in the second half, almost untouchable.

Yet even with the African Champions League victory and the Club World Cup prize money in excess of a million dollars, Al Ahly were in deep financial trouble. How any of the other clubs survived was a miracle. The club was forced to send out many of its best players on loan. Striker Gedo and right-back Ahmed Fathy signed for Hull City in the English Championship, Gedo's goals in particular helping them to secure promotion back to the Premier League. Aboutrika was loaned to Bani Yas in the UAE league for a huge fee. He went because he knew his club needed it and played with the number 72 on his back during his short time there.

Without their best players, Al Ahly was a different team, noticeably inferior. Bradley tut-tutted, sighed and shook his head, confiding in Zak Abdel, his Egyptian-American goalkeeper coach who had been with him in the MLS, the US national team and was now back in the country of his birth. 'It's funny,' Bradley says of Abdel, who wears a baseball cap pulled low over his brow and whose American accent seems less pronounced every time I have met him over the past year. 'He's been in America for years. Zak comes back to Egypt and he forgets it all instantly,' he chides, with a smile on his face. It is the only time during the match that he affords himself a smile. He is due to announce his next squad, for Egypt's third World Cup qualifier against Zimbabwe in six weeks' time, and he is not particularly impressed by what he has seen. He has done what he can to try and overcome his players' lack of match fitness, arranging five matches since the victory in Guinea and experimenting with as many different players as possible. They have won only one of those games, 3-0 against Congo in the United Arab Emirates. Most worrying of all were the heavy defeats to the Ivory Coast and Ghana. Ghana was something of a *bête noire* for Bradley. The West Africans, who were a Luis Suárez handball away from becoming the first African team to reach a World Cup semi-final at South Africa 2010, had knocked Bradley's US team out of the 2010 World Cup. Egypt would lose 3-0 to them in Abu Dhabi.

In a few days' time, after this match in Cairo, Bradley will take the Pharaohs to Madrid. He has arranged for Egypt to play Chile. The South Americans are looking strong in qualification for the 2014 World Cup. Argentina are running away with the group but Chile look as if they will join them, alongside a resurgent Colombia led by striker Falcao. Chile will provide a much sterner test for Bradley and give a clearer indication as to where Egypt really stands at the moment. But Chile and the World Cup feel as far away as ever in the empty Air Force Stadium. Ahly beat Ghaz el Mahalla 1-0, Dominique Da Silva's goal proving the difference. Only a handful of people have watched the game at the stadium, among them Khaled Mortagy, a board member of Al Ahly who sits next to Bradley. He has seen how Bradley has deported himself since taking the job. 'I don't think he's an American,' Mortagy says as we leave the stadium. 'I see him as an Egyptian.'

We drive back into the chaos and snarled-up traffic of Cairo. This time there are no sheep to blame for the gridlock. The return of the protesters to Tahrir Square has had a knock-on effect on the rest of the city. Aside from now being synonymous with protest and the revolution, Tahrir Square is also a major round-about and one of the busiest junctions in the city. When it is blocked, the effects can be felt for miles around. Near Bradley's apartment in central Cairo we go for dinner. The *maître d'* greets him warmly, ushering us to his usual table. Diners crane their necks to see the celebrity in their midst. Bradley has no security. He and his wife walk Cairo's streets without fear. They see a side of the city and country that no foreign coach has allowed himself to see before and he has been rewarded with genuine respect and love. The results help, of course, and victory against Zimbabwe in Alexandria would be a huge step towards Egypt winning the group. Outside his apartment Bradley is, as he is everywhere in Cairo, mobbed for pictures. One man grabs him around the waist. 'You are our captain!' he shouts. 'In America, we have Captain Crunch, Captain Hook, Captain Marvel,' Bradley replies as he stands to attention as the photo is taken. 'I am not your captain. I'm your friend.'

**

As Bradley prepared for only his third World Cup match with Egypt, Asia was coming close to the end of its qualification campaign. The final group phase was in full swing and Japan had virtually qualified for the finals already. I had stood by the side of the pitch at the Sultan Qaboos Sports Complex in Muscat, the capital of the Middle Eastern Sultanate of Oman, and watched as the Blue Samurai, now coached by former AC Milan coach Alberto Zaccheroni, scored an injury-time winning goal in sweltering conditions. Japan had not played well and Oman, who were coached by former France international Paul Le Guen, were unlucky not to win. But it was Japan's fourth victory in five games. They would need just a point now to qualify for Brazil. In the other Asian qualifying group, the campaign had not gone so well for Theo Bucker's Lebanon team. Bradley had met Bucker when he arranged a friendly between the two nations at Tripoli's Olympic Stadium, the same ruined pitch I had watched Hezbollah's team play on a year before. 'He's a crazy guy,' Bradley had laughed, with affection, when I asked him about Bucker.

Bucker's first match of the final group stage was against Qatar in Beirut. A huge crowd, buoyed by the optimism and unity of Lebanon's best ever World Cup qualification campaign, filled the Camille Chamoun Sports City Stadium. Lebanon were holding their own, keeping the Qataris at bay. Then, defender Ramez Dayoub hit a suicidal back pass between his defence and the goalkeeper. Qatar's Uruguayan-born striker Sebastián Soria, one of the team's many naturalised South American players, strode forward and stroked the ball home. Qatar won 1-0. Dayoub had played an absolute stinker and was substituted before the end. Despite the setback of this loss, there had also been moments of elation for Bucker. Lebanon had beaten Iran in a tense match in

Beirut and drawn against Uzbekistan. But they would need to beat Uzbekistan, South Korea and Iran to stand any chance of making it to their very first World Cup finals. As Bucker was preparing for the crucial match against Uzbekistan in Tashkent in March 2013, a scandal broke that would effectively destroy Lebanon's World Cup hopes. It was alleged that Ramez Dayoub's back pass was not simply down to a mistake. A match-fixing scandal had been uncovered in Lebanon and a host of national team players had been accused, including Dayoub, Mahmoud El Ali and Ahmed Zreik, the young winger who had left his uncle's restaurant in Michigan to return to Lebanon and play for the national team.

Theo Bucker was a broken man. 'We lost the first match of qualification 6-0 and this was very normal for everybody because this was the normal start for the Lebanon national team,' Bucker says when I talk to him on the phone to find out what had happened. 'We were suddenly showing astonishing performances. We were producing very good results. This was happening only because of me. The team and I worked closely together, everybody was listening to me. We were all believing in each other.' Bucker was angry. But it wasn't he who had noticed Dayoub's suspicious back pass. It was his Lebanese wife, his dentist, whom he had married when he took charge of Lebanon's team the first time a decade earlier. Sitting high up in the stands, Bucker recalls, she had spotted that Dayoub had tried to play the very same suicidal pass half a dozen times and alerted Bucker to it afterwards. 'Ramez Dayoub was playing weird,' he says of that Qatar match. 'I checked the match afterwards and he was trying three or four times to play very stupid back passes to the direction of the opponent forward. Finally he was successful. Everybody was astonished. But no one could come close to the idea that he could do it on purpose.' At first speculation in the local media swirled around the idea that perhaps the Qataris had paid the Lebanese players to throw the match, but that conspiracy was soon rejected. 'There was no other club, other team, other nation coming to our players and giving them money to lose the match,' Bucker explains. 'A couple of players were selling their matches to a betting company. That's it. There has been an investigation and as a result the federation has suspended twenty-four players.'

Bucker couldn't understand it. While the scourge of match fixing had become a huge issue in club football, World Cup qualification was a different matter. And the fixing of a World Cup qualification match in a country for whom the unity of the national team had transcended the sectarian divisions that had divided it and caused untold wars and misery seemed to be a different level of cruelty. 'I feel very, very BAD, very, very sad,' Bucker is shouting now. It sounds as if he's about to cry. 'There are players amongst them who were SELLING matches who I really trust and we were a very good group. And I never expected them to do this. And now everything is BROKEN.'

It wasn't just the back pass in the Qatar game that had made Bucker suspicious. He had also noticed that some of his players were living seemingly beyond their means. 'The proof for us here is that some of the players were living a life they are simply not able to afford due to their normal salary,' he recalls. 'If you are getting $1,500 [a month] salary, you are not able to buy a big BMW. You don't have two wives, five kids, two houses. You don't always have the best mobile phone and the best clothes. Since we know they didn't break into a bank the money must have come from somewhere.' FIFA's investigation into match fixing had uncovered a huge betting scam in Lebanon. Dayoub and Mahmoud El Ali, Lebanon's star striker, who I had seen score against the UAE in Abu Dhabi, rupturing a cruciate ligament in the process and having to be carried off the pitch on a stretcher, were both suspended by FIFA, initially for life. Zreik was initially banned for one season and fined $2,000. All three continue to deny involvement and have vowed to appeal but Bucker needed to pick a host of new players and lost the crucial match against Uzbekistan, effectively ending Lebanon's interest in the World Cup. When South Korea returned to Beirut, the site of Lebanon's greatest victory on home soil and one that had given the team and the country such hope, only a few thousand turned up for the game. It ended 1-1, with South Korea equalising in the seventh minute of injury time. No one trusted the national team any more. They had proved to be as disingenuous as every other lever of influence and power in Lebanese society. All their good work had been for nothing. 'In Lebanon they have destroyed that belief of unity,' Bucker says.

He would see out the qualification campaign and resign after Lebanon finished bottom of the group. Iran, coached by former Portugal manager Carlos Queiroz, would finish top of the group and qualify for their fourth World Cup finals. They would be joined by Japan, Australia and South Korea, the four highest ranked teams in Asia before qualification began. The two third-placed teams in the group stage, Jordan and Uzbekistan, would later play each other in a two-match play-off to reach a final round against the fifth-placed team in South America.

Now in his sixties, Bucker is unlikely to get as close to quali-fying for a World Cup finals again. 'If you make shit, it is very bad,' he says at the end of our phone call. 'But to steal the hope of a whole country? That is unbelievable.'

**

Even with the football league up and running again in Egypt, Bob Bradley had less than two months to prepare for his next World Cup qualification match at the Borg el Arab Stadium in Alexandria. This time, though, a few thousand fans were allowed into the stadium, even if the 70,000 empty seats swallowed any noise they made. Egypt had lost that warm-up match against Chile in Madrid, but by a creditable 2-1 scoreline. When Bradley returned he prepared his team for a match which, if they won, would put Egypt in command of their group. With ten minutes left the score stood at 1-1. Egypt were in control but a Zimbabwe goal would seriously jeopardise their chances. With two minutes left Mohamed Salah sprinted down the right, into the penalty box and, just as he was about to shoot, was wiped out by a Zimbabwe defender. The referee blew his whistle. It was a clear penalty. Mohamed Aboutrika stood before the penalty spot, whispered a prayer and drilled the ball to the goalkeeper's right-hand side. As he did after every goal he fell to his knees and kissed the turf. Bradley and Zak Abdel celebrated together on the touchline. They had won three out of three, with three still to play. Bradley and the Pharaohs were halfway there.

As Bradley celebrated his victory, the third round of matches in the African group stage spelled the end of Rwanda's chances of reaching Brazil. After an opening day 4-0 defeat to Algeria, the Amavubi could only manage a draw against the Squirrels of Benin. As Bradley's Egypt were beating Zimbabwe, Rwanda were losing 2-1 to Mali. It was the end of the road for Milutin 'Micho' Sredojović, Rwanda's intense Serbian coach whom I had met in Kigali during preparations for their opening World Cup qualifier against Eritrea. He was fired after the Mali game. 'We terminated the services of Sredojović Micho [sic] on grounds [sic] that he was not productive during his tenure,' a very blunt Michel Gasingwa, from the Rwandan Football Federation, gave in a statement by way of explanation.

Micho may have lost his job, and Bradley may have been excelling in his in tough circumstances, but there was one football team I had met so far during qualification that had perhaps overcome more than any other. Eritrea had departed from Rwanda after being knocked out of 2014 World Cup qualification. Eritrean football had been hit by a series of defections in recent years, but in Rwanda I had counted all the players back on to the team bus on the day of their departure. As had Negash Teklit, their coach. The World Cup match had seemingly stopped the rot – or so it seemed. Almost exactly a year later the same Eritrea team again travelled abroad to play at the CECAFA Cup, this time in Uganda. Seventeen of the players and officials went out shopping, never to return. Many of the players I had met in Kigali were part of Eritrea's 18-man CECAFA Cup squad in Uganda. The

Eritreans who had absconded in 2009 and fled to Australia had told me they believed more would follow, no matter what restrictions were put on Eritrea's footballers. They were right. In February 2013, Eritrea's players were finally granted asylum. 'This is very good news if they have finally been sorted by the relevant authorities,' Patrick Ogwel, vice-president of youth at the Uganda Football Association told the BBC. 'But next time teams should come and play football and return to their countries.' Negash Teklit once again returned home on his own with a lot of explaining to do.

11

BRAZIL, NIGERIA, SPAIN, TAHITI

Belo Horizonte, Brazil. June 2013.

Eddie Etaeta has everyone eating out of his hands. He holds a string of shells picked out of the Pacific Ocean in one, and with the other ushers a woman sitting in the small crowd in front of him to come forward. A dozen or so journalists in a small hotel conference room in the Brazilian city of Belo Horizonte watch on, happy and pacified. The woman, one of the journalists, coquettishly accepts his invitation as Etaeta places the string of white and pink shells over her head. They applaud in delight, unused to being honoured by coaches or footballers. In the Brazilian game they are more used to being harangued. Unlike the stars of the local league – some of whom will inevitably end up playing in top European leagues one day – no one here knows anything about the man sitting in front of them, nor the players he commands. 'We brought these all the way from Tahiti,' explains Etaeta in English with a thick French accent, delivered with a disarming smile. 'It is a traditional Tahitian welcome.'

Etaeta has, almost by accident, found himself at one of the world's highest profile football tournaments. As coach of the Tahiti national football team he hasn't needed to worry about the attentions of the international press before, most of whom almost certainly would not have been able to point out his home town on a map. The tiny Pacific island is part of French Polynesia, with a population of a quarter of a million spread across a sprawling archipelago. Football there is amateur in the purest sense. Some of the players hold down jobs as teachers and policemen and fishermen. One of them earns his living as a professional climber, clearing coconut trees and mountainsides for construction companies. Half of his team are unemployed. Crowds for games in the Tahiti league are counted in the dozens, rather than the thousands. Yet Etaeta, a teacher and former Tahitian international himself, had the previous year masterminded the greatest single moment in his island's football history.

The Confederations Cup is a chance for FIFA to make sure that everything is going to plan. It is held in the World Cup host country a year before the finals are due to take place. The World Cup is FIFA's sole source of income, and the Confederations Cup is a dry run for their big pay day. It gives the organisers the chance to prove that the country is ready for the greatest show on earth but there had been signs that Brazil wasn't anywhere near ready. Stadiums, infrastructure, hotels, everything was behind schedule. Only six of the planned twelve stadiums were ready. Stadiums in São Paulo and the odd construction at Manaus, a stadium built in a city in the middle of the Amazon rainforest that alternated between blasts of searing heat and torrential downpours in equal measure, were way behind schedule. The airports were not ready and there was no way of getting between the major cities without flying. The distance between one host city Porto Alegre, next to the Brazil/Argentina border, and Manaus is close to 2,000 miles, the same distance separating London from Beirut. But the Brazilians had patched things up just adequately enough to invite the world for a taste of what was to come.

Along with the hosts, Brazil, Spain, the winners of the previous World Cup, and the champions of FIFA's six confederations are also here. As Spain hold both the World Cup and the European Championship, Italy – whom Spain beat in the 2012 European Championship final – have been invited. African champions Nigeria are here. So, too, are Mexico from North and Central America, Japan from Asia and Uruguay from South America. The world's elite players will attend: Xavi, Iniesta, Neymar, Suárez,

Cavani, Pirlo. The final spot, from Oceania, is reserved for Tahiti. Previously it was always the same two nations that made it to the Confederations Cup from Oceania, but ever since Australia joined the Asian Football Confederation, the coast was now clear for New Zealand to dominate Oceania. They had, after all, qualified for the 2010 finals in South Africa, drawn all three of their matches and gone home the only team to maintain an unbeaten record. Even champions Spain couldn't boast that. Every tournament should have been a cakewalk for the Kiwis. But it didn't work out that way.

The 2012 OFC Nations Cup in the Solomon Islands doubled up as both the penultimate round of 2014 World Cup qualification and the path to the Confederations Cup. The semi-finalists would all go to the final round of qualification for Brazil, where the eventual winner would face an intercontinental play-off against the fourth-placed team from CONCACAF. The tournament began with a rank outsider among the underdogs. I had watched Samoa qualify for the tournament after beating American Samoa 1-0 in the capital of Apia. But things didn't go well for Samoa on the Solomon Islands. They played Tahiti first and lost 10-1. I thought back to Thomas Rongen, the Dutch coach who had almost – almost – taken American Samoa to the OFC Nations Cup instead after masterminding the team's first ever victory in thirty attempts. I imagined Jaiyah Saelua and Nicky Salapu playing in Samoa's place, and wondered how they would have fared instead. Something told me they wouldn't have been beaten by nine goals on Rongen's watch.

Tahiti were the surprise team of the OFC tournament, but there were also signs that they might be heading places. They had become the first Pacific island nation ever to qualify for a FIFA tournament when the Under 20s made it to the 2009 World Cup in Egypt. They conceded twenty-one goals against Spain, Nigeria and Venezuela but half of that team had gained some experience playing at an international tournament, even if that experience was only learning how to lose heavily. Now the four members of the Tehau family, three brothers and a cousin, who had played in that tournament were shining at the OFC Nations Cup. Between the four of them they scored fifteen goals on the way to the final. They would not, however, be playing New Zealand as tradition dictated. Somehow the All Whites had contrived to lose to New Caledonia 2-0 in the semi-finals. Tahiti clinched the title with a single goal from winger Steevy Chong-Hue. There were rumours that the New Zealand players were so sure of victory they had been out partying the night before but others pointed to the incredible heat and humidity in the Solomon Islands' capital of Honiara and the absence of their best player, centre-back Ryan Nelsen. Either way, they weren't going to the Confederation Cup. Tahiti were and they were drawn in a group with Spain, possibly the greatest international team of all time, Nigeria and two-time World Cup winners Uruguay.

The group couldn't have been any harder: the World and European champions alongside the champions of Africa and South America. The journalists being garlanded in Belo Horizonte aren't just there to find out about a team and coach about whom they know nothing. There is a macabre fascination, too. How much blood will be spilt? The three games will surely be massacres, won't they? There is only one question that remains unanswered: how many goals is too many goals? 'We want to score a goal or maybe get to half-time at 0-0,' Etaeta admits after we meet for the first time. The Brazilian journalists have all left now, each with their own string of shells. The Tahitians have brought hundreds with them, all neatly bundled up in large plastic bags and kept in a battered cardboard box behind the conference room door. Collecting friends was more likely than collecting goals. 'We are honest,' Etaeta says. 'Tahiti has not come to win.'

Etaeta holds an important honour in Tahitian football. He scored Tahiti's first ever goal in World Cup qualification, back in 1992. Another goalscorer during that (failed) attempt to qualify for USA '94 that day was Reynald Temarii, a former player for French team Nantes who would rise to become president of the Oceania Football Confederation and make it on to FIFA's powerful executive committee. He would later have to step down in disgrace when a British newspaper sting filmed him allegedly selling his vote over who would host the 2018 and 2022 World Cup finals in return for money to fund a football academy. He maintained his innocence but FIFA upheld its punishment, a one-year ban from 'all football related activities' and a 5,000 Swiss Franc fine. Temarii isn't here and no one mentions his name. Instead Etaeta talks about his team's status as underdogs and how he built his squad in the first place. 'I prefer to have good people than good players,' he says. 'Then we build step by step, tactically and then physically.' In Brazil the team has experienced many of the trappings of international football for the first time. Most of the players have never travelled this far from home before, or even stayed in a five-star hotel. Their preparations have been mixed. Etaeta watched Tahiti lose their final warm-up match against Chile's Under 20 team 7-0. The fear was, if Chile's Under 20s could do this to them, what would World and European champions Spain do? Although Nigeria are the first game, to take place at Belo Horizonte's Mineirão Stadium, Spain are the opponents that have been giving him and his team sleepless nights, both with excitement and fear.

Etaeta had to devise two solutions to two very different problems. The first was how to stop his players from being starstruck. Etaeta's ingenious solution involved a few hours on Google Images and a roll of Sellotape. 'I found pictures of Iniesta, Xavi and Torres,' Etaeta says, explaining how he would fix the photos on the dressing-room wall and make his players stare at them. 'I said to them: "Hey, look, look at him, take your picture now, don't take the picture when we play them in the Maracaná."' With Tahiti's weakness for a celebrity cured with some lo-res printouts of Fernando Torres in his blond-haired Liverpool glory days, Etaeta had a tougher time working out how to deal with the second problem. How could he acclimatise his players to the noise made by Brazil's notoriously vociferous crowds? Especially when they enter the famous Estádio do Maracaná. His solution was just as left-field: 'I put my players in a room with the recording of a crowd,' he recalls. 'I say: "Hey, hear this, this is what it will sound like in the Maracanã. They will shout, they will cry, they will whistle." In Tahiti we don't hear that. We play in front of a hundred, maybe two hundred people in the stadiums.'

With the recordings of a roaring crowd in their ears and their appetite for celebrity footballers satiated, Tahiti's players are ready to play the world's superstars. One player in particular is preparing for a game that has the potential to be as infamous as American Samoa's 31-0 defeat. Given what happened to American Samoa's Nicky Salapu after that game – the psychological torment, the bullying and the despair – I'd begun to worry about Tahiti's goalkeeper. Mickaël Roche is tall and blond. He was born on Tahiti to Tahitian and French parents. 'I have a job as a physical education teacher in Tahiti so I work every day with the children,' he says sweetly. The team has a few hours before their last training session. They should be resting but most of the players are in the lobby of their hotel, wanting to be seen by the press. Roche, though, is thinking of home. 'All the children, they are all really excited what's happening to their teacher. Their teacher is playing the Confederations Cup. I think maybe, maybe, they are a little proud!' The children, it turns out, were equally as star-struck by Roche's appointment with Spain's heroes as Roche himself. 'They always ask me: "Sir, please, get me the T-shirt of Iniesta" or "please get me the T-shirt of Xavi."'

Eddy Etaeta carries himself as if preparing for the worst. He talks quietly and is slight hunched, as if already defeated. He knows that the only victory Tahiti can win is the PR battle. A FIFA official has been parachuted in to manage their time in front of Brazil's unquenchable press, to hand out the shell necklaces from the box of hundreds, to produce a glossy brochure and DVD of the team, to regale people with stories about the working-class professions the players will return to. 'We want to win the hearts of the crowd and the citizens of the world,' Etaeta finally says before he takes the team for their last training session. 'Ninety-nine per cent of foot-ballers are amateurs. Just one per cent are professional. We represent this ninety-nine per cent of the world.'

At a football complex twenty minutes' drive north, the Tahiti team takes shooting practice. It is reminiscent of watching the US Virgin Islands train when I saw them prepare for their match against Haiti in 2011. No one hits the target. 'This is just amazing for them,' says Davidson Bennett, a Tahitian TV journalist who has travelled from French Polynesia for the game, as we watch balls balloon over the goal. 'A big football match in Tahiti has maybe two hundred in the crowd. This training field is ten times better than our best field in Tahiti. It's a kind of a Ferrari for them.' When they finish, the entire team and coaching staff gather in front of the lines of Brazilian TV cameras which are desperate for some scraps of information. The team begin singing.

Tahiti isn't a country. Rather, it is the biggest island that makes up French Polynesia. The issue of which anthem to play is complicated further by the fact that French Polynesia is still a French colonial possession. So Xavier Samin, another of the team's goalkeepers, wrote a song especially for the team, 'Chanson des Toa Aito'. Song for the Iron Warriors, Tahiti's nickname.

Play play together warriors
Friends, my brothers, play, play again
We will fight them
Wearing the colours of the country
Come on red and white
Come on the red of the Iron Warriors.

The FIFA man would later print copies of the song and hand them out to the press.

**

There were only two *bona fide* Tahitian supporters in the crowd at the Mineirão Stadium in Belo Horizonte – the mother and father of goalkeeper Mickael Roche – but Tahiti could now call on the backing of thousands. Military and civilian helicopters buzz overhead as 20,000 supporters make it to the match, the largest crowd the Tahitians have ever seen. When they enter the pitch the crowd chant Tahiti's name while mercilessly booing their Nigerian opponents. Brazil is a hugely ethnically diverse country, mixing the descendants of white settlers with those of the black slave trade that Brazil excelled in, along with its indigenous Indian population. On any street in Brazil, skin colour can range from milk-white to coal-black with every shade in between. Not that you would have guessed that from the crowd in the Mineirão, an overwhelmingly white sea of faces.

Parity lasts for all of three minutes. More goals quickly follow despite Nigeria contriving to miss chances with increasing wonder and ineptitude. The massacre that the world has expected is indeed coming to pass. Then comes the moment that Etaeta and his Tahiti team had dreamed of. A rare attack leads to a corner. The ball is sent over and Jonathan Tehau – one of the four-strong Tehau clan in the squad – rises higher than anyone else and heads the ball down into the goal. It is greeted by the crowd as if Tahiti have won the World Cup itself. The players celebrate by gathering together and mimicking the paddling of a canoe, something they have clearly practised. At half-time Nigeria lead Tahiti 3-1. Maybe they won't be thrown to the slaughter after all.

At half-time I speak to Igor, a young, mild-mannered Brazilian journalist from São Paulo who writes for ESPN. He is getting ready to leave. It isn't just the fact that the match has been a foregone conclusion, even with Tahiti scoring. There is still little chance of a second-half comeback given that Tahiti play a spectacularly open brand of football: attacking, brave and futile. Igor has heard that a protest planned to coincide with the match is bigger than many people had thought. The day before he had told me of a few small-scale protests that had been planned, one at a nearby church and another that would begin at the main square in Belo Horizonte and march on the stadium. A huge *manifestações* had erupted in São Paulo before the Confederations Cup began. The local government there had raised the price of public transport in the city, angering those relying on buses to get to work. Brazil's transport infrastructure is still stuck in the third world. People have to travel three or four hours on a bus to get to and from work, and now they will have to pay extra for the privilege. Many Brazilians, Igor explains, are deeply unhappy about the World Cup, especially the cost of hosting it. The Confederations Cup is supposed to be a dress rehearsal for Brazil's coming-out party: a World Cup, and, two years later, the Olympic Games in Rio, that will be the icing on the cake of an economic boom that, in 2012, saw Brazil overtake the United Kingdom to become the sixth largest economy in the world. Brazil had even been honoured by a now ubiquitous economists' acronym, BRIC, standing for Brazil, Russia, India and China, the economies of the new century. Under left-wing President Lula, Brazil had boomed. Millions were raised out of poverty and the confident middle classes had borrowed heavily to fund Western lifestyles. But the 2008 economic crash hurt Brazil, too, and the reality of preparing for the coming party had not quite met the expectations.

Billions have been spent on the stadiums while Brazil's infrastructure – transport, hospitals, schools in particular – was still stuck in the developing world. Corruption smothers everything. The cost of the stadiums themselves has tripled the original estimate. Solidarity protests have begun to spread throughout Brazil, but they are strongest in the cities that are hosting the Confederations Cup. Earlier I had seen banners being prepared in Belo Horizonte's main square denouncing FIFA, denouncing the World Cup and denouncing the government. They are, to the protesters, all part of the same problem.

The protest near the stadium has been styled as anti-World Cup, anathema to those who have been sold the cliché of Brazil's obsession with football. The media, especially those controlled by the all-powerful Globo media conglomerate, characterise these protestors as refuseniks, elitists, borderline communists even. A small, unwelcome voice spoiling Brazil's big day. Besides, the march from the centre of town to the stadium is six kilometres. I

protests since the end of Brazil's military dictatorship in the 1980s. A sign hung from a nearby balcony that read: '*Anti Copa*'. On the pavement the words '*A FIFA é Foda*' have been written in chalk: 'Fuck You, FIFA'. The roads have been blocked off by military police, who watch the protesters from afar. A bank of police horses chew on piles of hay left for them on the road, their dung covering the streets along all four exits.

Daniel Sanabria, a technician in his twenties, is standing nearby cradling his arm, an ice pack on top of a bloody bandage. He peels it off to reveal an ugly red welt on his left hand. 'A bullet,' he explains as a young woman tends to his wounds. 'Tonight this is about all of Brazil, we are moving against corruption,' says Tainara Freitas, a teacher, who is trying to rebandage Sanabria's hand. 'We have been suffering for too many years. This year we rise. We have woken up. We are on the streets like in Turkey and Greece. They have made us wake up about this. The World Cup in Brazil is about too much money. There are too many poor people suffering. The World Cup isn't good for Brazil. It will bring tourists and money but this is not good for poor people.'

They all told the same story. How the march had approached the barricades with military helicopters overhead. How the police responded not with warnings, but with tear gas, firing rubber bullets into the crowd, beating protesters who burned barricades in return. Igor isn't here. He is in hospital. 'The police came with a brutal force,' he explains when we speak on the phone. 'I didn't see the protesters do anything. The police threw a bomb and it explodes in the middle of the protest. Then police began to shoot.' It was then he was hit in the back by a rubber bullet, as he ran away. 'In that moment I just ran. I thought that if I looked back the police would probably shoot me again.' The rubber bullet that knocked him off his feet left a huge, multicoloured bruise on his back, but nothing more. He'd live, unlike one protester who died falling off a nearby overpass when the riot was in full swing. Igor wasn't a violent revolutionary, or a *favela* kid born into violence who wanted to rip up the world and start again. He was a thoughtful, articulate journalist just doing his job. So much so that he tried, if not to excuse, then at least to explain why the police opened with such violence. 'I don't think the police are well prepared,' he offers. 'They are badly paid. They have a bad life. They act like this because they are scared.' So why did the police shoot him? He is in no doubt. The Confederations Cup. 'I spoke to one of the highest ranked police guys in the state yesterday. He told me 3,500 policemen were on the streets because of the game. They are acting to avoid conflict near the stadiums. The police and FIFA don't want the protesters anywhere near the stadiums.'

FIFA, and in particular Sepp Blatter, have become the bad guys, too, complicit in what the protesters see as a financial stitch-up. They point to the fact that for Brazil to host the World Cup they have to agree not to levy any taxes on FIFA and also change the law to allow alcohol to be served at the stadiums. Previously beer had been banned because of violence in domestic Brazilian football. Some opposition MPs said the issue was about more than football violence and alcohol. It was about FIFA challenging the sovereignty of the Brazilian state. Blatter, alongside the Brazilian president Dilma Rousseff, was booed by the Brazilian crowd at the opening ceremony. 'People are using the platform of football and the international media presence to make certain demonstrations,' Blatter said after the incident. 'You will see today is the third day of the competition this will calm down. It will be a wonderful competition.' That was yesterday. Sanabria and Freitas, nursing their wounds on 7 September Square, instead now saw the Confederations Cup as an even more legitimate platform for protest. It was just the beginning.

What message do you want to send FIFA and the football world, I ask them both.

'Please, please, make more pressure on our government, on the Brazilian government to look out for us,' says Freitas before she makes her way back to the protestors, Sanabria still clutching his injured hand. 'They are looking out for people outside the country, they aren't looking for us, for the poor people.' They now had the world's attention.

**

Rio de Janeiro, Brazil

The Estádio do Maracanã in Rio de Janeiro has a special, rueful place in the Brazilian psyche. It is beloved by all who have seen it, even at its rundown worst. When it came to be renovated for the first time, it was feared it was an impossible task. So much human urine had been expelled over its concrete foundations that it had made the stadium structurally unsound. It was also the venue of an event that Brazilians had never forgotten, from the last time the country hosted the tournament: the 1950 World Cup final. Those who weren't born then have never been allowed to forget it either.

In 1950 the World Cup wasn't the mega-sponsorship event it is today. There were fewer teams and those that did make it had to travel for days to get there. 'In 1950 we played Besiktas of Istanbul, in St Louis,' explains former United States captain Walter Bahr, who played in arguably the second most famous match in the tournament: when the USA beat England 1-0 in Belo Horizonte. 'They [Besiktas] beat us badly, 5-0,' he recalls. 'It was a try out as much as anything, and then we faced an English select team with Stanley Matthews playing, in New York, and they won 1-0. Those were the first times the World Cup team played together. The next day we left for Brazil. It took us two and a half days to get down there!' There was a different format for the competition, too. The final was actually a final group game. Brazil merely needed to draw against their tiny neighbours Uruguay to become world champions. So convinced were the Brazilians that they would triumph several newspapers went to print convinced that Brazil were already world champions. *O Mundo*'s front page, printed that morning, read 'These Are The World Champions'. The Maracaná was full, with as many as 210,000 fans. They watched Brazil take the lead in the forty-seventh minute, too. Yet they somehow went on to lose the match 2-1. The catastrophe was so deeply felt that a word exists today in Portuguese from that game. *Maracanazo* means an unexpected victory for the underdog over one of the big teams in Brazil. Tahiti had walked on to the Maracaná pitch hoping that they, too, could channel the spirit of Uruguay 1950 before they took on Spain. It would be difficult to find a bigger mismatch in any sport anywhere on earth. Outside the stadium Spanish fans had arrived taking bets on whether it would be 10-, 11-, 12-0. Before the game Etaeta had said he didn't think Spain had any interest in destroying his team. 'I spoke with Vincente del Bosque,' he had happily told me. 'He is a good man, with good values that we share. He has no interest in humiliating us.'

The Spanish players didn't get the message. As in Belo Horizonte, the Maracaná crowd was brutally pro-Tahiti. Unlike in Belo Horizonte, though, where every black player who touched the ball was booed, only Fernando Torres received the same treatment. Before the game, goalkeeper Mickaël Roche, the PE teacher, had placed a garland of shells around Torres' neck. Torres responded by tormenting him, scoring at his near post within four minutes. When Torres scored Spain's third he left Roche on his backside, skipping around him and passing the ball into the empty net. David Villa nutmegged him. Torres scored a hat-trick. Villa's hat-trick came when Roche completely missed a ball over the top. Mata nutmegged him, too. Every goal was met with a disappointed shriek from the crowd. The biggest cheer, though, was reserved for Fernando Torres when he missed a penalty. It finished 10-0. It was a bloodbath, a record defeat in any major FIFA finals. Gone was the joyful expression from Etaeta's face, that a goal – no matter what else happened – was all that mattered. 'It hurts, it is really tough to take,' he says after the match, eyes on the floor, mumbling his answers. I wasn't sure whether he was more upset by the defeat or the fact that Vincente del Bosque *was* more than happy to humiliate Tahiti. Or at least his players were. Mickaël Roche was the player I worried about most. Spending time with American Samoa's Nicky Salapu had shown me the destructive power that a heavy defeat can have on someone's life, even on their long-term state of mind. Roche was the last player to leave the stadium. 'All the players had a hard job tonight,' he says sheepishly when he finally decides to go back to the hotel. He had spoken to his opposite number, Iker Casillas, but he wanted to keep the words between them to himself. 'It's really hard because I hate having goals scored against me, but ten? It really hurts. I've got to accept that. I just want to keep in mind the wonderful supporters. It was awesome. They don't know us and for them to be cheering us like this was awesome.' Tahiti's Confederations Cup journey ended against Uruguay, with a marginally better outcome. They only lost 8-0. Tahiti had finished the tournament with a record of played three, lost three, scored one, conceded twenty-four at an average of eight a game. *Maracanazo* was nowhere to be seen. At the end of the match the players did a lap of honour anyway, carrying a banner that read: *'Obrigado, Brasil!'* Thank you, Brazil.

The fireworks don't end at the final whistle in the Maracaná. Another protest has been planned to coincide with the Tahiti match. This time it is to be the biggest yet. More than 300,000 peaceful protesters have marched in Rio to coincide with the Spain–Tahiti kick-off. Just like in Belo Horizonte and the other host cities they denounce FIFA, the government, the president, Sepp Blatter, big business and the mayor. After the game I catch the tail end of the mass of people moving north. They are young, mostly university students. Many are with their parents. One sign catches my eye, cleverly segueing the country's poor state education system with its excellence on the football pitch.

'Brazil doesn't teach soccer in school,' it reads. *'That's why Brazilians are good at soccer.'*

The protest thins out the closer I get to the front. The movement is now in the opposite direction, as people leave to go home. It has been a long and exhausting march for them. At the front Rio's riot police are standing, two deep, in full body armour, shields up high with guns and water cannons behind them for back-up. A handful of protesters, half a dozen perhaps, no more, begin to goad the police, throwing bottles that crash metres from their feet. This police force aren't like their counterparts in Belo Horizonte. Rio's police are skilled in the art of *favela* pacification, an Orwellian term for local martial law where police effectively 'take back' areas of the city overrun by gangs and drug lords and patrol it with impunity until order is restored. As soon as they sense a provocation, they move forward, firing tear gas at first. I watch as they stop, fire, and move, blasting shotguns with rubber bullets into the backs of the fleeing crowd.

Hundreds of police march down Avenida President Vargas, past smashed out banks and shops, past burning barricades and cars. They fire at the slightest movements, or hurl stun grenades, three or four at a time, down side passages. One lands by my leg, temporarily blinding and deafening me. When the buzz of disorientation fades I'm breathing tear gas and retching into the gutter. I'm kneeling on the pavement with gunshots firing all around me, reaching for a bottle of vinegar I'd packed for just such an event. Having heard of Igor's experiences in Belo Horizonte I had gone that morning to a hardware shop and a supermarket. A gas mask was too expensive, but a painter's face mask was a good alternative. Seamus, a film maker who had shot the entire thing, and I huddled together, pouring vinegar on to our faces to counteract the tear gas. When our sight had returned, the streets looked like a war zone. A 300,000-strong largely peaceful protest had been pacified. The spotlight and downdraught of a hovering police helicopter moved along a now empty Avenida President Vargas, looking for anyone foolish enough to defy it. A last stand of protesters waited on the steps of Rio's beautifully grand municipal theatre. Tear gas had filled the square's surrounding restaurants and cafés, families and couples and friends trapped inside, crying, holding napkins and scarves to their mouths to keep out the gas.

But everyone here was cleared, too, by flash grenades, advancing police lines and, as a last resort, the crack of a baton.

It was made plain that night. If the football continued, so would the protests. Yet for all the problems off the pitch, Brazil had been enjoying a brilliant tournament on it. As the 1950 World Cup final proved, the national team – *A Seleção* – generally operated under almost inhuman pressure. Eyes were now elsewhere. And when it came to be asked about the protests the players took the side of the people, agreeing with their aims and the cause, while also denouncing the violence. Romario, one of Brazil's greatest ever players, also criticised FIFA and the government. Once an uncontrollable wild child blessed with almost supernatural talent, Romario is now one of the country's most upstanding politicians. 'We want and demand what is ours,' he said after the Rio protest. 'Enough robbery, lack of attitude, humiliation. Let's make the government understand that Brazil belongs to the Brazilians, and we will not tolerate in silence the absurd things that have been happening. Congratulations, Brazilians!'

Other former greats had not covered themselves in glory, however. Ronaldo and Pelé had both been castigated for suggesting stupidly insensitive things, such as stating that 'you can't play a World Cup in a hospital' or that Brazil 'should forget all the confusion' and just back the Brazil team. It was the age-old bread and circuses caricature that Brazilians were tired of. The military dictatorship used to think the same: with football, everything else is forgotten. But that has changed now. They can still love football, but also hate the extraordinary cost of hosting the World Cup finals.

Nearby a white and blue Brazilian police kiosk has been burned out. Only a few hundred protesters remain on the streets, dazed and walking in different directions. The police have returned, angrily pulling out the poles and burning tyres that had been thrown into their smouldering, melted workplace. This, remember, followed a group game between Spain and Tahiti. The Brazil team's progress has not been affected by the largest protests.

Their matches have proceeded relatively unmolested and the team have easily qualified for the semi-final after beating Japan, Mexico and Italy. They will play Uruguay, their tormentors from 1950, in Belo Horizonte. But the protests will finally follow them.

**

Belo Horizonte, Brazil

The morning of the Brazil v Uruguay semi-final begins in an almost carnival-like atmosphere at Praça Sete de Setembro, where I had seen the bedraggled last stand from the first protests to hit the Confederations Cup nine days earlier. Thousands have arrived here at midday for the six-kilometre hike to the stadium. Beautiful girls chant and sing as drummers beat out protest songs you could dance to. Mothers and fathers have brought their children to taste protest for the first time. Leftist political groups hand out leaflets that match their placards, calling for more education and less corruption. *Copa Pra Quem?* One leaflet reads: *Cup for Who?*

The police were there, too, showing a different face from the force I had seen crushing the protest in Rio. This time they have sent a dozen or so female officers, without riot gear, into the square to hand out leaflets calling on the protesters to denounce violence. *From the Military Police of Minas Gerais*, the leaflet begins, *Protest in Peace. Democracy, Yes. Vandalism, No*. On the flipside is a map to warn people where the police will be stationed and where the protesters will not be allowed to walk. 'FIFA, we don't want the cup to come to Brazil, because Brazil has many other problems,' shouts a sixty-three-year-old playwright with a wild grey beard and matching hair who calls himself Mao. 'The next cup, go to the United States. Brazil doesn't need you. Brazil needs other things.'

The march moves slowly along the main highway out of the city in the midday heat. Along the way the numbers swell. Gangs of agitated young men, shirtless, their faces already covered, join as the march passes two *favelas*. They don't want to talk, and they don't want to be photographed. By the time the 50,000 have walked the length of Avenida Antônio Carlos and reach the slip road to the Mineirão Stadium, volunteers and activists have formed a human chain to stop anyone from reaching the barricade where the police are waiting, like a black brick wall. They are shouting for the protesters to ignore the police, and move onwards. The sun is slipping towards the horizon now but it still burns as it sets over the metal barricades that separate the 50,000 or so protesters from the line of military police. I look at my watch. In a few minutes' time, one kilometre up the road the police in full riot gear are guarding, Brazil will play Uruguay in the Confederations Cup semi-final. There is no chance I'll make kick-off.

The activists' human shield makes no difference. Hundreds push past them, running to meet the police head-on. The protesters stand in front of the barricade, faces covered in football scarves, T-shirts and V for Vendetta masks, like a million other people who have gathered near stadiums in Rio, Fortaleza, Porto Alegre, Recife and Brasilia as the Confederations Cup circus moves from city to city. The protests are a long way from the sycophantic eulogies to smiling, barefoot *favela* kids splashing through sewers with a ball at their feet. This is Belo Horizonte's third and biggest protest so far. A single stone flies over the barricades towards the military police. A few others have been thrown before, but this one travels the furthest. A barely audible thlump replies, arching a trail of smoke high above the barricade. A tear gas canister lands at our feet, bouncing and spinning around, crazily spewing thick white plumes of smoke in every direction. The choking fog brings near total silence, save for the coughing and the wailing of those not wearing a gas mask. As it clears, the inexorable mechanics of revenge begin. The atmosphere changes from one of progressive idealism to violence. A small group has come prepared with fireworks, cherry bombs and slingshots. Activists in gas masks scurry around between them, picking up the freshly fired, still smoking tear gas canisters, placing them in empty plastic water coolers before jamming the lid on, neutralising the smoke instantly. Volunteer medics go from one prone protester to another, squirting a milky-blue coloured alkaline solution into the eyes of casualties screaming on the floor. Those who didn't come prepared scrabble at the dirt, yanking up cobblestones and slabs of concrete. 'They are crazy, they are poor people,' says Binho, a young protester. 'They do not know how to make protests and make signs and stuff. They are doing what they have to do.' I ask him whether that is really an excuse. Does he not think that the violence undermines the protesters' aims? But a stun grenade and gas canister land a few metres away, and we flee, going our separate ways before he can answer.

Within the hour the protesters own the street. The police are now trapped in their temporary quarters, a barracks they have set up, inexplicably, in a natural depression where the protesters can surround them from the higher ground. It has a single entrance and exit, which is blocked by burning tyres and cars. Young men demolish the streets around them. Flash grenades, rubber bullets and tear gas no longer work. A Kia car showroom is ransacked and set ablaze. Its vehicles are pushed through the windows and into the street, before being rolled over and set on fire. Unlike the police of Rio, Belo Horizonte's forces are easily bested. There are no guns or weaponry other than rocks, slingshots and the sheer numbers of protesters. I watch, hidden under a corrugated roof, as hundreds of rocks are thrown by boys no older than seventeen into the place where the police are sheltering. When one building is destroyed, another is set upon, and another, and another. It is only a matter of time before the crowd move towards the VW garage opposite: a huge glass building that the staff have bolted shut. They are now hiding behind their desks but, given that the whole building is effectively a big glass box and the lights are blazing inside, it's easy to see where they are. The building is surrounded as 200 people pelt the glass with rocks. 'I don't give a fuck,' shouts one man, his top off, a black scarf around his head and face as he moves past me. He is holding a rock in his hands. 'Fuck the police, the bitches!' he shouts, turning and throwing his rock in one graceful movement. It sails into the pane of glass with a crunch. The terrified staff can be seen hiding in a back room now. Gunshots are fired back, seemingly from inside the showroom, scattering the protesters. They are only permanently pushed back when a military police helicopter swoops low, using its downdraught to knock those beneath it to the ground. But it also activates the tear gas and broken glass, swirling it around us into a vicious cloud. We dive to the floor and cover our eyes. When I open them again the riot police have broken through and are surrounding the garage.

The streets outside the stadium are empty now. The protesters, the rioters, whatever you want to call them, have fled, burning out shops and cars along the way. They have left their barricades behind, which now burn untended. Among the flames are the charred remains of two motorbikes, a car and an upturned plastic swimming pool that has been dragged from a nearby shop. In the ashes the corners of plastic signs can be seen poking out, half-formed words of solidarity and splashes of handwritten slogans. The banners of the protesters had also been thrown on to the fire. It is a long, tiring six-kilometre walk back to the city. No taxi will come here or dare stop nearby. The only vehicle that moves down the empty road back towards Belo Horizonte is a police riot van with loudspeakers blaring. They warn residents to stay inside. Bandits are on the prowl, they say. It takes over an hour to walk back. Only then do I remember the match. No one at the protest had thought to ask, but Brazil had beaten Uruguay 2-1. They would play Spain in the final.

**

Rio de Janeiro, Brazil

On the day of the final the Maracanã is surrounded by a ring of steel. Horses, dogs, batons, armoured personnel carriers, guns, tear gas; the full arsenal of the military police is on show. There are a few small protests nearby but the final passes largely peacefully. The arriving fans are more interested in having their pictures taken in front of the thousands of security personnel stationed outside. For once, football takes precedence. The Maracaná is full, singing the national anthem. When the band stops, the Maracaná sings the second verse, unscripted. It isn't a show of blind nationalism, or a snub to the protesters. The protesters have reignited a pride and a hope that things don't always have to be this way any more. The president Dilma Rousseff was genuinely shocked by the protests. A leftist who had been tortured under Brazil's military dictatorship and who felt some kinship with the street protests, Dilma promises to ringfence Brazil's oil profits and pour them into education. She also promises to recruit thousands of foreign doctors as a stop-gap measure to improve healthcare until more Brazilian doctors can be trained to take their places. A flurry of reforms to politicians' perks, transparency over their spending and the promise to drop a law that will make it harder to prosecute corrupt politicians all follow.

Only time will tell if it will be enough. There will be two important tests to judge whether the president has successfully appeased her people: a presidential election next year and the World Cup finals itself. If things haven't measurably improved by then, the protesters and the violence and the tear gas will return. FIFA's reputation has taken another hit, too. Throughout the tournament they had been wrong-footed and on the wrong side of almost every argument. As the protests grow, Sepp Blatter urged Brazilians not to use football to protest for improved social conditions. Yet Blatter was due to speak at a conference in Belo Horizonte during the Confederations Cup that would showcase how football could be used to further social goals. In any event, he left Brazil on an unscheduled trip before the conference was due to take place. Journalists were banned from attending it.

Every team that played at the Confederations Cup qualified for the World Cup finals. Every team except Tahiti. They wilted in the final Oceania qualification stage as the normal order of things returned. New Zealand won the group and with it an intercontinental play-off against a team from CONCACAF. At the Confederations Cup final Brazil destroyed Spain. Brazilian football may be revered throughout the world, but even the most rabidly pro-Brazil Brazilian concedes it does not have a team to compete with the greats of the past, of 1970, 1982, 1994 even. Yet against Spain, and with a crowd full of pride and energy behind it, they crush the world champions 3-0. Neymar finally came of age, giving Brazil a new hero to hang its hopes on. The 2014 World Cup finals will be a chance to lay to rest the ghosts of 1950, to finally win on home soil the World Cup that Brazil had prematurely awarded itself sixty-four years ago and pull the word *Maracanazo* back from infamy. The question is: how much tear gas will be fired on their route to the final?

12

ROMANIA, HUNGARY

Bucharest, Romania. September 2013.

The Animal is angry and The Animal wants to make them pay. Outside the brand new Arena Națională in Bucharest a group of perhaps one hundred men, maybe more, are marching purposefully down a green, tree-lined boulevard towards the enemy. At the front the shorter, younger members of the group proudly grasp a large Romanian flag – the red, yellow and blue tricolour – while others hold aloft burning red flares and chant:

> *Ro-ma-ni-a!*
> *Ro-ma-ni-a!*
> *Ro-ma-ni-a!*

In less than an hour Romania and Hungary will play each other in a World Cup qualification match. Ever since the European qualification draw for Group D was made, this game has been highlighted by both sides as the most important of the campaign. As expected, the 2010 finalists, Holland, dominated the group and had already virtually qualified after winning all six of their first matches. Finishing second would clinch a play-off spot. It was all the rest could realistically hope for. Hungary currently occupy that space but there are just four games left and they only lead Romania by a single point. But that isn't the sole reason for the outpouring of nationalistic pride. The Animal is here on other business. Revenge.

The chants of the mob are drowned out by the passing heli-copters and piercing wails of sirens as police riot vans screech past in the same direction The Animal is heading. Muffled explosions can be heard in the distance as Romanian fans run in the opposite direction, grown men tripping over the kerbside as tears stream down their cheeks in temporary blindness. A familiar acrid stench, one that I had become acquainted with in Egypt and then Brazil, follows them: the unmistakable smell of tear gas. Not that The Animal is too concerned by that. *Animalu'*, as he is known in his native Romance tongue, is the leader of the Steaua Bucharest ultras, the organised fan group of Romania's biggest club and current champions.

The Animal is short but powerfully built, in his late thirties with a shaven head and arms covered in tattoos. He coolly watches his parade from the back as the men and boys march towards the helicopters, the explosions and the gas. 'Between Romania and Hungary there is a lot of tension, we cannot stand each other,' he says in a measured, almost polite tone. Around him his younger followers jump up and down excitedly, screaming anti-Hungarian invective. The Animal calms most of them instantly with a raised arm. Except for one, The Little Animal, a teenager who is missing several teeth and spits in my face as he shouts. 'When we played them in Hungary it was with no supporters,' The Animal explains, as if he is reading from a manifesto. 'Now the Hungarians come here and cause a lot of destruction on the streets.'

He had watched it all unfold on TV. When the first night train from Budapest arrived the evening before – pulled by a golden engine adorned with the faces of Hungary's glorious foot-balling past; the Mighty Magyars Puskás, Kocsis and Czibor from the 1950s – hundreds of Hungarian fans hung out of its windows and doors, lighting flares and chanting against the *țigani*, an extremely derogatory word used by the Romanians for the Roma gypsies, which the Hungarians had, in turn, borrowed to insult all Romanians instead. Hundreds of Romanian riot police, dressed as if expecting a war, waited at the Gara de Nord station for the train to arrive. A stream of skinheads poured out of the carriages, most wearing black T-shirts. Some gave Nazi salutes as they passed by. One fan spat in the face of a waiting policeman. The police replied by beating them with their batons, breaking up their numbers and frog-marching small groups of supporters into the city. When they arrived they rampaged through the historic centre, smashing up cafés and restaurants as confused tourists and Romanian citizens looked on. Rumours spread on TV that a waitress had been attacked, that a café had been set on fire, that the police had lost control of the centre of the city. They replied by firing tear gas into the streets to control them, the first time anyone can remember the police using it since the revolution that toppled Nicolae Ceaușescu in 1989. The Animal and his ultras were now hell-bent on payback.

'We go to find them, to fight with them,' The Animal explains. 'But the police are so crazy! They stop us but they don't stop them?'

'FUCK HUNGARY! FUCK HUNGARY!' The Little Animal shouts, louder than before, as he stomps up and down on the concrete.

'They want Transylvania,' The Animal replies when I ask him why there is such tension between the two neighbouring countries. 'But they can't have it, it is Romanian land!'

'WE HAVE TO KILL SOME HUNGERS!' The Little Animal screams. The conversation continues like this; The Animal calmly talking, The Little Animal shouting death threats.

'After the game in Bucharest there will be a lot of fights. That is sure.'

'HUNGARIA IS SHIT!'

'There will be a lot of Hungarian people in Bucharest after the match. Be careful.'

'SUCK MY DICK HUNGARIA!'

The Animal finally loses his temper with his lieutenant. '*Shhhh, 'n mortii ma-tii,*' he says in an almost paternal manner. The Little Animal shuts up immediately. It's only later I find out that '*'n mortii ma-tii*' is one of the most horrific putdowns in the Romanian language, a shortened version of the expression which translates as: I fuck your mother's dead family. 'It's our history together,' The Animal says of the Hungarians, now that he has the floor to himself. 'They want Transylvania. They want Romanian land. These Hungarian people,' he says, before stopping to correct himself. 'These Hungarian FUCKS need to go home.' The police helicopter is now hovering above the northern entrance to the stadium, over where the muffled explosions are coming from. The Animal and his crew of Steaua Bucharest ultras stop and wait for more men to swell their numbers.

**

Romania and Hungary have a complex and fractious history, one that had been largely frozen under communism but which has come to the fore in recent years. The relationship between the two countries has see-sawed as empires have risen, crumbled, and borders have been redrawn around the rubble. The root of this enmity can be found in the post-First World War settlement that carved up the defeated Austro-Hungarian Empire. Hungary lost almost three-quarters of its territory to its surrounding countries, including Slovakia, Serbia and Ukraine. But it was the Romanians who benefited most from the 1920 Treaty of Trianon, when they achieved their long-held aim of seizing the region of Transylvania. More than 1.3 million Romanians of Hungarian descent – many of whom speak Hungarian as their first language – still live in Romania. Many Hungarians view Trianon as a catastrophe, a national tragedy forced on a kingdom that had existed for a thousand years. Romanians view it as simply righting a historical wrong. Even under the Ottomans, Romanian speakers were the overwhelming majority in Transylvania, but were treated as serfs by the largely Hungarian upper classes. There were even laws that prevented Romanians from living within the walls of many cities in Transylvania.

Still, nationalistic and patriotic concerns were largely buried behind the Iron Curtain and the tensions kept in check. But in the 1990s the sense of injustice began to creep back. In 2010 the election of a more nationalistic government in Hungary – the right-wing Fidesz party – succeeded in reigniting the issue. One of the Fidesz party's first laws handed citizenship – and with it voting rights – to Hungarian populations abroad, angering its neighbours for encouraging their citizens to look towards Budapest rather than their own capitals. Behind Fidesz was an even more radical group. That election saw Jobbik come third with close to a million votes. Jobbik is an ultra-nationalist, radical right-wing political party that has been accused of following anti-Semitic policies and which calls for the return of a 'Greater Hungary'. You can usually spot a Jobbik march in Budapest. The party's politicians might be young, articulate and clad in expensive suits, yet a Jobbik rally is made up almost exclusively of the same white, male skinheads in black T-shirts who now dominate Hungary's football terraces. The first World Cup match between Hungary and Romania the previous March, a 2-2 draw, was played behind closed doors because of anti-Semitic chanting when Israel played a friendly in Budapest in 2012. 'That empty stadium was a clear sign of radicalism in Hungarian football,' says Vörös Szabolcs, a foreign correspondent for the conservative *Magyar Hirlap* daily newspaper, who was at the game. 'Twenty thousand people were outside the stadium, we could hear voices, we could hear the screams of the trainers. Sadly there were anti-Romanian chants, as usual.'

In the weekend before the Romania–Hungary match in Bucharest three Hungarian league teams were fined a total of 1.2 million forints (£3,000) for anti-Romanian and anti-Slovakian chants. In a warm-up match against the Czech Republic the fans chanted 'Transylvania is Hungarian!' They promised to mount an 'invasion' of Romania before the game in Bucharest and flew the Székely flag, the flag of a historically ethnically Hungarian area that is now marooned in the centre of

Romania and that many Hungarians would like to see gain autonomy. 'The people on and around the football field, I wouldn't say they are all radicals, but I would say 80 per cent are,' says Szabolcs of the changing nature of both Hungarian politics and football. 'Decades ago families went to football matches. Now it is not the case. Football is the sphere of telling our hurts, telling our problems in a radical way.' So radical in fact that even Romania's foreign minister had intervened over the anti-Romanian chants being used in the run-up to the match. 'Such words should be condemned, they do not belong on a football pitch. Let's not hide behind the finger here, extremist attitudes exist everywhere, they happen in Romania as well,' Titus Corlăţean told the country's Antena 3 news channel a few days before the Hungarian fans invaded Bucharest. 'The best answer will be to beat the Hungarians at football.'

It is a high-stakes game that no one can bear the thought of losing. Not the players, the coaches, the supporters, the politicians and not The Animal himself. I leave the Steaua ultras to regroup and follow the hovering police helicopter that marks where the Hungarian supporters are to be found. The road in front is blanketed in smashed glass, turned-over tables and chairs. The juddering hum of rotar blades becomes louder as I walk towards the stadium. The shouts are indecipherable over the noise but become clearer the closer I get. They are only interrupted by the periodic bursts of explosions and breaking bottles.

Ria!

Ria!

Hun-ga-ria!

On either side of the road frightening looking Jandarmeria Română, a military faction of Romania's police forces, stand guard with their weapons in hand. Some have nightsticks, some merely riot shields. Scattered among their number are several officers carrying what look like oxygen tanks with a rubber hose attached to the nozzle. It doesn't spray water or foam but tear gas. Rather than simply hurl a canister into a riot, Romania's police prefer administering the gas at close quarters, preferably, it seems, at face level. By the sulphuric smell in the air it has recently been used, too. One officer sprays a burst of gas on the ground as I walk past, raising his one free hand to imitate sniffing under his arm. 'Deodorant,' he laughs. His colleague next to him shakes his head, looking at the angry mob he has just helped to quell. 'Why?' he asks in perfect English, 'why are they so angry?' Behind a final line of police a few thousand identical looking, angry men are penned in like cattle, singing nationalist songs and flying nationalist flags. Around them dozens of Romanian film crews are perched on fences, TV vans and kiosks. They, too, are wondering the same thing, incredulous at the alien army that has just invaded their capital. *Why are they so angry?* Thankfully, The Animal and his group are nowhere to be seen to complicate matters yet. Instead, the Hungarian fans have arrived flying the Székely flag, denouncing all Romanians as *ţigani* and fighting any non-Hungarian who gets in their way. Which is something of a problem for me. The Romanian Football Federation has refused to accredit me for the game. I'd only managed to get a ticket for the sold-out match after the Hungarian federation agreed to give me one. I was to watch one of Europe's most inflammatory fixtures sitting with the Hungarian fans. Five metres away they are still throwing flash bombs, smoke grenades and flares at the police. As the police advance on them to force them into the stadium, I weigh up my options. I am clearly not Romanian, but neither do I look Hungarian. Do I play it safe and watch the game from the comfort of a nearby bar, or jump into a crowd of people who hate foreigners and journalists in equal measure? I take a vow of silence, hide my camera and microphone and slip through the police line, joining the crush towards the stadium gate as another chant against the gypsies rises.

**

appropriated the term. They lost only one game between 1950 and 1956, and that was the 1954 World Cup final, the so-called Miracle of Berne. Yet even that defeat isn't what it seems. Hungary had already beaten West Germany 8-3 in an earlier round, but the Golden Team contrived to throw away a 2-0 lead in the final to somehow lose 3-2. The victory was met with euphoria back in Germany. It was just nine years after the end of the Second World War and the newly divided country was still examining its conscience after the horrors of the Nazi regime. The World Cup, though, saw the national anthem played in public for the first time and victory witnessed an outpouring of national pride. Several German academics have suggested that the Miracle of Berne was a crucial psychological moment in the history of the country, the moment when West Germans collectively began to look forward rather than back. But how did Hungary lose? Several theories were posited. For one, Puskás had suffered a fracture on his ankle early in the tournament. He still played in the final, and scored the first goal, but was hampered throughout. That final, though, has since been dogged by accusations that the West Germans had relied on a little extra help. After the defeat Puskás was fuming, accusing the West Germans of injecting drugs that fuelled their incredible second-half comeback. The Germans insisted they had merely been injected with Vitamin C and that Puskás was a sore loser.

In 2013 Puskás and Hungary's anger was largely vindicated. A report by Berlin's Humboldt University outlined an enormous government-funded programme that was involved in doping sportsmen and women. The use of performance enhancing drugs had been well documented among East German sportsmen and women, but the report alleged that it had been widespread in the West, too. Far from being Vitamin C, the substance was likely to have been Pervitin, a methamphetamine. As the German newspaper *Der Spiegel* pointed out in a 2005 report, Pervitin was the Wehrmacht's wonder drug. Millions of tablets were sent out to soldiers, pilots and sailors during the Second World War. Between April and July 1940 alone over thirty-five million tablets were shipped to the German army and air force. It was, as *Der Spiegel* continued, a 'Blitzkrieg fuelled by speed'. The 1954 World Cup final, it turns out, was a miracle fuelled by speed, too. 'That the West German World Cup-winning team of 1954 beat Hungary in the final enhanced by drugs is something we have known for a long time,' the legendary football writer Brian Glanville wrote in *World Soccer* magazine shortly after the report was released. 'It was plain soon after the final itself with tales – not least from an enraged Puskás – of German players vomiting in their dressing room. When more than half that team succumbed to jaundice and were out for months it was plainer than ever that their remarkable second-half rally against the Hungarians had a chemical basis.'

Puskás and the Golden Team would never play in another World Cup final. In fact, that final marked the beginning of the end of that team. True, Hungary went on to qualify for the 1958 World Cup finals, but Puskás and many of the Golden Team would not be in Sweden for it. Puskás was playing for Budapest Honvéd in the European Cup when the Hungarian uprising took place in 1956. The team refused to go home and many eventually found their way into top European clubs. After serving a two-year ban from UEFA for not returning to Hungary, a now thirty-one-year-old Puskás signed for Real Madrid, where he shone, famously scoring four goals in the 7-3 defeat of Eintracht Frankfurt in the 1960 European Cup final. He would never play for Hungary again. For the next thirty years the Hungarian national team delivered ever diminishing returns. Their last appearance at a World Cup finals was in Mexico 1986, more than a quarter of a century ago. The current crop of players is no Golden Team – who, realistically, could ever match that team? – but in the race for Brazil 2014 Hungary were second in their group and a victory against Romania would make them favourites to secure a place in the play-offs with a chance to see one of the historically great national teams of world football return to what many Hungarians see as their rightful place at football's top table. The legacy of

Puskás and his Magical Magyars had, understandably, weighed heavily on the shoulders of every team and coach that followed.

**

A half-hour bus ride outside Budapest, at a training complex near the village of Telki, the current Hungarian team is about to start its last training session before leaving for Bucharest. Their coach is sixty-three-year-old Sándor Egervári. He got the job after taking charge of the Hungary Under 20 team a few weeks before they were due to go to the 2009 Under 20 World Cup in Egypt. Miraculously, he took them to a third-place finish, reviving memories of an age when Hungary could compete with the world's best. His face and bald head, ringed by tufts of silver-white hair, are tanned, a permanent legacy from his time coaching in Kuwait and Saudi Arabia. 'As you say in football language it is a kind of a six-point game,' he says in the lobby of the swanky hotel, glasses perched on his nose. 'Turkey, Romania and Hungary are going for the second place. The game is important for us because of the two nations' historic past. It was full of problems.'

Egervári avoided the ignominy of losing to Romania at home, even if that was replaced by the greater shame of having to play the match behind closed doors after the fans had been heard making anti-Semitic chants. The return match in Bucharest will be different as Romania have a significant advantage. 'We know that the atmosphere will be very special,' he nods. 'More than fifty thousand Romanian and maybe three, four, five thousand Hungarian fans will be there. For sure it will be a very, very exciting atmosphere. But we have mental training so that the Hungarian players don't think about the atmosphere.' None the less, the press on both sides have been hyping up the game, evoking old slights and perceived historical wrongs. The report on doping in West Germany and its role in the 1954 final had only just been released as well. Egervári played for Budapest Honved as a young man, the same army team as Puskás, but he was too young to have played with him. He had long ago defected by then. 'I am sorry but the 1950s and the 1960s is the past already,' he says when I ask about the Golden Team and its effect on subsequent generations of players. 'But in the past twenty years football has gone really down and only now has it tried to get up again. More than hundreds of pitches have been lost. They built buildings and petrol stations and shops. So we have lost not just our pitches but our values.' Nor did he have much time for the report on doping at the 1954 final. 'We don't care. We knew at the time that the Hungarian team was the best in the world,' he says, echoing the view of many Hungarians that, regardless of what the record books say, the Mighty Magyars were the true world champions in 1954. 'We don't care about whether it was true or not. This is history. We know the Hungarian team was the best in the world. That is important to us.'

Hungary's twenty-five-year-old, flame-haired goalkeeper Ádám Bogdán, on the other hand, doesn't remember anything other than Hungary losing. His generation of international players has no memory of the national team competing in international tournaments. 'Well, we haven't been to a World Cup since 1986 so qualifying means everything,' he says as his coach impatiently waits for the rest of the team to leave for training. 'I was born in 1987 so I don't remember anything when I was growing up. I was watching different teams in the World Cup, supporting different teams like England. It means everything for football fans in Hungary. We have to take it as a motivation and keep on fighting.' According to Bogdán, the constant search for any signs of a new Golden Generation has been something of a hindrance to Hungarian football, but now they have a good mix of players appearing in top European leagues, even if many of them aren't playing regularly. But in the Arena Naţională form will probably have little bearing on the result. 'It will be hostile,' Bogdán replies when I ask him how he thinks Hungary will be received. 'It is no secret that we don't have the best relationships between the two countries. But it is the biggest derby against Romania. The problems were only eighty years or so ago. But that's politics and life and that is a rivalry. I know it means a lot to the people in Romania because when we lost a part of Hungary a lot of people are stuck outside the country. Those people still live there, still speak Hungarian and live as Hungarians so this match must mean a lot to them as well.' Egervári, though, sees the game as a chance at least to partially right the failures of the past on the pitch while trying to avoid the political arguments off it. 'For us we don't care about the political situation. It is not war,' he says as he finally ushers his players towards the exit. 'It's just football.'

Not everyone agrees. 'The right wing is so strong now, there are ultra-right-wing parties like Jobbik and they get into the stadiums,' explains thirty-eight-year-old Szabó Szilárd, a sports journalist for Kossuth Radio who has seen Hungary's terraces become more intolerant and inward looking as the country has moved increasingly to the right. 'Because of one hundred or two hundred stupid people Hungarian sport can be damaged. That is what politicians, sportsmen, everyone wants, we want to get them out of the stadium.' Although the right-wing Fidesz party is in power, it is the ultra-right wing Jobbik party that has made the greater advances. They gained almost a million votes in the previous election by articulating an insular vision of Hungary's future by parading a largely distorted history of its past. The biggest enemy of all is Romania. 'Transylvania was part of Hungary, yes,' Szilárd explains. 'There are still a lot of people who think that Transylvania should be part of Hungary. There are voices like that. In every country there are radical thinkers who are not able to accept the history so that is the primary reason for the rivalry.'

The run-up to the match had worried Szilárd. The chants against the Israel team, the supporter ban for the first Hungary–Romania game in Budapest, the anti-Romania and Slovakia chants that had been heard, and punished, at the previous week-end's league matches all pointed to a potential car crash. 'We are all afraid that anything can happen,' he says. 'I have some friends who will go to Bucharest. They are going to Transylvania in a mini bus and then changing into a Romanian one. It is just not possible to go to Bucharest for this game with a Hungarian vehicle. I was told in Serbia [where a large Hungarian minority live in Vojvodina] they burned a whole bus.' Transport was indeed a problem. Despite being neighbours with a shared history, and having been at peace for decades, few flights could be found between Budapest and Bucharest. There was one sixteen-hour night train that left, almost completely empty, every evening. I said goodbye to Szilárd, took his number and promised to meet him in Romania, in Bucharest. 'Oh no,' he says, laughing, as he packs up his radio equipment. 'I'm not going … I'm not crazy.'

**

Hungary's parliament sits on the eastern banks of the Danube in the heart of Budapest. The magnificent Gothic building is one of Europe's oldest parliaments. Márton Gyöngyösi's office is found two blocks further down, in a dull, modern block allocated for the daily grind of parliamentary work. His desk overlooks the river and is cluttered but tidy. On one chair sits an old hardback copy of an exposé on the workings of Mossad, Israel's national intelligence agency. Tall, youngish and wearing bookish glasses, he looks more like a bank manager than an ultra-nationalist firebrand. 'In this case there will be a football match that is only partly about sport,' he says as we sit down. 'It is about history and politics. It is not only winning a football match. It is also about beating Romania.' Gyöngyösi is an MP and the foreign affairs spokesperson for Jobbik, the party that has been most vocal in its condemnation of Romania in recent years. The rise of Jobbik has been seen by many as one reason why relations between Hungary and Romania have deteriorated in the past few years. Since its success in the 2010 elections it has been accused of following a radical nationalist agenda, including certain policies that have been labelled anti-Semitic. Gyöngyösi himself was rebuked last year for suggesting that Hungary's Jewish population should be catalogued in a list. He had reasoned that Jews might now pose a security risk to the Hungarian state post-Arab Spring. 'I think such a conflict [the Arab Spring] makes it timely to tally up people of Jewish ancestry who live here, especially in the Hungarian parliament and the Hungarian government who, indeed, pose a national security risk to Hungary,' he was quoted as saying. He was roundly condemned and later apologised, claiming he was mistranslated. 'Jobbik has moved from representing medieval superstition to openly Nazi ideologies,' the chief rabbi of the United Hungarian Jewish Congregation, Slomó Koves, had said following the uproar. Still, Jobbik could well hold the balance of power in the next election in six months' time. 'I'd love to live in a world, I dream about a world, where Hungary regains the territory we have lost and I think every Hungarian should think that way,' he says when I ask him about Romania, Transylvania and the run-up to the match. 'Reality is a different question. We always have to cook with what we have.'

Football has become something of a battleground in Hungarian politics in recent years. The country's prime minister is Viktor Orbán, leader of the Fidesz party, who has been criticised by the European Union for his overly dictatorial style in altering the country's constitution. He is also a huge football fan who has invested billions of dollars of public funds into the game, including a massive stadium-rebuilding programme. Critics have mocked him for funding the building of a brand new stadium in the village where he grew up and where his summer house can be found. And last year the government assumed all the debt of Budapest's six football clubs, while agreeing to subsidise their operation for the next seven years. Both MTK and Ferencváros, two of Hungary's biggest teams, had been promised huge amounts of money to renovate their stadiums. That included $160 million alone for Ferencváros. The presidents of both clubs are high-ranking members of Fidesz. But why is Fidesz investing so heavily in football? For Gyöngyösi, the answer is simple: votes.

Football, it seems, is Fidesz and Jobbik's natural constituency. 'If you go to any Hungarian football match you find patriotic people there. It is not a group of people you have to give a boost to,' Gyöngyösi explains. 'They are by nature open to these patriotic and nationalistic feelings. They are groups of people generally closer to patriotic and nationalistic sentiments than liberal and left-wing sentiments.'

Like most countries under communism in Eastern Europe, in fact like most countries under *any* form of dictatorship, football has developed a deeper political identity in Hungary. In many countries – be they Yugoslavia, Romania or Hungary itself – the terraces provided a rare outlet for views impossible to air in civil society. Each team assumes a distinct political personality. 'Football under communism was one of those areas where some kind of statement about the regime could be made in a different way,' Gyöngyösi says. 'It was not explicit. But if you supported Ferencváros, that was 99 per cent sure you were patriotic, nationalistic and 100 per cent anti-communist. It is very rare I hear of a liberal left-winger supporting Ferencváros.' Many in Hungary believe that Orbán and Fidesz are investing in football to shore up voters ahead of the 2014 elections, including Gyöngyösi. 'Under pressure from Jobbik, Mr Orbán has been taking on a very patriotic and nationalist approach, at least in rhetoric,' he says. 'There's a battle for right-wing votes in the country. Mr Orbán has been wanting to pick up some voters from Jobbik. The double citizenship laws ... that was our idea.' The government's huge investment in football – at a time when the country is experiencing economic austerity, when the average crowds at Hungarian league games has slipped below 3,000 and when the game has been continually marred by high-profile cases of racism and anti-Semitism – has not been popular with everyone. But Orbán hasn't turned back. After the first Hungary–Romania World Cup qualifier earlier in the year Orbán was asked his opinion on FIFA's decision to ban fans from attending because of the anti-Semitic chants. 'It is better if I keep my opinion to myself,' he replied cryptically. Gyöngyösi is also angry that FIFA intervened. 'There has always been some kind of double standards in the world,' he says. 'Go to a Tottenham or Ajax or Livorno match [teams with either a traditional Jewish or left-wing identity] and see what is chanted there. I am sure it is not extraordinary to what is happening in Hungary. Romanians write out texts [banners] that are just as nasty. I think it was a very unjust and crazy ruling by FIFA.'

With the money pouring in, Hungary now has its best chance of qualifying for a World Cup finals in a quarter of a century, made all the sweeter if it can beat its arch-rival along the way. 'It is not just a World Cup qualifier because beating Romania in this match is more important than reaching the World Cup finals,' Gyöngyösi admits. He won't be at the game. Jobbik is hosting a three-day retreat in eastern Hungary to finalise its legislative plan before the next session of parliament. But on the final day all of its members will gather in a log cabin to watch the match. 'I am sure there will be a lot of Jobbik fans at this match,' he says. Will there be any trouble at the game, I ask him. Will the Hungarian 'invasion' of Bucharest be a peaceful one? 'If anyone expects the Romanian and Hungarian supporters to sit with their popcorn and their Coca-Cola and watch the match in silence then they don't know what football matches are all about,' he laughs. 'This is the nature of football matches, we should be more tolerant when it comes to expressing opinions in football matches.' He says this without a hint of irony.

**

Bucharest, Romania, match day.

As the upper echelons of Jobbik settle down in front of a television at their retreat somewhere in eastern Hungary, 3,000 Hungarian fans turn their backs on the pitch, raise the middle fingers of both hands and boo the Romanian national anthem.

The Arena Naţională is a riot of red, yellow and blue as 'Deşteaptă-te, române!' (Wake up, Romanian!) is sung by seemingly every Romania fan in the stadium. The anthem is seen as particularly offensive to Hungarians as it is thought the first verse refers directly to the Hungarians who used to rule so harshly over them until the mid-1800s:

> *Wake up, Romanian, from the sleep of death*
> *Into which you have been sunk by barbaric tyrants*
> *Now, or never, make a new fate for yourself*
> *To which even your cruel enemies will bow.*

The Hungarian anthem has already been given the same treatment. Thousands of Romanian fans hold banners with the year 1918 on them, the year the First World War ended and when Transylvania declared its union with the Kingdom of Romania. The Treaty of Trianon two years later sealed the deal. Some supporters chant '*afara, afara, cu ungurii din tara*'. Out, out, with the Hungarians from our country. It had been a frightening experience entering the stadium. I had kept my mouth shut and camera hidden as we inched towards the gate, hustled and harassed by the police along the way. Yet when I get to the entrance I am turned away. My ticket is, in fact, with the Romanian supporters. A panicked policeman bundles me away from the crowd in case the combustible atmosphere is set alight by a suspected Romanian in their midst. The Hungarian fans view me suspiciously as I am ushered into the next stand. My seat is in the middle of a completely empty square of stadium, left as a firebreak between the two sets of fans. I am now in no-man's land.

It takes just ninety seconds for Romania to take the lead. Hungary defender Richárd Guzmics dawdles on the ball, slips and allows Ciprian Marica to race through. Marica stumbles when one on one with Ádám Bogdán in the Hungary goal, but somehow he manages to chip the ball into the bottom right-hand corner. The stadium explodes. A quiet middle-aged couple who have also been sitting in no-man's-land go berserk, running towards the Hungarian fans, screaming as they flash their middle fingers. The Hungarians respond by ripping up their seats and throwing the metal barriers at us over the security guards' heads. I move as far away from them as I can get.

Romania destroy their great rivals. Thirty minutes later Mihai Pintilii receives the ball on his right foot and curls a sensational shot into the top right-hand corner of the goal. Bogdán can do nothing about either goal. Wave after wave of Romanian attacks crash on to the Hungarian defence. With each feeble reply, the Hungarian fans become quieter and more menacing. I fear a Hungarian defeat. I am supposed to be on the same night train home as most of the away supporters, now stewing in a potent brew of defeat, humiliation and alcohol. At half-time the Romanian fans taunt the opposition from behind the safety of two fences and lines of riot police. The chants end when two flash grenades, somehow smuggled into the ground, are thrown over and explode by our feet. In the second half Bogdán makes two incredible saves to prevent utter humiliation. It could, and should, have been 6-0. With two minutes to go Romania score again, leaving the 40,000 Romanian fans ecstatic. Hungary have been abject, humiliated by their biggest rival. After the match the UDMR, the biggest political party that represents the interests of Romania's Hungarian minority, lodge a complaint with FIFA over 'anti-Hungarian' sentiments and chanting during the games, as well as what they see as the police's heavy-handed treatment of the away fans. The humiliation, though, does not end there. A few days later Romania contrive to lose to Turkey and Hungary smash Estonia, leaving second place in the group wide open again. Hungary need a good showing in Holland in their penultimate match for a chance to qualify. Holland destroy them 8-1. It is the joint biggest defeat in Hungary's history. Within three games Hungary have gone from anticipating a potential trip to Brazil that would revive the memories of the Golden Generation of the 1950s to perhaps falling to its lowest ever ebb. To make matters worse, Romania will go on to finish second in the group and qualify for the World Cup play-offs.

Incredibly, there is no trouble in Bucharest that night. The Romanian supporters quickly hurry home, perhaps sensing that revenge might be on the cards, while the Hungarians are kept back in the stadium. A fleet of buses with barred windows waits for them under the stadium, ready to transport them all back to the railway station under police escort. The night train back to Budapest is full but peaceful. The Animal and his group of ultras from Steaua Bucharest were nowhere to be seen, before or after the game. The Romanian media later report that, far from confronting the Hungarian fans for their behaviour in Bucharest, they had found a group of Dinamo Bucharest ultras and fought with them instead. When the night train arrives back at Keleti station in Budapest the next afternoon, hundreds of black T-shirted Hungarians stumble drunkenly down the platform, waving their flags and singing their songs about Hungary's glorious history, past the golden coloured engine painted with the smiling faces of the Magical Magyars.

13

BOSNIA AND HERZEGOVINA, SLOVAKIA

Žilina, Slovakia. September 2013.

On the pitch in front of me the Bosnia national football team is training in silence ahead of their next World Cup qualifier against Slovakia in twenty-four hours' time. The match is taking place in Slovakia's third largest city, close to the Low Tatras Mountains, the natural border with Poland. The cold wind and rain hint at snow and winter's early arrival. Even in a wet and empty stadium the fear is palpable. Their coach, Safet Sušić, buried deep in a thermal jacket and hood, is being soaked by a nagging drizzle. The fifty or so Bosnian journalists watching in the stands shuffle their feet and chain-smoke to keep warm. But they, too, watch in silence. No one – not the players, the coach or the journalists – looks as if they want to be here.

Which is strange. Bosnia are currently top of Group G in World Cup qualification. It has been an incredible campaign so far. They have scored more goals than anyone else, smashing twenty-three in six qualifiers, at almost four a game. They are unbeaten and cruising towards their first World Cup finals since Bosnia became an independent nation. Bosnia's first eleven would not be disgraced at any World Cup finals either. Up front they have Manchester City's Edin Džeko and Stuttgart's Vedad Ibišević to score the goals, Roma's Miralem Pjanić provides the midfield guile and, in defence, captain Emir Spahić and goalkeeper Asmir

Begović have raised a formidable barrier. For a coach whose attacking philosophy is merely to score one more goal than the opposition, no matter how many they concede, Safet Sušić's Bosnia have been remarkably miserly, too, conceding just four times. Then, a few days earlier in the central Bosnian city of Zenica, in front of a home crowd desperate for The Dragons to plant one foot in Brazil, they conspired to lose 1-0 to Slovakia. Greece, who have stuck to them like glue, moved level on points. The Greeks knew what every team in Europe has come to suspect: that against the Bosnians their chance will come. It always does. The fear has set in. Every Bosnian in the Štadion pod Dubňom – not to mention the millions spread across the world – have good reason to be unhappy. History is beginning to repeat itself. Bosnia are about to choke.

Bosnia have been this close to qualifying for a major tournament twice before. There was little they could do in coming second to Spain in their qualification group for the 2010 World Cup in South Africa. Spain had won all ten of their matches, after all. It was also bad luck to draw Portugal in the play-offs. They lost both legs 1-0. Worse still, they again drew Portugal in the play-offs for the 2012 European Championships two years later. This time the result was more emphatic – 6-2 over both matches – but it was the final group game against France that had made Bosnians question whether they would ever see their team at a major finals. At the Stade de France in Paris, Bosnia took an early lead through a brilliant curling right-foot shot by Edin Džeko. France only led the group by a point before the game, meaning Džeko's goal would have put Bosnia through to their first major finals. But a late penalty by Samir Nasri took France to the finals instead and consigned Bosnia to their fruitless play-off against Portugal. Goalkeeper Asmir Begović played that day after coming on as a half-time substitute. 'We've been on such a journey to qualify for these tournaments and we've always fallen short,' he says, now sitting on the second floor of the team hotel after training. 'It's almost the story of the country. No matter what the sport, they always fall at the last hurdle.'

Downstairs the bar is full of Bosnia fans drunkenly singing sad old songs at the top of their voices. Žilina is full. It is impossible to get a room in the city as almost every ticket had been bought by travelling Bosnia fans. The stadium can hold 11,000 and it is thought at least 8,000 will be Bosnian. It has been the same at every away match in qualification. 'The love people have for their country is amazing,' Begović says. The Bosnian war has much to do with the attendance. Back in 1992 Bosnia declared independence. It was always a multi-ethnic nation within the Yugoslav republic; half-Bosnian Muslim and the rest largely Serb and Croat. But during the subsequent war it tore itself apart from the inside as communities turned on each other. As many as 100,000 people died in two and a half years, leaving behind familiar names for ever associated with bloodshed. There was, of course, the siege of Sarajevo, the longest in modern European warfare, and the massacre of Srebrenica, where 8,000 Bosnian men, from boys to pensioners, were murdered by a Serb militia. The country's name is synonymous with tragedy and every player and every fan has their story. Begović left his town in eastern Bosnia, where the worst massacres took place, when he was four years old. 'My parents and grandparents who had built a life in Bosnia had lost everything,' he says of that time. His family ended up in Germany and then in Canada. 'We lived in a Bosnian way wherever we lived, whether that was Germany or Canada,' he says. He speaks now in a broad North American accent. 'We took everyone's culture on board but we were always Bosnian.' Begović got out but Džeko stayed, in Sarajevo. 'I was six when the war started,' he told football writer Jonathan Wilson in 2012. 'It was terrible. My house was destroyed so we went to live with my grandparents. The whole family was there, maybe fifteen people, all staying in an apartment about thirty-five metres square. It was very hard. We were stressed every day in case somebody we knew died.'

When the war finished, football resumed, but only after the pitch of the city's biggest club, Željezničar Sarajevo, the club Džeko would go on to play for, was cleared of mines. 'When the war finished,' Džeko believed, 'I was much stronger, mentally.' Which is why Begović believes the national team is so important to Bosnians. Other than the legitimacy that a World Cup finals infers – former Croatian president Franco Tudjman told then Croatia captain Igor Štimac that the national team had done more for the state than any single politician – the Dragons have become a rallying point for the refugees, and the sons and daughters of refugees, displaced by the war. War destroyed Bosnia but it also spread Bosnians far and wide. 'The war took people all over Europe, all over the world,' Begović says. 'When we have this game it brings people together and they travel from far away to support us. It gives us an extra edge and a push. Every game this qualifying we've pretty much been playing at home, even when we're away.' The duel immigrant identity had caused a dilemma for Begović. Before Bosnia he had previously represented Canada's Under 20s. In Canada Begović's 'defection' didn't go down well. 'I had to get on with my life as it was,' he recalls of his decision to represent Canada. 'When the opportunity came it was a difficult decision. But I never had family getting to watch games. My family comes to every Bosnia game home and away. Uncles, aunties; that's where your identity is and that's what makes you feel proud to represent your family and represent your country. It does mean a little more. I didn't take playing for Canada for granted but it was a stronger pull to play for Bosnia.' Bosnia now had a choice. If the team lost again it was to be the play-offs again. Safet Sušić – himself considered both the greatest Bosnian and the greatest Paris Saint-Germain player of all time, who represented Yugoslavia at the 1982 and 1990 World Cup finals – had been in charge of that game at the Stade de France. It's unlikely he'll survive another near miss. 'We've never qualified for a major tournament before so we don't know how we do it, until we do it,' Begović admits. 'Once we get there we'll know how we'll do it and do it again.'

With a population of under four million, Bosnia is punching above its weight even getting this far. Eighteen years ago Bosnia didn't even have a team, as such. The Dragons played their first where you come from. Since the war there are so many people across the world. There will be people here from USA, Canada. Asmir Begović grew up in Canada. Ibišević grew up in America. Most of our players did.' What will it mean, World Cup qualification, for such a new country, I ask. 'Look at the expectations of people, there are seven thousand here,' he replies. 'Some people here will probably earn £350 a month in Bosnia. They will put most of their monthly budget into this game. They killed our people for so long and we want to show them what we are made of.' Fahrudin is less happy. 'We are not a new country, mate. We are not a new country,' he puffs angrily, getting red in the cheeks as he shakes his head. 'We are a very, very old country. We are the oldest country in the Balkans. NEVER SAY THAT AGAIN,' he shouts. 'Never say that again. We are older than Serbia and Croatia.' He is the only Bosnian I had seen get remotely angry all day. 'We love our country,' he apologises, holding me by the shoulder in an iron grip. 'We will beat them tonight 2-0. We are very proud.'

As planned, the Štadión pod Dubňom is full of Bosnian supporters. A small square of Slovaks in white shirts fills a corner of the stadium, but they can't be heard. The Bosnian team's hotel has been full of hundreds of Bosnia fans waiting to see the players leave for the game. Inside a dozen fans are watching another football match on the television in the bar. In Tashkent, Uzbekistan are playing Jordan in the final Asian qualification play-off. The two teams finished third in their respective groups. Uzbekistan had been particularly unlucky, having led the group until being overtaken by Iran and South Korea after the final match. For Jordan it was the closest the tiny Middle Eastern kingdom had ever got to the World Cup finals. The first game in Amman had ended 1-1, as had the game the Bosnian fans were watching. The winner, who would then contest a final intercontinental play-off with South America's fifth-placed team, would have to be decided by penalties. Uzbekistan missed an early one. The Jordanian player ran up to take his kick and then ... nothing. The screen went dead. Every screen in the world went dead. The global feed had somehow wearing the Stars and Stripes, having just watched the US beat arch-rivals Mexico 2-0. It was the fourth time they had beaten Mexico *dos a cero* in the same stadium and the victory put the US on the brink of qualifying for their seventh World Cup finals in a row. But they needed a draw in Tegucigalpa to make it happen. I had seen the US begin its campaign against Antigua and Barbuda in Florida, when they squeaked through 3-1. They had easily qualified for the Hexagonal, a final group stage of six teams. The top three qualified automatically for Brazil 2014 while the fourth-placed team would play the winner of qualification from FIFA's smallest confederation, Oceania. That had long been known to be New Zealand. The US and Mexico were clear favourites, but CONCACAF qualification has been a popular route for the underdog. Haiti qualified for the 1974 finals, Jamaica in 1998 and Trinidad and Tobago, the smallest nation ever to qualify, in 2006. Jamaica had made it to the 2014 Hexagonal, along with Honduras, Panama and Costa Rica.

The US had a tough start, away to Honduras. Many complain that CONCACAF World Cup qualification gives Mexico and the US an easy ride, but those who do probably haven't considered what the US faces when it goes on the road in Central America. Aside from the usual anti-American sentiment, Honduras can also claim to be one of the most dangerous countries on earth. As Andrew Keh in the *New York Times* pointed out before the game, the game's host city, San Pedro Sula, 'was the most violent city on the planet. According to the United States Department of State, there were 159 homicides for every 100,000 residents in 2011. The area's population is about one million.' Troops with machine guns guarded the team's every move. On match day itself 45,000 people would cram into the stadium. The Honduran government declared a national holiday to ensure the match was full. It's not unusual for players to be pelted with objects ranging from bottles full of urine to rocks. 'In terms of batteries being thrown at me, I think I've seen it all,' US striker Jozy Altidore told Keh before the game. In CONCACAF qualification at least, the United States is everyone's worst enemy.

Sure enough, with 45,000 screaming home fans – and only fifteen official away fans – Honduras won 2-1. Life on the road might have been tough for the United States but their home form was exemplary. They won every game at home, without conceding a single goal. More importantly the crowd had, for once, been an advantage. 'Any time you can play in a stadium when you have more fans rooting you on is better, you have that home field advantage,' midfielder Clint Dempsey said before their first home game, in Denver, against Costa Rica. 'It's difficult sometimes being an American player. You find times even in your own country when you feel like you are playing away.' Yet it all nearly went very wrong. A blizzard hit Denver during the Costa Rica match, dropping so much snow that it was almost impossible to distinguish between the white shirts of the American players and the pitch. Conditions were so severe that the referee took the players off the pitch. When they returned, the US won the game with a goal from Dempsey. The Costa Ricans, who had tried to get the match postponed, were livid. 'I asked them to stop. They should suspend the ref,' Costa Rica coach Jorge Luis Pinto told the press after the game. 'It was an embarrassment. It was an insult to Costa Rica.'

The Costa Ricans would get their revenge. When the US team arrived in the country they were made to wait in line at immigration along with everyone else, every request for a training pitch was turned down, they weren't provided with any balls to practise with and, best of all, the nation's cab drivers had agreed a 'go-slow', ensuring that the US team coach would be stuck in traffic when it arrived. They ended up losing 3-1. But their home form was enough to carry them to the top of the group, to Columbus, Ohio, and another *dos a cero* against Mexico. The result left Mexico in deep trouble. *El Tri* was enduring the worst World Cup qualification campaign since they failed to make it to Italia '90, itself a rare event given their World Cup pedigree. They had hosted the tournament twice and appeared in the finals a further twelve more times. They were fifth in the group after drawing five of their early games and the 2-0 defeat to the US meant they could lose out on a play-off spot to Panama. They had only two games to sort it out. But, back in Columbus, the US fans waited for the result, chanting 'We are going to Brazil' to each other, and 'You're not going to Brazil' to the Mexicans. When the match in Honduras finished in a 2-2 draw, the US had qualified for Brazil. The US players, who had also been watching the Honduras match on TV in the dressing room, ran out to the pitch and sprayed the delirious fans with champagne and beer.

Six days later, back across the Atlantic in Cairo, one American was still unsure of his plans for next summer. Bob Bradley, who had taken the US to the last sixteen at South Africa 2010, was sitting in an auditorium alongside the national coaches and football officials of nine other nations. Well, eight other nations. Inexplicably the Nigerian delegation had not turned up. The ten teams had finished top of their qualification groups and were now waiting to see who they would be drawn against for the final, two-leg Brazil 2014 play-offs. There had been many shocks along the way. Two teams had a chance of qualifying for a World Cup for the first time: the tiny West African state of Burkina Faso and, incredibly, Ethiopia. The Walias had made it to the final round of qualification despite being one of Africa's lowest ranked teams. They had begun their journey in the preliminary round two years before, the same round that saw Rwanda play Eritrea. Ethiopia had drawn their first game against war-ravaged Somalia 0-0 but won the return 5-0 before going on to top a group that contained 2010 hosts South Africa.

Bob Bradley's Egypt had bigger issues to contend with. As well as having to come to terms with events in Port Said, he also had to deal with the fallout of both the revolution and its counter-revolution. Since we had met there had been a coup in Egypt, deposing the country's president, Mohamed Morsi. It was rumoured to have caused problems in the camp. Morsi was a leading figure in the Muslim Brotherhood and the team's beating heart was Mohamed Aboutrika, a devout Muslim and a supporter of Morsi. According to *Sports Illustrated*'s Grant

Wahl, who wrote a profile of Bradley, as Muslim Brotherhood supporters were killed in their hundreds on the streets after demonstrations Aboutrika took to Twitter to express his dismay. He spoke out against the coup which had divided the country between those who supported the Brotherhood and those who had seen the army's takeover as necessary to stop the clumsy process of Islamification that Morsi and his followers had tried to push through:

> *I supported Dr Morsi out of complete conviction,* Aboutrika tweeted. *In light of the success of the January 25 revolution and the freedoms and expression of opinion that followed ... I think there will be a real democracy and respect for other opinions, but unfortunately this hasn't happened. So I decided not to talk politics. But when it has to do with reputation and dignity I will not be quiet.*

Such was the reverence in which Aboutrika was held on all sides of Egyptian society that few called for him to be banned, as had happened with other players who had expressed unpopular or contradictory views to whichever government or army general was in power at the time. 'Look, Trika has had the strength to always stand behind his beliefs and say what he thinks, and that doesn't always work here,' Bradley told Wahl before the draw. 'I will defend that part of him for ever, because he is a good man and cares about Egypt. In order to focus on doing everything to get to the World Cup, he's picked up on the need to not be high profile at the moment.' Despite the coup and the divisions, the team kept winning. In fact, they were the only team in World Cup qualification that, up to that point, had won every single game, six out of six. Aboutrika and the lightning quick winger Mohamed Salah had starred in the campaign, having scored eleven goals between them. They finished top of the group and with it secured a seat at the draw alongside the Ivory Coast, Senegal, Tunisia, Algeria, Ghana, Nigeria, Cameroon and, of course, Ethiopia and Burkina Faso.

Aside from Egypt's battles with itself, African qualification had been beset by ineptitude elsewhere. Qualification campaigns had either been saved or ruined by a series of administrative blunders over the use of recently naturalised players and even accidentally fielding players who had been banned. Ethiopia believed they had qualified for the play-offs with a game to spare, only to have a 2-1 victory over Botswana changed to a mandatory 3-0 defeat for fielding a player who should have been suspended. It brought South Africa back from the dead, but Ethiopia managed to beat Central African Republic in the final game to qualify for the last round.

In Group L Togo were punished for fielding an ineligible player against Cameroon, who had themselves been briefly suspended by FIFA. Togo had won the game 2-0, but transforming that into a 3-0 victory for Cameroon completely changed the calculus for the group. Libya were top and had only needed a draw against Cameroon to make it to the final round. The country had survived the downfall of Colonel Gaddafi and a qualifier was played in Tripoli. In fact, many of the players had left football to go and fight for the rebels on the frontline. FIFA's decision, however, meant that Cameroon were now top and handed a huge advantage. They beat Libya 1-0.

In Group J Liberia were punished for the same offence but it made little difference. The top two teams, Senegal and Uganda, played their final game knowing victory for either would be enough to qualify. Uganda were now coached by Milutin 'Micho' Sredojević, the gruff, hard-talking Serbian coach I had met in Kigali when he was in charge of the Rwanda team. Rwanda had finished last in their group and sacked Micho over the team's poor run of form, but Uganda drafted him in for the end of their campaign and the do-or-die game against Senegal. Senegal won 1-0, too.

But the most egregious errors had both elevated and condemned the tiny Cape Verde Islands. The West African state, which has a population of just 500,000 people, had been on the verge of World Cup elimination. The Blue Sharks is a team made up of players from the local league in the West African islands, mixed with pros from the Portuguese-born diaspora. Their part-time coach, Lúcio Antunes, has a day job as an air traffic controller at Cape Verde's biggest airport. They had managed to finish second in their group to Tunisia, but were thrown a lifeline after another team in their group, Equatorial Guinea, selected striker Emilio Nsue, a former Spanish youth international, for a game the previous March. Nsue's goals helped Equatorial Guinea beat Cape Verde 4-3, but it later emerged that he had been deemed ineligible by FIFA and the result was reversed, bringing the Blue Sharks' campaign back to life. They were now within striking distance of Tunisia, who they played in the final game. And, sure enough, Cape Verde won 2-0. Tunisia, though, knew that wasn't the end of the story. After the game they too examined the paperwork and immediately appealed against the result. The Tunisian federation had discovered that defender Fernando Varela was technically still banned. Varela had been sent off against Equatorial Guinea and, with the match result annulled, Cape Verde had believed the red card would also be annulled. Not so. A 2-0 victory to Cape Verde had been transformed into a 3-0 victory for Tunisia. 'It is a nightmare, it is incredible, incredible,' the deputy president of Cape Verde's federation, Lena Vasconcelos, told me on the phone. 'Lots of people have phoned up to tell us we are right, that when a match is forfeited all the red and yellow cards are taken away.' The appeal failed and Tunisia prevailed. All in all seven African teams were penalised for getting the rules wrong.

Even given the chaos going on in Egyptian football, its FA had at least managed to get their paperwork in order, and Bradley had negotiated the group stage of African qualification with aplomb. As he sat in the room waiting for the draw there were two teams that almost everyone wanted to avoid: Algeria and Ghana. Four years earlier, Egypt had played Algeria in one of the low points of African football. The violence surrounding that fixture has been well documented and Bradley, and the Egyptian authorities, wanted to avoid a repeat of that circus.

Ghana, on the other hand, posed a different set of problems. They were, by most people's calculations, the best team in Africa. Bradley had had his own bad experiences playing them. When he was coach of the US in South Africa, he had seen his team top their group and secure a last-sixteen knock-out match against Ghana. A solitary goal early in extra time by Asamoah Gyan, the same striker who would miss the penalty that would have seen Ghana later qualify for the semi-finals, eliminated the US and Bradley.

In the end, the draw in Cairo came down to the last few balls. Egypt were drawn against Ghana. It wasn't great news, but Bradley wasn't giving anything away. 'We are the strongest team in the group,' he said afterwards. 'We are not afraid of confronting Ghana.'

**

There is no party in Žilina after the Slovakia–Bosnia game. Due to the huge number of Bosnians in the city, the match has been deemed high risk and almost every bar has been forced to close early. I walk back from the stadium through the empty cobbled streets, past the discarded flags and banners. The main square and the stage are silent. The only people left on the streets are the odd gaggle of bored riot police, left behind just in case, and a few stray packs of Bosnian fans. They hug the side streets furtively looking for a bar to call home for a few, final hours. Bosnia, on the whole, didn't deserve to beat Slovakia. But the comeback, at one down, was something new for most of these fans. The team didn't crumple even if they had made things harder for themselves. The Dragons did what they had to do. Now their destiny is in their hands. They have two final group games, against Lichtenstein and Lithuania, home and away. The fans who had come to Žilina from every corner of the world agreed. If they failed to beat either team, they didn't deserve a place in Brazil.

Down one street, bumping along a wall, hands in pockets, red fez perched on his head, Fahrudin is walking home after failing to

14

ICELAND, NORWAY

Oslo, Norway. October 2013.

It is 11 a.m. and Eidur Guðjohnsen is standing with his team-mates in a nightclub. At least, it looks like a nightclub. The room's walls are painted colourfully; spotlights illuminate a stage and what could pass for a small dance floor. In the centre a strangely shaped bar offers beer and nuts while the low clattering of dance music plays over the PA system. The Iceland national team are politely waiting in a line, hands behind their backs, in the Ullevaal Stadium in Oslo. Tomorrow Iceland play Norway in the final round of matches in European World Cup qualification. Regardless of the competition, the match would always have aroused some local interest. Iceland was settled by Vikings in the ninth century AD and changed hands several times before gaining full independence from Denmark after the Second World War. Its tiny population, cold temperatures, inhospitable winds and remote location – Reykjavik is the most northerly capital city in the world – means that a match between Iceland and pretty much anyone has usually been a foregone conclusion. Its league, for example, is ranked among the worst in Europe. But then something strange started to happen. Iceland had been drawn in Group E with top seeds Norway, Switzerland and Albania. They had been drawn from pot four, the lowest ranking possible in European football. UEFA considered Iceland to be on a par with San Marino, who had never won a competitive game, and Andorra. Not much was expected of them, but when Iceland beat the group favourites Norway in their first game it was clear that they had been massively underrated. 'I think it's the first time in the history of Iceland where we've not had just three or four quality players but we have a whole generation,' Guðjohnsen says as polite Norwegian journalists nudge past. 'We are a nation of 360,000 and look at the quality of footballers we have right now.' He points over to Gylfi Sigurðsson, Iceland's midfield general who plays for Tottenham Hotspur, and striker Kolbeinn Sigþórsson who plays for Ajax. 'It's extraordinary.' Even more extraordinary is the fact that Iceland is on the verge of becoming by far the smallest nation ever to qualify for the finals. It was a record that, if they broke it, was unlikely to be broken again. Iceland would forever be the ultimate underdog.

Guðjohnsen has become used to being Iceland's only star. For over a decade he has played at the highest level, starting out at PSV alongside a then unknown Brazilian kid called Ronaldo. He then scored over seventy goals for Bolton and Chelsea before signing for FC Barcelona. He's thirty-five now, playing in Belgium, and this campaign with Iceland is likely to be his last. But it could end in Brazil, even if just a few weeks earlier the campaign had looked like it was all over. While Romania and Hungary were throwing insults at each other in Bucharest, Iceland had gone 4-1 down to Switzerland with only half an hour left to play. In the previous game they had been hammered 4-2 by Slovenia in Reykjavik, too. But then Iceland launched perhaps the most extraordinary comeback in World Cup qualification. Coach Lars Lagerbäck threw on Guðjohnsen to play deeper in midfield. It is all his legs can manage these days. Sigþórsson coolly slotted home Iceland's second but it was the young AZ Alkmaar winger Jóhann Guðmundsson who scored with two blistering left-foot shots, one in the ninety-second minute, that secured a 4-4 draw. At just twenty-two, he had scored a fine hat-trick and salvaged what proved to be a vital point.

Now it all comes down to this, a final group game against Norway. Win, and Iceland will reach the play-offs for the first time in their history. A draw might even be enough if Slovenia fail to beat Switzerland. The question was: how had Iceland managed to put together a team of young, talented players who were all now playing at good European teams with such a tiny talent pool to draw from? The answer was quite simple. 'The first full-size indoor pitches were built thirteen years ago,' Guðjohnsen explains. 'So this is the first generation of players that has played the whole year through which wasn't always the case before. We had the league for three or four months and the rest was pre-season.' There was also the coach. Iceland had hired Lars Lagerbäck, the veteran former Sweden manager who had coached at three World Cup finals himself. With the Swedish team he'd had to control the mercurial talent, and volcanic temper, of Zlatan Ibrahimović. After that he was in charge of Nigeria at the previous World Cup before taking the Iceland job. 'He came in before this campaign and did extraordinarily well,' says Guðjohnsen. 'He gives you a lot of freedom but is very disciplined.'

You cannot imagine Lars Lagerbäck disciplining anyone with any menace. A few hours later we are sitting in a café talking amiably about Icelandic society. 'Besides football the character amongst the players and people in general is very, very good,' Lagerbäck says, dressed in a blue Iceland tracksuit. 'They are not spoilt and they are taking care of themselves. I like the country and the society as a whole.' Lagerbäck is sixty-five now, affable, and aware that this is likely to be his last job in international football. He spotted, on taking the job, that Iceland was on the verge of something very special. 'That is why I took it!' he beams. 'When I looked into it, the Under 21s qualified for the [2011] European Championships in Denmark. They are all twenty-three or twenty-four years old now and I thought that looks really interesting to work with young, talented players and some of the other players that were older, too.' The decision to build seven full-sized indoor sports halls, just before the 2008 financial crash that bankrupted the country, allowed young players to train and play competitively in two seasons all year round. 'I think the only chance for smaller countries is to develop youth players so they can go to top, bigger leagues,' Lagerbäck says when I ask him what other smaller nations can learn from Iceland. 'With all respect to smaller countries, and also Sweden is a small country, if the Swedish national team or the Icelandic national team didn't have their best players in a good league, the national team couldn't do well. That is the only advice that counts: that you educate young players so they can get out to the bigger leagues in Europe.' Iceland is producing so much talent that they have got this far without, potentially, one of their best players. Aron Jóhannsson was born in the US but raised in Iceland, by Icelandic parents, and nurtured by Iceland's youth system. He even played for Iceland's Under 21 team. But that didn't stop the US national team from offering him the chance to play for them, which he took. It was still something of a sore issue in Icelandic football circles.

Even a few years ago the entire Iceland national team was amateur, with part-time players working as fishermen or journalists or studying for master's degrees. Now the entire team plays in Holland, Denmark, England and beyond. All except one, who's keeping Iceland's spirit of amateurism alive. Goalkeeper Hannes Halldórsson isn't sure whether he's a goal-keeping film director or a film-directing goalkeeper. 'My first film was a small action comedy when I was twelve with a group of friends,' he says of his early life in Iceland. He has a shaven head and stands to attention, both hands behind his back, when he speaks. 'I wasn't the action hero. I made the film in 1996. It was a very simple technique. I managed to make it with a VCR and a video camera. It was like *Superman* but we called it *Swimming Man*. He was wearing a stupid outfit.' Halldórsson was obsessed with film making and football as a kid and decided to pursue both, playing part-time for the Icelandic champions Knattspyrnufélag Reykjavíkur while making music videos and advertisements. His most famous film was the video for Iceland's 2012 Eurovision Song Contest entry. 'I was a little irritated I hadn't been asked before,' Halldórsson says bluntly. 'I'm one of those names that is mentioned as things have been going well in directing commercials, so my name pops up. I was a Eurovision fan as a kid.' 'Never Forget', by Greta Salóme & Jónsi, is a thumping, operatic metal boy-girl duet. The song came twentieth in the final with Norway awarding it five points. Still, it reached number two in the Icelandic charts and a more modest number ninety-four in Belgium. 'She's an elf, a mysterious figure,' he says, explaining the video. 'We have this elf belief in Iceland that goes back many centuries. It's about a haunting woman this guy can't forget. A mystic woman trying to entice him to the other side. It's when he's young, and he doesn't go. When he's older he goes all the way.'

Halldórsson has been ever-present in the Iceland team and every bit as important as Kolbeinn Sigþórsson's incredible scoring record of twelve goals in eighteen matches. The World Cup is one dream that he has. He has another. 'It is my dream, to make one feature film before I quit football. I can only be a footballer and a commercial director because you can shoot for two days and then train for one. A film is forty days in a row.' What kind of film is it, I ask. 'It's a horror film. Not a zombie film. It's a supernatural, low-key ghost thriller that takes place somewhere in an isolated part of Iceland.' His next job might have to be closer to home. Victory against Norway and then in the play-offs might require Halldórsson to shoot the video for the team's official World Cup song.

'I'd have to see some videos to see what you are talking about because I have no idea what that is,' he says, confused.

You know, like New Order's 'World in Motion'. You know New Order, right?

'No, I've never heard of them,' he says but thinks for a few moments, visualising what a World Cup music video would like if he *did* have to shoot one. 'I would make some mix of maybe training videos and showing the nation taking part in it,' he offers. 'Er ... children running around in national outfits? Maybe a guy in a small store wearing an Iceland shirt?' He gives up. 'I don't think it would be a horror video.'

Halldórsson will start tomorrow night against Norway. He and the team mooch around in the lobby of the hotel. They have free rein to do pretty much whatever they want. There's no press pack harassing them, no paparazzi looking to catch a glimpse of a WAG. 'If people don't take that responsibility they don't belong in the squad I am coaching,' Lagerbäck says. 'I have very few examples where players haven't responded with that. Look at now. After training the players are free to go out after lunch if they like. You have to treat them as normal people and players respond to that on the pitch, too.' He had learned this, he says, after coaching perhaps the most strong-willed and talented of modern players. 'When you compare it to Zlatan when he came into the team you had to find a role for him, he is that kind of player,' Lagerbäck recalls. 'That is basically what I changed in my philosophy when I started coaching national teams and working with world-class players. With skilful players you have to give them as much freedom as possible inside the team. You can't run everything.'

**

Approximately 0.28 per cent of Iceland's population have arrived at the Ullevaal Stadium on match day. Some of the 1,000 or so fans did not have far to travel. Norway is home to one of the biggest communities of Icelanders outside the country, but most have flown in for the day. 'They have extremely good talent, the Icelanders, so we are not surprised. Icelanders are always optimistic about things,' says Petur, a gruff middle-aged fan accompanying his daughter to her first away game. He talks slowly and says the word 'optimistic' as if telling the punchline of a joke. 'Lagerbäck changed the team, extremely, I think. He has a lot of experience and before he came we had a bad run. It was not so good. I think we'll win 3-1.' Petur won't be here for long. He returns to Iceland after the game to get back to his job as a fisherman. 'I'm on a fishing trawler so you work twenty-four hours a day, twenty-five to thirty days at a time at sea.' How do you catch up with the football, I ask him, on a boat that has to negotiate forty-foot waves? He looks at me pityingly. 'We have satellite TV. And internet,' he says, as if speaking to an idiot. 'Sometimes the conditions are not so good. But most of the time it is ... tolerable.' There are few Norway fans to be found. Although they started the campaign as top seeds in the group Norway's campaign soon fell away. The legendary Egil Olson had been reinstalled as coach. 'Drillo' had been in charge of Norway during the greatest period in the national team's history. His scientific approach in the mid-nineties was years ahead and his methods wrung the maximum return from what was a modest amount of talent. He led the team to two World Cup finals. At one point, Norway were ranked the second best team in the world by FIFA. He had left to find fame abroad and had garnered a reputation as something of an eccentric for taking training in his famous green wellington boots and being one of the few figures in football who had something of a political past: at one point he'd been a member of Norway's communist party. Alas, Drillo failed at then English Premier League club Wimbledon, where he was sacked, and later with the Iraqi national team, where he was removed without warning as the country sank deeper into conflict. Still, he had returned to Norway with much hope, but the results didn't change. A defeat to Switzerland saw him leave – although Drillo later claimed he felt he had no choice but to resign – and he was replaced by Per-Mathias Høgmo. Even that change made no difference. Høgmo lost his first match in charge, against Slovenia, and Norway were promptly eliminated. They now had nothing to play for.

As the night draws in and the temperature plummets, the stands fill up with Icelandic flags. At the same time, thousands of miles away in the northern Ghanaian city of Kumasi, Bob Bradley is standing on the touchline at the Baba Yara Stadium in white shirtsleeves, arms folded, as Ghana play his Egypt side in the first leg of their African World Cup qualification play-off. Bradley knew this was arguably the most important match of his long career. It was about more than just winning a game. Bradley had seen World Cup qualification as his contribution to the revolution, a chance for the national team to be a symbol of some kind of unity at a time when Egyptians were more divided than ever. The whole campaign came down to this. A few thousand Egyptian fans had even travelled to Ghana for the match. Given the spectator ban in Egypt, it was a rare chance to see Egyptian players in the flesh.

But within minutes of the start of the game the script has changed. Ghana score within four minutes and quickly go 2-0 up. Mohamed Aboutrika, the man Bradley calls his 'blood brother' because of the strong bond the two enjoy off the pitch, scores a penalty to give Egypt an away goal and some kind of hope. As half-time approaches smoke hangs so heavily over the pitch at the Baba Yara Stadium that it is impossible to see the ball fly into Egypt's penalty area. So many flares have been lit during the first half that even the players are hard to pick out. But Abdul Majeed Waris has no problem seeing the ball; he rises higher than the rest and powers the ball down and into the net. Ghana now lead 3-1 at half-time. In the second half, Ghana go on the rampage. Egypt's players appear to give up as Ghana score three more. The game ends 6-1 and Bradley's hopes of finally breaking Egypt's World Cup curse are all but over. There will be a return leg in Cairo, but they will have to win 5-0 against the best team in Africa.

In the stands the Ghanaian police wade in to stop any trouble breaking out, not between rival fans but between the Egyptians themselves. Those fans, who had put their political differences to one side to support the same team, as the players had done, quickly turned on each other. A yellow flag with a black hand and four fingers had been flown. It is the 'Rabaa' sign, which means 'four' in Arabic: the symbol of the Pro-Morsi, anti-coup movement. To many Egyptians showing four fingers is a sign of support for the Muslim Brotherhood and akin to treason. The ugly confrontation is quashed and the flag removed. With the national team's hopes for the World Cup all but gone, so, it seems, has the underlying need for unity. 'The dream of going to the World Cup is what kept our team united,' a disconsolate Bradley said after the game. 'But we've seen that become nearly impossible.'

**

In Oslo it is only the Iceland fans who are making any noise. A drummer is leading the 1,000-strong group in song and dance as the match begins. 'We don't want to get our hopes too high,' admits Kolbeinn Tumi Dadason, a football journalist covering the Norway game for an Iceland sports website. 'They call it Eurovision fever. Every time we send a song to the Eurovision, we believe that it will win it and usually finish sixteenth. So we shouldn't take anything for granted.' But soon Iceland are 1-0 up thanks to Kolbeinn Sigþórsson, the Ajax striker, who has just scored his thirteenth goal in nineteen games. If they win it doesn't matter what happens between Slovenia and Switzerland. But Norway's dominance tells and they equalise fifteen minutes later. And that is it. Norway attack but Iceland easily contain them. When the full-time whistle blows no one knows whether it will be enough. Lagerbäck had said he would make sure there would be three ways of finding out the score in the other game in and around the dugout, but they'd all seemingly malfunctioned at the same time. Players and officials mill around in the centre circle talking. And then the news comes through. Switzerland have won, and Iceland have made it to the play-offs for the first time in their history. The squad sprints along the pitch in a long line towards the celebrating Iceland fans. They don't jump into the stands – that's not a very Icelandic thing to do – but dance and sing in front of the ecstatic crowd. One supporter stands out at the front, a huge bear of a man with a big beard and horned helmet, wearing nothing but a Superman onesie and wrapped in an Icelandic flag. He is crying like a baby and being held up off the floor by two men nearly as big as him. 'We're two games from the World Cup. HOW DO YOU THINK I FUCKING FEEL?! I'm from little Iceland!' shouts Arni (as I later learned he was called) after I find him and ask him how he feels. 'Do you hear my voice?' he yelps. 'I'd give it ALL. I'd give it *all* for this country.' Thick tears splatter into my face. 'I'm so fucking proud. We can stand tall! AGAINST WHOEVER!' He finally breaks down, sobbing in my arms, soaking my cheek and the lapels of my jacket with his tears. Later Arni promises to travel to wherever Iceland plays its away play-off match, and wear his Superman onesie at the game. It is good luck now.

**

Across Europe, World Cup qualification is coming to an end. There have been few shocks. Spain have cruised home, as have Belgium, Italy, Holland and Germany. Switzerland, with its contingent of Kosovar players, have made it to Brazil without losing a match. Xherdan Shaqiri is by far the best Swiss player of the campaign. England have left it late to secure their place in Brazil, having won back-to-back matches against Montenegro and Poland at Wembley. Russia win their group, forcing Portugal into a play-off spot. It is left to Bosnia to try and become Europe's only debutante at the 2014 World Cup finals. After the Slovakia game, where I had seen The Dragons fight back from 1-0 down to win in front of a home crowd of former refugees, Bosnia easily disposed of Lichtenstein 4-1. Four days later they travelled to Kaunas in Lithuania knowing any mistake would be punished by second-place Greece. In Slovakia players and fans had said the same thing. After everything the country had gone through, after every choke en route to a major tournament, they believed defeat now would be hard to recover from. As expected, it was like a home game for Bosnia and midway through the second half Vedad Ibišević received the ball six yards out all on his own in front of the Lithuanian goal. For a split second he didn't seem to know what to do with it, given that he had so much time and space. But he poked the ball home and Bosnia had finally made it. Back in Sarajevo, 50,000 people were on the streets celebrating the proudest moment in the country's short life. 'I really can't believe that we made it,' Ibišević tells the *New York Times* after the win. 'Definitely a dream coming true for me and the whole team. It took a little time to sink in. When we arrived back in Sarajevo, the people were in the streets and all so happy. The people didn't really have many occasions over the last twenty years to celebrate anything. They kind of forgot what it was like. It was a great atmosphere and just a big party.'

A few days later the European play-off draw will be made. France would play Ukraine, Romania will play Greece, Portugal will take on Sweden. And Iceland? They will play Croatia. 'You never know in November you can have snow and minus temperatures,' Lagerbäck says before he leaves the stadium. The weather is so bad in Iceland in November that a football match has never been hosted then. It could be minus ten. Lagerbäck gives a self-deprecating half-smile when I ask him where this achievement ranks in his long career. 'This is a special thing,' he replies. 'Because this was a team that nobody really believed could do it.'

15

JORDAN, URUGUAY

Zaatari refugee camp, Jordan. November 2013.

As the car speeds north through wide open desert, passing caravans of domesticated camels and Bedouin shepherds marshalling their flocks of goats, the Zaatari refugee camp slowly rises into view. It is a vast complex, ringed by 8.3 kilometres of white concrete walls and wire. Buildings and huts can be seen inside, as well as electrical wiring and satellite dishes that hint at a creeping permanence. As many as 150,000 people live here now. When times are bad a thousand more are added to the numbers every day. During quieter periods, only a few hundred arrive. Within eighteen months the Zaatari refugee camp has become Jordan's fourth biggest city. It isn't going anywhere any time soon.

Zaatari had been a nondescript hamlet, housing no more than a few hundred people, until 2012. Syria's bloody civil war was by now one year old and hundreds of thousands of refugees had fled to neighbouring countries: north to Turkey, east to Iraq, west to Lebanon and, most of all, south across the border to Jordan. Zaatari lies just ten kilometres from the Syrian border and a further fifteen from the small city of Daraa, where the uprising against President Bashar al-Assad's rule began in March 2011. The local infrastructure couldn't handle the huge influx of people, many of whom were carrying horrific injuries and had witnessed unspeakable savagery. In July 2012 Zaatari opened and quickly filled. Life restarted, too. At the main gates Jordanian merchants peddle fruit and vegetables to their new and ever-expanding market. Young boys, no older than ten years old, weave around the legs of the adults pushing wheelbarrows as they keep an eye on the horizon. They are Syrians on the lowest rung of Zaatari's new mercantile hierarchy, earning no more than one dinar a day ferrying the meagre possessions of the new arrivals into the camp. In just eighteen months a new social structure has sprung into life with a corresponding explosion in prices, the premium the poor have to pay in any disaster economy. There are satellite TV 'shops', caravans and tents converted into makeshift showrooms; a taxi service operates in the camp charging five dinars, just over £4, for a three-kilometre ride. Before the war, in fact even today anywhere in Jordan expect in Zaatari, five dinars would get you from the capital Amman to the Syrian border. Down one road in the camp, chris-tened the Champs-Elysées, 685 shops can be found: neatly arranged kiosks selling tinned food, barbers selling haircuts, importers selling TVs and mobile phones; a pet shop that sells small birds. There is even a baker that specialises in wedding cakes and, nearby, a wedding dress shop. There are fifty-six mosques in Zaatari. Even in war and in exile life, and love, continues. In little over a year the camp has gone from being a sleepy and ignored mark on the map to one of the biggest refugee camps in the world with an economy worth an estimated £100 million a year, according to the UN.

At the end of the Champs-Elysées, on the very edges of the camp, a group of young men are sitting at desks in their football kit taking notes. One of them is Omar al Taleb Bassam. He is thirty-one but looks older. Bassam used to be a footballer, a striker for a local amateur team in Daraa. Home is just twenty-five kilometres away but it is impossible for him to return. Instead he has built a new life in Zaatari and is using football to help the children and young adults who have arrived, shattered by war, to move on as best they can. He is a coach now, organising matches and tourna-ments to teach the young men a little more about fitness, tech-nique and discipline. 'It's rehabilitation through football,' Bassam explains after his lecture. Outside half a dozen young children are kicking a ball in the air and chasing it as one pack on a sandy pitch with goalposts. 'The children arrive completely devastated. They have seen their family members killed before their eyes and the journey to Jordan is a difficult one for them. Through football at least we try to remove the sense of fear and give them some sense of normalcy. Football is the most popular sport. It plays the role of the mother. It is the only outlet many have.' Bassam had, like every single person, come to a tipping point where staying in Syria was no longer an option. 'I could not take life in Syria any more,' he says quietly. 'My life was threatened on a daily basis. Basically we are Syrian people asking for freedom under a repressive regime. They did not choose between an elderly person, a child or a woman. They were targeting everybody. They were bombing homes, villages. It became unliveable so we fled to Jordan.' It wasn't just the children who had been helped, or distracted, by football. It had been good for Bassam, too. The camp was orderly, it had electricity – even if most of it was illegally taken from a wire hooked up to the power lines outside – but Zaatari wasn't without its tensions both between its occupants and its hosts. 'They, the Syrians, are all after maximising their own benefits so basically food, goods, vouchers they all want to maximise what they can get,' Bassam says of life in the camp. 'Outside things are OK. With the Jordanians outside the camp in the towns there is some exploitation. It is not across the board against all Jordanians because the five fingers on one hand are not the same. But that is the general sense they get.'

For Jordanians the Syrian crisis was another wave of refugees for the country to deal with. The war in Iraq had seen over a million Iraqis flee westwards. Before that the creation of Israel in 1948, followed by wars in 1967 and 1973, had seen huge numbers of Palestinians move east. Jordan was long known as the quiet man of the Middle East, an oasis of relative calm as countries degenerated around it. Of the one million Iraqis who had come, almost 400,000 still remained. And the Palestinians now made up the vast majority of the Jordanian population. The tensions and, sometimes, the hatreds between the two communities was Jordan's dirty little secret, something the authorities covered up and which the local press could not report on. 'The Jordanian authorities consider any talk about a Palestinian–East Bank Jordanian division to be a threat to national security,' Professor Yasir Suleiman from the University of Cambridge had told me. 'East Bank Jordanians tend to be more vocal about the issue publicly: they feel that they are the indigenous population and that the state is more theirs than the Palestinians'.' There was only one realm in Jordanian society in which the tension was allowed to become vocal: football. Jordan's two biggest teams are Al Wihdat and Al Faisaly. Wihdat comes from the Al Wihdat refugee camp outside Amman. That, too, was supposed to be a temporary refugee camp. Now, after more than sixty years, it has become merely a suburb of the capital. The club has always had a strong Palestinian identity. Their club badge has Jerusalem's Dome of the Rock on it. Yasser Arafat once even referred to Wihdat as the national team of Palestine, long before the Palestinians had their own proper national team. Al Faisaly, on the other hand, has roots in the country's Jordanian East Bank population. When they play each other the resentments come to the surface; how the Palestinians controlled the levers of business while the Jordanian East Bankers dominated the government, military and police. Al Wihdat's fans would chant about a free Palestine: 'One, two, three, Jerusalem for the Arabs!' The Al Faisaly fans would urge King Abdullah to divorce his wife, Queen Rania, who is a Palestinian. Rioting at the teams' games has been commonplace in recent years. I had been to a derby between the two on the last day of the 2007–8 Jordanian season. It was played at an isolated stadium in Zarqa, not far from where the Zaatari camp would later be founded. Al Wihdat had won the league the week before, meaning that no Faisaly fans had turned up. That didn't matter much. Wihdat's fans, who had been peaceful throughout, were set upon and beaten by the Jordanian police. Every Wihdat fan I spoke to believed they had been attacked because they were Palestinian. 'In the heat of the game, where large crowds gather, repressed feelings may be vented in the public sphere,' Professor

Suleiman said. 'The authorities know this, but as long as the vents are not overloaded, they tend to tolerate the political in football.'

But, in 2009, one such vent let a little too much pressure out, sparking an incident that made it to a diplomatic level. A cable released by the WikiLeaks website, titled 'Jordanian Soccer Game Halted Amidst Anti-Regime Chants, Hooliganism Toward Palestinians', detailed how a league match between Wihdat and Faisaly was abandoned:

```
S E C R E T SECTION 01 OF 02 AMMAN 001689

SIPDIS

E.O. 12958: DECL: 07/23/2019
TAGS: PGOV KDEM SOCI JO

SUBJECT: JORDANIAN SOCCER GAME HALTED AMIDST
ANTI-REGIME CHANTS, HOOLIGANISM TOWARD PALESTINIANS

Classified By: Charge d'Affaires Lawrence Mandel for
reasons 1.4 (b) and (d).

Faisali 0, Wahdat 0, PPD (Riot)
--------------------------------

2. (C) Jordanian police intervened to stop fan
violence and the chanting of anti-regime slogans
during a July 17 match between Amman soccer clubs
Faisali and Wahdat in the industrial town of Zarqa.
The unrest began when Faisali fans started to chant
slogans against Palestinian-origin Jordanians,
including Queen Rania. Some Faisali fans threw bottles
at Wahdat players and their fans. The coaches of both
teams ordered their players off of the field in the
middle of the game for their own safety, and the
remainder of the match was cancelled. (Note: It ended
in a scoreless draw. End Note.)
```

The cable went on to say 'There is broad recognition throughout Jordan that the Faisali–Wahdat incident exposed the uncomfortable gap between East Bankers and Palestinians, one that most would rather keep well hidden for the sake of political stability.'

That tension had proved problematic for the national team. With few players playing abroad, the Jordanian team's best players came from both Wihdat and Faisaly. The country had enjoyed virtually zero success until this World Cup campaign. An hour's drive south from Zaatari, in the capital Amman, Jordan will soon play two-time World Cup winners Uruguay in the first of a two-match intercontinental play-off with the winner clinching a place in Brazil. Al Nashama, 'The Brave Ones' in Arabic, began their campaign to reach Brazil in the summer of 2011. At the Amman International Stadium, where the first Uruguay game would be played, they beat Nepal 9-0. The team was led by legendary former Iraq coach Adnan Hamad. Hamad was a former Iraqi international who had taken a path towards coaching when injuries ended his career early. When the Second Gulf War broke out, and German coach Bernd Stange quit, Hamad took over. His greatest achievement was coaching the Iraqi Olympic team at the 2004 Athens games. He had taken his young squad there just as Iraq was disintegrating into a vicious war. Yet the team went out and shocked the world. In their first game they beat Portugal 4-2, a team that contained the likes of Cristiano Ronaldo, Hugo Viana, Hugo Almeida, Bruno Alves and José Bosingwa. The Lions of Mesopotamia topped their group and beat Australia in the quarter-finals before losing to Paraguay in the semis. They lost their bronze medal match 1-0 against an Italian side captained by Andrea Pirlo. Iraq went home empty-handed, but Hamad's multi-confessional and multi-ethnic team, containing Shia, Sunni and Kurds, would go on to win the 2007 Asian Cup. Of that championship-winning side goalkeeper Noor Sabri, striker Hawar Mulla Mohammed, midfielder Nashat Akram and captain Younis Mahmoud all cut their teeth in Athens. It was Mahmoud's goal against Saudi Arabia in the 2007 final that clinched the title for Iraq.

Jordan won its first four games in the group stage of qualification for Brazil 2014, defeating Iraq in Iraq, China and Singapore. In the second group stage they defeated both Australia and the current Asian champions Japan, finished third, beat Uzbekistan on penalties and were now preparing for Uruguay. Except that Adnan Hamad is not here. After the final group game against Oman he quit and was replaced by former Egyptian international Hossam Hassan. Hassan played in Italia '90, Egypt's last appearance at the finals. The former striker had gone into coaching after retirement. His last job was as coach of Al Masry.

Jordan's opponents were lucky to be here. Uruguay had struggled in South American qualification. The single group stage format of qualification in CONMEBOL is not forgiving for the underdog. Or perhaps it is. Every country in CONMEBOL had qualified for the World Cup finals. Except one. Venezuela had been on course to clinch at least a play-off spot after their finest ever qualification campaign. Six South American teams could qualify: Brazil as hosts, the top four in the group and a play-off spot against weaker Asian opponents for finishing fifth. Until the last five games it looked as if Venezuela would push out Uruguay. The 1930 and 1950 World Cup winners had been in miserable form. Despite having finished in the semi-finals at South Africa 2010, then winning the Copa America, Uruguay lost heavily to Bolivia and Colombia. A team that contained Luis Suárez and Edinson Cavani and coached by Óscar Tabarez looked as if it would watch the finals from the other side of the border. It was only a run of four victories in their last five games that secured their play-off spot. An Argentina featuring Lionel Messi and Sergio Agüero qualified as group winners, to be joined by Colombia, Chile and Ecuador. Ominously for Jordan, Uruguay beat Argentina 3-2 in their final group game.

Bassam, even after the tensions between the Jordanians and Syrians inside and outside the Zaatari camp, is still rooting for Jordan. 'Unfortunately we can't go to the stadium as it's full,' he says. He is right. The day before tickets were being sold outside for fifty dinars, more than a week's salary. 'We might not be able to watch it as it is on Al Jazeera TV and we can't afford the Al Jazeera cards. But we will support the Jordanians and hope that Al Nashama will do their best.'

We leave the Zaatari refugee camp, past the pet shops and cafés and arcades full of young kids playing computer games. With every passing day an average of 400 people will join their numbers. The UN has to plan as if they are in charge of a permanent city. Which, in a way, Zaatari is. Metered electricity is on the way. A police force is being assembled and trained by the British. Consultative councils headed by community leaders have been set up to prevent the protests and riots that have broken out periodically over food and conditions. The prospect of elections and a seat in the local Jordanian municipality has been mooted. The Jordanians after all feel aggrieved that the Syrians are creating business and using resources without paying tax or rates. One shawarma stall, according to a UN representative I talk to, was bringing in $13,000 a month. Every day the roots of Zaatari grow a little bit deeper. One day a Zaatari football team will be formed. A stadium will follow. The caravans will be upgraded to single-floor concrete huts, then two-floor buildings. Just as with the Palestinians and the Wihdat refugee camp in Amman, what started out as a stop-gap will become permanent. As we leave, a ragged group of refugees arrive, placing their belongings into the wheelbarrows of the young Syrian boys at the entrance. For the first time I notice that the entrance is guarded by armed Jordanian troops. It's not clear who they are keeping out and who they are keeping in.

**

Amman, Jordan

Jordan's past, present and future look down on the pitch at the Amman International Stadium as Al Nashama train for the game of their lives. Three huge colour portraits dominate one stand. On the left King Hussein, the revered former king who negotiated the country through wars and internal Palestinian insurrection and who had made peace with Israel in 1994. In the middle is King Abdullah II, Hussein's eldest son who replaced him when he died in 1999. In it he is wearing a Jordanian football shirt with the number 99 on the front, celebrating a goal. To the right is a picture of Hussein bin Abdullah, the king's teenage son and crown prince. In the dugout another member of the royal family is watching, too. Prince Ali has arrived with his security escort. A crowd of Jordanian fans desperate for tickets meet him outside, chanting his name. The stadium already feels like match day. A few thousand Jordanians have turned up, not to see training – which is closed – but to try and get tickets. Smoke hangs in the air from the street vendors cooking maize for passing trade. The taxi driver who dropped me off had asked one of the touts the price of a ticket. He sped off angrily without giving a reply when he was told it would cost fifty dinars, close to £50. 'This is the biggest match we have had in our history. That is a reality,' the prince says as we watch Hossam Hassan put his players through their paces. 'We are on the verge of qualifying for the World Cup. There's been a lot of hard work from players and officials and coaches to get here. Remember, Jordan is a country that has very limited resources but at the same time with the spirit and hard work we managed to get here.'

Many of these players had played at the 2007 Under 20 World Cup, where they faced Uruguay. Jordan lost but it gave the Jordan Football Association enough confidence to invest in training centres for both boys and girls. Now both senior teams, for men and women, had a chance of making it to their next respective World Cups. The men's team had as tough a match as it was possible to get. But at least it had overcome its traditional divisions. I ask Prince Ali about Faisaly and Wihdat and the rivalry between Jordan's East Bankers and West Bankers. 'I think there are rivals on the pitch and I think, to be honest, that rivalry has helped us because there's so much emotion behind it,' he says, a little uncomfortably. 'The emotion that has got us to that level. Our players on national team duty are all united, they are all one. I'd like to emphasise our players all come from very different backgrounds across the country. The reason they are playing is they love the sport. I don't think there's anything political, our clubs right now all realise and support each other. We are one family and that's a reality so I am not concerned at all.'

Hossam Hassan, too, believes the divisions are something of the past, even if that seems hard to accept. 'You have a bad idea about Faisaly and Wihdat, there is no problem here,' he says pitchside. 'It's like in Spain with Barcelona and Real Madrid, there's a rivalry, but now we are all in the national team. We are all Arabs together under Allah.' Hassan had appeared to solve the vexed issue of political division by choosing fewer players from both teams. Jordan's recent success had seen a few players leave for the much higher level Saudi league. Half a dozen players had been chosen from the two teams, although many more had started their careers at either club. But with his meagre choice when compared to Uruguay's riches Hassan had big problems even before the game. Their goalkeeper Amer Shafi, who had been in goal during that incredible penalty shoot-out in Tashkent against Uzbekistan, was suspended. Midfielder Amer Deeb, who had made his name at Wihdat and was arguably Jordan's best player, had been omitted from the squad. But Ahmed Hayel, the striker who had scored the decisive goal in Jordan's qualification victory against Japan, was fit. 'It is big especially for Jordanian and Arab football, we are very ambitious and we know that Uruguay is a real team and very difficult to overcome,' Hassan explains. Training has finished and night has set in. 'But we will make the Jordanian dreams come true and take our chance and give our all by fighting on the pitch. We are going to win the match tomorrow in front of the Jordanian crowd. The crowd has been a huge part of Jordan's success.' Prince Ali, under the shadow of his father, brother and nephew, leans on one knee as the team – and his security – gather round. He offers softly spoken words of encouragement before the players leave, to be replaced by Luis Suárez and the rest of the Uruguay team. Suárez is the player every Jordanian wants to talk about. The gate at the end of the stadium is opened and more than a hundred people crash through, tripping, falling over each other, jumping hoardings to get closer. And that is just the photographers.

Outside the front of the stadium, a hundred or so Jordanian fans have remained to sing songs in honour of the royal family. As they sing Prince Ali walks over to them and talks to their leader, a young man with a beard and a voice hoarse from shouting who has been standing atop a metal barrier. He bursts into tears. 'Praise God! I spoke to Prince Ali!' croaks Khaled Ziqawe, a twenty-nine-year-old bank clerk. 'Suárez and Cavani are nothing! There is no Suárez, no Cavani, only Ahmed Hayel!' I ask them all who they support: Faisaly, Wihdat or someone else? No one replies at first. 'Tomorrow, there will be no Faisaly, no Wihdat,' Khaled finally says. 'The Arab world will be behind us and, tomorrow, Al Nashama will be one team, all the people from Jordan will come together. Even Wihdat and Faisaly.'

**

It is just three hours until kick-off and the roads that lead towards the Amman International Stadium are awash with noise. Security has swamped the area. It is rumoured that King Abdullah II, his wife and the crown prince will be coming to the game. Police riot vans and motorcycles move up and down the highway that passes the stadium, their sirens screaming at a painful volume. Lines of riot police in full body armour ring the stadium, stopping anyone from walking even an inch down the route they are guarding. Street vendors hand out posters of the Jordanian team and plastic versions of the traditional red and white headscarf, just in case it rains. A line of men sell a stack of Jordanian flags to a group of women in full black *abayas* and *niqabs*. Female police officers hang around by a wall nearby, wearing their trouser uniforms with the specially designed head covering under their caps. Groups of young men, *shebab*, run around, excitedly predicting a huge Jordanian victory. As ever in the lead-up to an important match in Jordan, it is chaos, like a thousand cats running in a thousand different directions. For the Uruguayans who had made it to the game, it was likely to be the furthest, most expensive and most alien away trip they would ever experience. 'We just arrived, I don't know how far it is,' says Luis Castillo, a sixty-five year old doctor, who has flown from Uruguay. 'We flew Montevideo–Rio, Rio–Dubai, Dubai–Amman. It's a long journey. We don't know anything about the Jordanian team but people have been friendly. Unusually friendly.' He says the last words suspiciously, given that caustic reception away fans get in Brazil or Argentina. 'They want to take pictures with us,' he says. 'That is very unusual. We'll be cautious: 1-0 and win it in Montevideo.'

They will be the only Uruguayans from Uruguay that I meet. Busloads of fans dressed in blue and white line up to get inside, speaking in an accent that sounds familiar. 'This is my grandfather Miguel and he is the King,' says Eran, a Uruguayan supporter with a thick, rolling, unmistakably Israeli accent. Although Jordan and Israel have a peace treaty, few Israelis risk travelling to Jordan, especially given the deteriorating security situation in most of the region. Almost everyone in the line is from Israel. Eran had been born in Israel but his grandfather Miguel had made *aliyah*, the Jewish return to the land of Israel, from Uruguay in the 1950s. Miguel was in his eighties now, clutching an old flag in his hands. He has not seen Uruguay play since he travelled to Rio to watch the 1950 World Cup match between Brazil and Uruguay at the Maracanã. He had witnessed the *Maracanazo* first-hand and had bought a flag on the morning of the game, the same flag he had in his hands today. 'I bought this when I was at the Maracanã,' he says in Hebrew, Eran translating for him. 'It was wonderful.'

'We have come from Israel to see La Celeste,' Eran admits finally. His brother is here, too. It is the first time either had ventured into Jordan. 'We have never been here before because it's dangerous for us,' he laughs. 'We are going under cover.' The hundreds of Uruguayan fans push past, through the single concrete door, the police unaware of the crowd's true identity. 'We came with all the family who are from Uruguay,' explains Romi, a female fan who has also travelled from Israel. 'Uruguay is too far. It has been OK. We've been fine so far.' What do you think the score will be? 'I think it'll be 5-0 to Uruguay.' Won't it perhaps be best to hope for a draw? So the atmosphere isn't too tense. Romi laughs in my face. 'It won't happen! I'm sorry. Go Celeste!'

**

Romi is, of course, correct. The stadium is full two and a half hours before kick-off as Jordan's fans throng to see an upset. The rules of the underdog have been turned on their head for the evening. Uruguay may have all the stars and two World Cup wins behind them, but they are by far the smallest country ever to win it and still one of the smallest countries ever to participate in the finals. In population terms, Jordan is twice as big as Uruguay although both are giants next to Iceland. Still, it is Jordan that come out strongest. For the first five minutes they burst down the right wing time and time again. Jordan's right-back Oday al Saify almost manages to squeeze the ball past Uruguay's goalkeeper Martin Silva. Al Nashama are, at the very least, ahead on corners. But, soon enough, Uruguay slowly but effectively constrict Jordan, and go ahead. After several terrible misses, one by the strangely quiet Suárez, Maxi Pereira slides in almost on the line to put Uruguay into the lead. When half-time comes it is 2-0.

At half-time the game's special guest, King Abdullah II, arrives wearing a red Jordan T-shirt with the number 99 on the front under a black blazer. The quiet crowd is reignited and the players respond. For the first ten minutes of the second half Jordan are a different team, pouring forward knowing that a goal might change the course of the game. The ball is crossed in from the right and

Ahmad Hayel, the hero against Japan and the player whom Jordan's fans believe will outshine Uruguay's world-class strikers, splits La Celeste's centre-backs. He is free with an open goal but somehow he fires wide. He lies on the turf with his head in his hands. His team-mates lie on the turf with their heads in their hands. King Abdullah jumps into the air thinking Jordan have scored and then slumps back into his seat. He is holding his head in his hands, too. A few minutes later Uruguay go 3-0 up, then 4-0. By the time Edinson Cavani scores, an immaculate, curling free-kick into the top right-hand corner to make it 5-0, the Jordanian supporters can do nothing but applaud. Jordan's World Cup hopes are all but over. After the final whistle a few supporters blame the defeat on Hossam Hassan and his young and experimental line-up, one he says he was forced to make, but there is no anger directed at the players or anyone else. Uruguay's fans quickly leave the Amman International Stadium, slipping over the West Bank border that night, taking their secret home to Israel with them.

16

THE LAST THIRTY-TWO

Zagreb, Croatia. November 2013.

Iceland and Croatia are standing in line for the national anthems in the middle of a misty, freezing and miserable Maksimir Stadium. A sleety rain that has been falling most of the day has only just abated and the stadium is almost full. There is none of the euphoria that had greeted Croatia when I was last in Zagreb eight months previously. On the way to the stadium a few hundred Croatian fans filled beer tents that had been set up along the street, huddling together for warmth as a DJ played national-istic rock songs that the crowd bellowed back. In March, when Serbia came to town, things were different. It was early spring and the sun shone in Zagreb's main square as it filled with tens of thousands of Croatia supporters drinking and singing. The roads up to the stadium had been closed by the police and turned into one big open-air bar full of supporters of all ages carrying flags with the names of their home towns written on them.

Croatia had beaten their old enemy that day. The teams' two coaches, Igor Štimac and Siniša Mihajlović, had buried the hatchet that day, too, and embraced on the pitch after the game, even as the crowd chanted 'Kill the Serbs'. Both men met once more, this time in Belgrade. As expected, the atmosphere was equally as electric and loaded with history. It finished 1-1 but two players were sent off. When Croatia's Josip Šimunić was shown a red card for a vicious professional foul, he nearly caused a riot. As he walked to the tunnel he was pelted with chairs and missiles.

Flares were thrown, too. 'We didn't pay too much attention to what was going on in the terraces because that happens a lot in Croatia, too, and I can only hope that fans in this part of the world start behaving themselves soon,' was all Štimac had to say about the sending-off after the game. Eight months earlier he had promised a lifetime ban for any Croatian player making any inflammatory tackles against Serbia. But the result had secured Croatia second place in a group Belgium easily won, and with it a play-off spot. It was an added bonus that they had eliminated Serbia in the process. But this wasn't enough for the Croatian press, who had grown increasingly unhappy with Štimac's reign, especially his tactical tinkering. When Croatia lost to Scotland Štimac's days were numbered and he was replaced with young and inexperienced former international midfielder Niko Kovač for the play-offs. Mihajlović, too, had been moved on after his unsuccessful campaign.

There was no euphoria, yet Croatia were now just ninety minutes away from Brazil. They had been drawn against Iceland in the European play-off, the lowest ranked team left and the team everyone wanted to draw, but the first leg in Reykjavik had not gone well. The snow and the wind that Iceland's Swedish coach Lars Lagerbäck suggested might arrive had not materialised but his team had managed to grind out a 0-0 draw, even after playing most of the second half with only ten men. Now they, too, were only one game away from qualifying and becoming the smallest nation to appear at a World Cup. If Iceland succeeded they would prove to be one of the greatest underdogs of all time.

World Cup qualification was coming to an end across the globe. In every continent the final group positions had been calculated. All that was left was the play-offs in Europe, Africa and the two intercontinental matches between Uruguay and Jordan and Mexico and New Zealand. Mexico had just managed to scrape fourth place in their group but they needed the help of the Americans to do it. The US beat Panama 3-1, meaning Mexico qualified for their play-off even after they lost their final game.

And when it mattered, *El Tri* turned it on, smashing New Zealand 5-1 in the first match in the Azteca and virtually securing their place in Brazil, too.

It is largely left to Iceland to upset the odds, and the home match has given them confidence. 'It's going to be a busy game,' Iceland's film-making goalkeeper Hannes Halldórsson admitted the day before. 'We always have ambition to go further than the size of the population allows us to do. They are one of the best teams in the world so it's a David and Goliath scenario. But now the pressure is on Croatia.' Iceland are missing their top scorer after Kolbeinn Sigþórsson was seriously injured in the first game but there is an experienced replacement in Eidur Gudjohnsen. Everyone in the team believes that their time has come, even the cautious Lagerbäck. 'I think we have a good chance,' he says, explaining that Iceland's success offers a blueprint for other small nations on how to take on the bigger teams. 'Even if you are a third division team, if you put in a good performance maybe you can beat a first division side.'

The teams sing their national anthems and take their positions at opposite ends of the pitch. A banner is unfolded across one stand thanking, in English, the Icelandic nation for being the first country in the world to officially recognise an independent Croatia state. For once, no one is threatening to kill anyone.

**

On the top floor of a nearby hotel a few hours before kick-off, the Icelandic federation is hosting a crash course in Croatian football. The room is crammed with Iceland fans wearing horned helmets and blue national team jerseys. Former Iceland international turned sports journalist Guðmundur Benediktsson is standing at the front with a flipchart open, furiously drawing lines and numbers to show where the Croatian players are likely to run. The supporters politely raise their hands to ask questions about tactics and formations:

What will be the Croatia team?

They haven't told us yet.

Will it rain?

We don't know.

Who is Luka Modrić?

Er ...

Benediktsson is momentarily thrown by the question. It isn't a normal football crowd. The match has become a thing of national pride regardless of whether or not you like or know anything about the game. 'I was first of all announcing the starting line of the Iceland team and maybe the probable line of the Croatia team,' Benediktsson explains after his one-man show holding the crowd. 'But mostly I was telling them about a meeting with the national coach explaining what the Croatian team does a lot so I was just explaining to them what to expect today.' It would be unthinkable for a national team coach to hand out the team's starting line-up and formation days before the match to keep the fans informed. Unthinkable anywhere but Iceland. The team still retains its rapport with its supporters, even as they come close to making history. 'I played my games between 1994 and 2001 but it was nothing like this, nothing like this,' he says of the atmosphere that has surrounded not just the team but the country since the team's incredible run. Benediktsson had played for Iceland in the 1990s, a different age, when virtually all the players were amateur and Iceland was one of the very worst teams in Europe. He was a student back then when he played for the national team but defeat hadn't dimmed the experience. 'I didn't have a low point with my time,' he says. 'We didn't win many games. But at that time it didn't matter. It was just the honour of representing the national team.'

Iceland's Cinderella run isn't quite the same as the United Arab Emirates making it to Italia '90, or the Zaire team in 1974. They weren't unknown amateurs who had taken holidays from their jobs as policemen or civil servants to shine briefly and brightly before fading into obscurity. They hadn't overcome a war or a revolution. Iceland was a triumph of playing the professional game better than anyone else. Money had helped to build the facilities that any country would envy. Yet their run still mattered, and it still proved that, given the right conditions, anybody still has a chance of qualifying for a World Cup finals. Without that hope, the international game would wither and die.

More than 1,500 Iceland fans had made it to Zagreb, over 0.5 per cent of the population this time around. Here, too, was Arni, the huge bearded man in a Superman onesie who had cried on my shoulder after the Norway game. They all believed, and the rest of the world hoped, that Iceland could give the World Cup some of the magic only the underdog can bring. The Croatian team were the exception. 'I am aware they have high expectations, full of enthusiasm, but to be honest, I have no idea where their optimism comes from,' striker Ivica Olić said before the game. 'We are a better team, we will score more than once and we will win and go to Brazil.' Benediktsson was not impressed. 'I don't think this Croatia team is as good as the team of Prosinečki and Šuker. I don't think they are a better team than us,' he says as the army of blue shirts with horned helmets head to the Maksimir for Iceland's last shot at Brazil. 'We have been saying, the whole nation has been saying: "When will it stop, when will it stop, it must stop now." But it hasn't. It's still going on. Why not? Why not?'

**

The match begins as everyone expects it to. Croatia attack from the start, punishing Iceland's every loose pass. For the first half an hour they grimly hold on. At one point they even have the ball in Croatia's net but it is ruled offside. Just as it seems that Iceland might hold on until half-time, Bayern Munich striker Mario Mandžukić arrives at the far post and rattles a deflected pass into the net. The goal shouldn't make much difference for Iceland. They are away from home and away goals count double. If they score they will still qualify. But they are a shadow of the team that came back against Switzerland when 4-1 down, or even the team that held Croatia 0-0 a few days ago. Maybe it is the tiredness of playing with ten men for forty-five minutes in Reykjavik, or the absence of Kolbeinn Sigþórsson. Guðjohnsen has barely touched the ball. Maybe the occasion and the pressure have simply become too much.

Even though they have played badly, they are handed a route back into the game when Mandžukić crazily stamps down on Jóhann Guðmundsson's thigh near the halfway line and is shown a straight red. Yet, even against ten men, Iceland can't string a pass together. Just a few minutes into the second half Croatia kill Iceland's dream. Their captain Darijo Srna collects a pass on the right and fires the ball into the bottom left-hand corner. Croatia, it turns out, play better with ten men. Goalkeeper Hannes Halldórsson was right when he predicted he would have a busy night, and makes a string of fine saves to prevent a whitewash. As the minutes tick down, and the Croatia fans sing louder as the ninety minute mark approaches, the life drains from the Iceland team. The full-time whistle is a relief.

The Croatian players run on to the pitch as the Iceland team lie on the deck. After all the controversies and ghosts of the Yugoslav civil war Croatia have at last fulfilled their promise. But there is to be one more moment of madness. Josip Šimunić grabs the stadium announcer's cordless microphone, turns it on and runs across the pitch towards the still celebrating crowd. 'For the homeland!' he shouts. 'Ready!' the fans shout back. The chant is that of the fascist pro-Nazi Ustaše regime that brutally ran Croatia during the Second World War. Šimunić claims it is was simply an innocent expression of love for his country. FIFA slap him with a ten-match ban for stoking religious or ethnic hatred. Šimunić's World Cup is over, even if he doesn't know it yet.

The Iceland team are devastated. That night, live on Icelandic national television, Eiður Guðjohnsen will break down in tears as he announces his international retirement. 'Nobody said anything in the dressing room, we all definitely thought we were going through,' Halldórsson says outside the stadium after the game. The Iceland bus is waiting with its engine on as the rain begins to fall again. The players can't bring themselves to board it. 'This was the worst game we played in the competition,' he says, staring at the floor. 'I don't have an explanation. Now all I see is disappointment. Maybe some hope will come later. But this was a once in a lifetime experience for most of these players.' He will go back to Iceland, he says, and work on his horror film.

The last doubt over who will be present in Brazil is resolved that night. Portugal overcome Sweden in their play-off while Romania could not match the power and certainty of the Greeks. France managed to turn a 2-0 deficit against Ukraine into a 3-0 victory in the second match. Even in Africa the favourites all won. Burkina Faso and Ethiopia both lost out. The very same African teams that qualified for the 2010 World Cup would be heading for Brazil. Bosnia will be the only debutante in 2014. Goliath had won. David was vanquished

'The future is still great for Icelandic football,' Lars Lagerbäck says optimistically as he finally leaves the stadium. A man pushes past us with a trolley laden with crates of beer for the celebrating Croatia team. 'I have to look at myself in the mirror and see if I am too old to continue or stay as a coach but it has been a fantastic journey for me.' He would later sign on for two more years with Iceland, until the 2016 European Championships. He is one of the few coaches I had met in three years who has not been sacked. Lagerbäck finally gathers his distraught players. He ushers them towards the waiting coach as celebratory songs rise from the open window of the Croatia dressing room, over the Iceland team and out into the night.

POSTSCRIPT

Most Serene Republic of San Marino. December 2013.

The headquarters of the San Marino Football Association can be found on the edge of Mount Titan. A brand new, angular building stands guard over an artificial football pitch where a group of teenagers are playing a game. Inside, the shelves of its corridors are adorned with pennants, medals and trophies although very few of them are for winning anything. San Marino is a micro-state near the Italian city of Rimini. It has a population of just over 30,000 and claims to be the world's oldest constitutional republic. As you enter San Marino, before the road climbs steeply around the mountain that dominates this tiny territory, you are greeted by an arch bearing the words: 'Welcome to the Land of Liberty'.

Giampaolo Mazza is almost smartly dressed in blazer, shirt, tie and faded blue jeans when we meet inside. For sixteen years he has been the coach of the San Marino national team. During that time he has never won an official game, although they did once beat Lichtenstein in a friendly. In most games they would be lucky to score a goal. 'When we play the matches,' he says as we sit down in the boardroom, 'we already know it is impossible for us to win or to get a positive result.' Mazza has just finished taking charge of San Marino's 2014 World Cup qualification campaign. It hadn't gone well. They had been drawn in England's group along with Ukraine and Poland. That they lost all of their games wasn't a surprise. They are ranked 207th, and last, by FIFA, and have been for years. What was surprising was their goal difference, which finished at minus fifty-three. They had conceded fifty-four times and scored just once, against Poland in a 5-1 defeat. They had also lost 8-0 to both England and Ukraine. Although it has been worse. 'My lowest moment was the match against Germany in 2006 when we lost 13-0,' he recalls. Lukas Podolski scored four that night just down the road from Mazza's office at the Stadio Olimpico di Serravalle. 'We had many critics and many people questioning our presence in the group.'

San Marino's players are amateurs with full-time jobs to go back to after their inevitable defeats. The toughest part of the job over the past sixteen years, Mazza believes, has been dealing with the mental toll on the players during and after the qualification campaign. 'The most important job in San Marino is the psychological state of the players,' he says. 'Our players know we will have negative results so it is important to reconstruct the spirit the day after the game so they can go back to their jobs.' Mazza's entire working life as a football coach has involved preparing for defeat in the least damaging way. 'For us the positive remains with the satisfaction of playing famous teams from all around the world,' he says. 'Usually its teams we only see on TV and they're pretty famous. We don't feel defeated every time we play with the team; we try and get good results even though we know it's impossible.' Which begs the question: why do it? And why do it on the biggest stage of all? Mazza doesn't even miss a beat. 'At the last Olympics in London Usain Bolt was in the final and won the gold medal,' he replies. 'Before then he had to pass through qualification. Following the same reasoning San Marino should participate in these competitions. The powerful competitors meet the weaker ones. This is a question of sport.'

**

At the Estadio Centenario in Montevideo, Jonas Eriksson blows his whistle to bring the final match of 2014 World Cup qualification to an end. It finishes Uruguay 0 Jordan 0. The result means that Uruguay have made it to Brazil, even if all the hard work had taken place in Amman a few days before. Between the first match of qualification – in which Jay'Lee Hodgson scored twice for Montserrat in a 5-2 loss to Belize – and the last, 820 matches had been played, 2,350 goals scored and 100 red cards issued. I had travelled to every continent to watch the qualifiers, following match fixing in Lebanon, riots in Brazil and ultra-nationalism in the Balkans. In Rwanda I had learned how the national team of Eritrea had become a vehicle to escape an appalling dictatorship. The players I had met in Kigali had chosen to return to Eritrea. But a year later most of them had fled – and were granted political asylum – after playing in a tournament in Uganda. More players defected after a tournament in Kenya in December 2013.

In Samoa I had seen how one match, Australia's world record 31-0 defeat of American Samoa, had affected the lives of everyone involved for a decade. I'd also seen two pieces of history: the first was American Samoa's maiden victory in any competition. The second was watching the world's first transgender player start a World Cup match. After the 2-1 victory over Tonga, Jaiyah Saelua had played in the 1-1 draw with the Cook Islands as well as the final 1-0 loss to Samoa. 'I don't want to say regrets, but I wish I had played it differently against the Cook Islands,' Jaiyah says when we speak on Skype. 'I feel like it haunts me sometimes. We could have made it if only we didn't score that own goal. I think about it all the time. Every time I see a park. Every time I see people in uniform [football kit] or see a ball. It doesn't even have to be a soccer ball.'

Jaiyah returned to Hawaii but discovered that she had been kicked out of college. They claimed she hadn't told them she was leaving. Instead she took a job as a security guard. The money was good, and college got further and further away. There was some good news, though. Jaiyah had made an important decision. 'I have decided to start my transition,' she says excitedly. 'I'll be taking hormones and testosterone blockers, using laser hair removal. I've already made enough to start my breast augmentation.' All she needs now is a start date. But there is one last thing she wants to do, something that would be impossible to do afterwards. 'I want to play in the World Cup qualifiers for 2018,' she says. 'It would mean everything. I've been preparing for it mentally. Learning from 2011 I'll play harder and play smarter. But I'll play.' That qualification campaign is likely to begin in 2014 or 2015. 'My only worry is that my hormone treatment might get in the way,' she says. 'And I don't want to jeopardise my team-mates because of my transition.' If American Samoa fail to reach the 2018 World Cup finals, Russia will be a poorer place without Jaiyah Saelua.

Unlike Jaiyah Saelua, the Kosovo national team was unlikely to be allowed to even dream of the road to Russia. When I'd last spoken to Fadil Vokrri and Eroll Salihu, two former players who now ran the Football Federation of Kosovo, they had proudly shown me a petition they had gathered. The petition was filled with the signatures of players who had their roots in Kosovo but who now represented Switzerland and Albania instead. Without full UN and FIFA recognition, Kosovo had haemorrhaged its substantial talent to other countries that *were* members. The petition wanted to show support for Kosovo's footballing recognition, but it appeared to have had little effect. After Sepp Blatter promised an agreement on whether Kosovo could play other FIFA-recognised countries, the move appeared to have been quietly dropped.

But in January 2014, FIFA finally agreed to allow Kosovo to play with some restrictions. A first match was organised against Haiti in March. Edson Tavares, the Brazilian coach I had met in Port au Prince, was, of course, long gone. No Kosovo flags would allowed to be flown, nor national anthem sung in the northern city of Mitrovica. Rather than play the game in the capital Prishtina, as most had assumed would happen, the Kosovars had symbolically chosen a city that was divided between ethnic Albanians and Kosovo's Serbian minority.

All eyes, though, were on who would play for the Kosovo team. Would any of the Swiss players appear? The Swiss had easily qualified for Brazil, and were considered top seeds no less, largely thanks to the team's Kosovar players. But their presence, even in a successful team, was still controversial. At least to some. In February the Swiss had voted in a referendum to restrict the amount of immigration into the country. German newspaper *Die Welt* highlighted the absurdity of the anti-immigration mood by tweeting a picture of the national team with the immigrants blanked out. Only three Swiss players remained.

When I met the Swiss team before their World Cup match against Albania, and watched as the Kosovar players signed Eroll and Fadil's petition, Bayern Munich's Xherdan Shaqiri was the focus of the media's attention. Now, attention had shifted somewhat to 19-year-old Manchester United prodigy Adnan Januzaj. Januzaj was Belgian born, with Kosovar parents, and an unseemly tug of love had broken out between Belgium, Serbia, Turkey and England as to which national team he should represent. At the waterlogged Adem Jashari stadium, in front of an ecstatic 17,000 strong crowd, Eroll watched as Haiti held Kosovo – minus Januzaj and Shaqiri – to a 0-0 draw. But it was a start.

In Egypt Bob Bradley had stayed in the country as coach of the national team as it fell apart around him. But there would be no fairytale ending, at least not a conventional one. The 6-1 thrashing by Ghana in their first World Cup play-off was too much to overcome. 'It just seemed like a day everything came together in the worst possible way,' says Bradley when we speak. 'Emotions, nerves, a bad start, that is what it was like. Ironically the last words from me before going out were: "You don't win a game in the first minute, but you can put yourself in a bad position." After the game the knives were out. There was talk that he would be fired. The Egyptian FA suggested that it might be too dangerous for him to go back but that turned out to be a lie. The return match in Cairo was to be Bradley's first in front of a full stadium of home supporters. The Ghana Football Association had desperately tried to move the game but to no avail. Still, before the game Bradley felt the need to clear the air. 'I took responsibility for that game,' he says. 'Before the second game I did a TV show, the most popular show in Egypt. It runs from 11.30 p.m. until 1.30 a.m.

but went all the way to 2 a.m. I wanted to make sure the players got the respect they deserved from the Egyptians.'

Having now spoken directly to the nation, Bradley was sure the crowd would get behind the team in Cairo for the return game. He still believed that a comeback was possible. 'For two years we represented Egypt and Egyptian football at the highest level,' he says, recounting the team talk he gave. 'We still have one chance in Cairo, finishing it in a right way whether that's a miracle or not. Maybe we can pull it off.' With better luck, Egypt would have had a chance. In the second game they went in at half-time 1-0 up. Bradley thought they should have been 3-0 up. The game ended 2-1 to Egypt. Bradley had finally beaten Ghana, the team that knocked his US side out of the last World Cup. It seemed desperately unfair. The Pharaohs had won seven out of eight qual-ification matches and were drawn to play Ghana, Africa's best side. In contrast, Mexico had won just two out of ten games and played New Zealand in a play-off.

Bradley is now in Norway, where he was hired as coach of top division side Stabæk. When the season kicks off he'll be the first American to coach in the top division of a European league. 'You couldn't find two more different ends of a spectrum: you can breathe the air, there is structure to everything and everyone's blond.' Egypt will never leave him, nor will his abiding memory of his time there: his relationship with midfielder Mohamed Aboutrika. 'As a man there's none better than Trika. Meeting him was as great an experience as you can have.' He has a few months until the start of the season to prepare his new team and get used to his surroundings. He has also been approached by someone wanting to make a film of his life. We toss around some ideas about who should play him in the story of his life. Bryan Cranston is mentioned. 'I'm not sure about that,' he laughs as we discuss how Cranston might approach the role. 'My fifteen minutes were up half an hour ago.'

**

World Cup qualification had offered me a snapshot of the world, but the campaign had meant many things to many people. Unity, reflected power, revenge, redemption, even escape. The campaign had shown how, in the age of football's rampant commercialisation, something as old-fashioned as international football, patriotism even, was still alive. It had also shown the world is changing quicker than we realise. The mass migration of people because of wars, famine, revolutions or, simply, the desire to find a better quality of life had further blurred the boundaries of identity and belonging. In many places the national football team was the last institution left that still preserved it, even if 'it' was fluid, a reality that had long ceased to be. The idea of a national team representing a nation had become more stretched and more diffuse than ever. But it still mattered, which is why people go to extraordinary lengths to play, and support, international football, with the World Cup at its apex.

San Marino was arguably the one place where that blurring of boundaries hadn't happened, and the result was accepting perpetual defeat. 'We cannot take a player from a different state and give him citizenship because the law will not support it,' says Giorgio Crescentini, the president of the San Marino FA. He is a big man who speaks slowly from behind a large desk where he keeps a small replica of the World Cup. 'We have to build our players from the age of six until they reach the national team. In a country with only 30,000 inhabitants what we do *already* is a miracle.' It takes ten years to get a passport from San Marino. As recently as 1982 a referendum was held over whether women should lose their citizenship (and with it their right to live in the country) if they marry a foreigner, as had been the case since the 1920s. Fifty-seven per cent of the population voted to keep the law.

'On the one side I am proud of this special characteristic: we are pure and perhaps the only ones. This gives us pride,' he says. Although even Crescentini concedes that some new blood would be useful. Several Serie A players have married women from San Marino. But the applications for the players' passports were rejected.

'Of course, if that was possible, we would do it.' As every team from Palestine to Haiti realised, without fresh blood it's hard to get much better. 'We are weak,' Crescentini agrees. 'But we are pure.'

**

After sixteen years of losing almost every game Mazza resigned after the final World Cup qualifier, the 8-0 loss to Ukraine. Up to that point he was the longest serving national coach in Europe. 'It has nothing to do with the defeats,' he says. 'But I think that after sixteen years it is time to leave and give the job to someone with a different approach.' He believes that, whoever is coach, San Marino is unlikely to win a match or ever appear at a major tournament. He laughs out loud when I suggest the possibility. 'I believe this is a dream,' says Mazza. 'I would be very happy if my successor wins a match. But I know that this will be almost impossible. At least from the experience I had. At the least, I wish there will be some better changes and we will not lose eight, nine, ten, eleven-nil.'

Outside football Mazza is a PE teacher in a local school but he won't be going far, even for such a small place as San Marino. He'll still help coach the youth team, who are having their best ever year after the Under 21 team beat Wales recently, San Marino's first competitive victory at any level. He'll miss the foreign travel and the chance to coach abroad. He'll miss Wembley. But most of all he'll miss the reception San Marino received after every match regardless of the heavy defeats. He'll miss thousands of opposition fans cheering them off. What is it in human nature that makes us appreciate a team like San Marino in a completely different way, I ask. Why do we gravitate towards the underdog? 'We prove we can play against world champions even though we are small.' But perhaps the answer is even simpler than that. 'Everyone who is normal,' he says, 'sees themselves in us.'

ACKNOWLEDGEMENTS

Thirty One Nil has been a huge undertaking, one that was far bigger than I had originally intended. It took me to six continents and to over 20 countries. Along the way I met hundreds of people, many of them unsung heroes, who have helped me. Without them this book would not have come to life. I apologise in advance for anyone I have forgotten.

In the West Bank and Tajikistan I'd like to first thank StephaneFloricien, without whom I'd probably still be a in a jail cell somewhere in Russia, as well as Jerome Champagne and Susan Shalabi from the Palestinian Football Association who allowed me to follow the team wherever they went.

I'd also like to thank the football associations of Haiti, Rwanda, Lebanon, Antigua and Barbuda, Croatia, Serbia, Hungary, Bosnia, Iceland, Norway, Belgium, Oman, Jordan and San Marino for allowing me to come into their worlds. In particular, Bonnie Mugabe, Omar Smarason, TomislavPacak, AleksandarBoskovic, AbdulrahmanMagdy, TamasSztancsik, JurajCurny, Mark Bowers, Priscilla Duncan, SaraiBareman and Daniel Markham.

On the road there have been many people who have shared in these adventures, many of them journalists, who have also given me contacts and generally did their best to keep me out of trouble. In particular Mala Roche and everyone doing great work with Trocaire in Haiti; James Corbett in the West Bank; AleksandarHoliga, SašaIbrulj and Rory Smith in Croatia; Igor Resende and Seamus "El Grande Perro" Mirodan in Brazil; Kenny

Laurie and Karl Baz in Lebanon; Gail and Thomas Rongen, KristianBrodie and the whole crew from Agile Films in American Samoa; AmrFahmy, Hany el Haridy, and Bob and Lindsay Bradley in Egypt; huge thanks to Merissa Khurma, ReemaAsendar and Jonathan Wilson in Jordan; and, finally, thank you Enzo Marino Frisoni, Amalia-Maria Rosoiu and DadianaChiran in San Marino for putting me up and sharing Marino's incredible memories of the 1968 Olympics.

Many of these chapters found their nucleus in my reporting and it would not have been possible to travel so far and so wide without the commissions given to me by various editors. Most of all I'd like to thank Richard Padula at the BBC World Service, Jason Stallman and Andrew Das at the New York Times, Gavin Hamilton from World Soccer, everyone at Delayed Gratification, Jonathan Heaf from GQ, Ben Wyatt, Dylan Reynolds and John Sinnott at CNN and Louis Massarella from FourFourTwo.

Of course, *Thirty One Nil* was only a pipe dream without the continued support and help from my agent Rebecca Winfield, who dragged me over the finishing line, as well as Charlotte Atyeo at Bloomsbury who took a gamble on this even as the sound of deadlines whooshed by.

Without the support of my mum and dad I'd probably be living on the streets by now. They have put up with more chaos than a 34 year old should really be putting his parents through. Equally as supportive have been Laura Montague, Rob Reddy, Alina, Silviu and OdettaTotti and, in the early part of the book, Ana Piferrer Garcia and family.

Finally, I do not have names for many of the people who helped me. But two in particular stand out. The volunteer medic who wiped the effects of tear gas from my eyes in Brazil and the young man who sheltered me from gunfire in Port Said. You never told me your names but I will never forget what you did.

James Montague, January 2014.

INDEX

Abbas, Mahmoud 34
Abdel, Zak 215, 221
Abdullah II, King of Jordan 302, 304, 305
Aboutrika, Mohamed 134, 135–6, 141, 143, 146, 147, 214, 221, 275–6, 288, 318
Abu Dhabi 123–5
Adu, Freddy 150
Advocaat, Dick 99
Afewerki, Isaias 74–5, 77, 83
Afghanistan 23–5, 30–3
  diaspora 31–2
  Palestine first leg match 15–17, 28–9
  Palestine second leg match 33–6
  security situation 24, 25
Africa Cup of Nations 63, 64
Akram, Nashat 297
Al Ahly SC 209, 210–11, 212, 214–15, 216
Al-Ahed 115, 117, 118–23, 126–7
Alazar, Samuel 72, 79
Albania
  Bosnia and Herzegovina match 270
  Switzerland match 168, 182–9
Alexandre, Jean-Marc 57
Algeria 81, 142–3, 278
Ali, Mahmoud El 117, 121, 126, 218–19
Ali bin al-Hussein, Prince 300–3
Allenby Bridge, Jordan/West Bank 32
Al-Shabaab militia 63
Altidore, Jozy 273
Alyan, Murad 28, 36
American Samoa 88–94, 98–101, 225, 315–16
  Australia match 2001 9, 89–90, 96, 100–1, 104–5
  Cook Islands match 101–6
  fa'afafine 91–3

J. S. Blatter Stadium 94
  Samoa match 103–6, 106–10
  Tonga match 91, 93, 94–8, 107
Amman, Jordan 30–3
Amour, Ismail 29
Anderson, Viv 2
Andorra 13
Anguilla 3
Animal, the 246–9, 251
Antigua and Barbuda 45, 49, 61, 149–50, 152–8, 158–62, 162–4
  Haiti match 61–2, 155–6
  Jamaica match 167
  United States of America match 151, 164–7
anti-Semitism 259–60, 261–2
Antunes, Lúcio 278
Arab Spring 128, 131–2
Arafat, Yasser 34
Argentina 298
Aristide, Jean-Bertrand 47, 51
Arja, Khodr 119–20
Arkan 196, 199, 202
Arni (Iceland fan) 289, 290, 310
Aruba 3
Asian Football Confederation 18
Australia 298
  American Samoa match, 2001 9, 89–90, 96, 100–1, 104–5
  Eritrean refugees 84–7

Bahamas 3, 13
Bahdari, Abdelatif 19
Bahr, Walter 235
Bahrain 128–9
Bangladesh 113, 116
Bangoura, Alhassane 147
Bassam, Omar al Taleb (Syrian refugee) 293–4, 298–9

Begović, Asmir   266–7, 267, 268, 269,
   270, 271
Behrami, Valon   183, 183–4, 186, 188
Beirut   111–12
Belgium   290
Belize, Montserrat match   3–4, 10–13,
   49, 315
Bell, Charles   105–6
Benediktsson, Guðmundur   308–9
Benin   81
Bennett, Davidson   229
Bermuda, Montserrat match, 2006   5
Bezaz, Moussa   15, 17–18, 19, 22–3,
   23–5, 26, 27–8, 28–9, 34–5, 36
Bičakčić, Ermin   272
Bilić, Slaven   201, 205
Bin Laden, Osama   21
Bishara, Roberto   16, 19, 22–3, 35
Blackstock, Dexter   159, 163, 165, 166
Blatter, Sepp   34, 170, 177–82, 189,
   234, 244, 316
Boban, Zvonimir   199
Bocanegra, Carlos   166
Bogdán, Ádám   257–8, 264
Bokšić, Alen   195
Bosnia and Herzegovina   266–70, 312
   Lithuania match   290–1
   Slovakia match   270–2, 279–80
Bosnian War   268–9
Botswana   277
Bowers, Mark   161
Bradenton, Florida   149–51
Bradley, Bob   133–9, 139–41, 143–5,
   146–7, 148, 209–10, 215–17, 220,
   275–6, 278, 287–9, 317–18
Bradley, Michael   150, 165
Brazil
   1950 World Cup final   235-6
   economic slowdown   231
   ethnic diversity   230
   infrastructure   224, 231
   protests   231–2, 232–5, 237–40,
      240–3, 244
   Spain match   245
   Uruguay match (2013 Confederations
      Cup)   240, 243
British Virgin Islands, US Virgin Islands
   match   3–4, 48–9
B'Tselem   39
Bucker, Theo   112–18, 120, 122–3,
   125, 126, 129–30, 217–20
Budapest   250, 253, 258, 259, 260,
   265
Burkina Faso   312

Byers, Peter   149–50, 151, 160, 162,
   165, 166

Cahill, Tim   104
Cairo   134, 139
   Tahrir Square   131–2, 136–7,
      211–12, 216
Cameroon   10, 277
Cana, Lorik   171, 185–7
Cape Verde Islands   277–8
Castillo, Luis   303
Cavani, Edinson   298, 305
Central African Republic   136, 147, 277
Central Midlands Football league (South
   Division) (England)   2, 13–14
Ceus, Steward   46, 47–8, 51, 55, 61, 155
Champagne, Jerome   24
Chelyabinsk, Russian Federation   29–30
Chile   216
China   37
Clifton All Whites FC   1–3, 13–14
Cochrane, Justin   158–60
CONCACAF   3, 13, 44, 48, 157, 225,
   245, 273,
Confederations Cup   224–32, 234,
   236–7, 240, 241, 243, 243–5
Congo, Democratic Republic of   63
Cook Islands   90, 100–1, 107
   American Samoa match   101–6
Corlăţean, Titus   251
Corruption   129, 177, 181, 218–19, 227
Costa Rica   274
Court of Arbitration for Sport   174
Cranston, Bryan   318
Crescentini, Giorgio   319–20
Croatia   190–3, 194, 201, 269
   footballing heritage   190–8
   Iceland match   291, 306–12
   Serbia match   194, 197, 203–8, 306–7
Curaçao   45, 55–62, 154
Curtis, Tom   62, 151–8, 161–2,
   163–4, 164–5, 166, 166–7

Da Silva, Dominique   214, 216
Dadason, Kolbeinn Tumi   289
Dayoub, Ramez   217, 218–19
Deeb, Amer   301
Defoe, Jermain   6
Dempsey, Clint   165, 273
Dominican Republic   13
Dominique, Henry Robert   155–6
Donovan, Landon   150, 166
doping   254–5
Duvalier, François 'Papa Doc'   41

Dyer, Kenny   4–6, 11, 12, 13
Džeko, Edin   266, 267, 268–9

Eddine, Noor   23
Egervári, Sándor   256–7
Egypt   132–7, 137–8, 141, 143–5,
   209–17
  Algeria match, 2009   142–3
  Arab Spring   131–2
  Borg el Arab Stadium   139–40, 145
  Chile match   216
  coup   275–6
  elections   140, 210
  England Match, 1990   141–2
  Ghana match   278–9, 287–9,
    317–18
  Guinea match   147
  Mozambique match   138–9, 145–7
  Port Said massacre   132–3, 135–7,
    140–1, 210–11
  Port Said verdict   212–13, 214
  World Cup performances   141–3
  Zidan banned   147–8
  Zimbabwe match   215, 220–1
El-Abd, Adam   143–4, 145
El-Hadary, Essam   146
Embaye, Kahsay   74–5, 79, 83
England   141–2, 290, 313
Equatorial Guinea   278
Eran (Uruguay supporter)   303–4
Eric the Eel   12
Eritrea   64, 67, 72–8, 81–2, 83–4, 85,
   221–2
  comparison with Rwanda   83
  defections   64, 73–6, 76–8, 83,
    84–7, 221–2, 315
  Ethiopian war   74–5, 77
  Human Rights Watch report   77
  Rwanda first leg match   70–2
  Rwanda second leg match   63–4,
    78–82
Etaeta, Eddie   223–8, 230, 232, 236–7
Ethiopia   74–5, 77, 81, 312
European play-off draw   291
Eusébio   147

fa'afafine   91–3
Faisal al-Husseini Stadium, Al-Ram, near
   Ramallah   23, 33–6
Fakhouri, Fahed Al   26–7, 38, 39–40
Falklands War   8–9
Fathalla, Mahmoud   146
Fathy, Ahmed   215
Fayyad, Salam   35–6

FIFA   127, 176–7, 181, 224, 227
  elections, 2011   178
  recognition of Kosovo   169–70,
    174–6, 178–82, 185–6, 188–9,
    316
  recognition of Palestine   17, 34, 177–8
Forde, Olson   149–50, 151
foreign players, nationality rules   159–60
France   267, 291, 312
Freitas, Tainara   233, 234–5

Gakuba, Abdul Jabar   70–2
Gebrehiwet, Samuel   86
Gebremeskel, Nevi   86–7
Gebreyesus, Tesfaye   68
Gedo   215
Gemayel, Nadim   124–5
genocide   65, 67–8, 70–2
Germany   290, 314
Ghana   215, 278–9, 287–9, 317–18
Ghanem, Jamal   38–9
Gibraltar   174
Glanville, Brian   255
Goitom, Daniel   79–80, 80, 81
Gomez, Herculez   166
Greece   266, 272, 290, 312
Guðjohnsen, Eiður   281, 282, 283,
    308, 311, 311–12
Guðmundsson, Jóhann   282
Guinea   147
Gyöngyösi, Márton   259–60, 260–2

Haile, Ermias   84–7
Haiti   10, 43–8, 56–7, 58, 154, 316
  Antigua and Barbuda match   61–2,
    155–6
  Curaçao match   45, 55–62
  earthquake, 2010   42, 44–5
  Stade Sylvio Cator   41, 42–4, 52–5
  Tonton Macoutes   41
  US Virgin Islands first leg match
    42–4
  US Virgin Islands second leg match
    50–5
Hajrović, Izet   272
Halldórsson, Hannes   284–6, 308, 311
Hamad, Adnan   297, 298
Hamšik, Marek   272
Harbi, Ahmed   36
Hariri, Rafic   114, 115, 118
Hariri, Saad   120
Hassan, Abbas   126, 127
Hassan, Hossam   298, 300, 301, 305
Hayel, Ahmad   301, 305

Hegazy, Ahmed 143, 146
Heidenrich, John G. 65
Hezbollah 111–12, 114, 117, 120, 121, 127
Hijazy, Ali 120
Hodgson, Jay'Lee 2–3, 4, 6–8, 10–11, 13–14, 315
Høgmo, Per-Mathias 287
Holland 13, 246, 264, 290
homophobia 93
Honduras 272–3, 273–4
hooliganism 135–6, 246–9, 251–2
Howard, Tim 165, 166
Huckerby, Darren 2
Human Rights Watch 77
Hungary 253–6, 256–9, 259–60, 264–5
    anti-Semitism 260, 261–2
    Golden Team 253–6, 257
    nationalism 250–1, 261
    relationship with Romania 249–50
    Romania match 246–9, 250–2, 262–5
    uprising 1958 255

Ibišević, Vedad 266, 271, 290
Iceland 281, 282, 283–6, 308, 311–2
    Croatia match 291, 306–12
    Norway match 281–2, 282–3, 286–7, 289–90
    Switzerland match 282
India 37
Indonesia 128–9
Iran 129, 130, 217–18, 220
Iraq 10, 127, 297–8
Islamic Jihad 39
Italy 290
Ivanović, Branislav 207

Jamaica 10, 167
Jamal Ghanem Stadium 38–9
James, Molvin 166
Jamieson, Tony 102
Januzaj, Adnan 317
Japan 217
Jarun, Omar 16, 17, 18, 20–1, 21, 26, 27, 35, 37–40
Jean-Bart, Yves 44–5
Jenas, Jermaine 2
Jóhannsson, Aron 284
Jordan 37, 127, 293–4, 295–9, 300–2
    Al Wihdat refugee camp 295–7
    Amman International Stadium 299–300
    Palestinian refugees 294–7, 300–1

Uruguay match 297, 302, 302–5, 314–15
    Uzbekistan match 271–2, 298
    Zaatari refugee camp 292–9
Joseph (Haitian fan) 60–1
Joseph, Marc 165, 166

Kabul 15–16, 25
Kagame, Paul 65, 69–70, 71–2, 83
Karekezi, Olivier 80
Kargar, Mohammad Yosuf 24
Keh, Andrew 273–4
Keshkesh, Ahmed 22–3, 23–5, 28–9, 34
Kigali, Rwanda 68–9
Klinsmann, Jürgen 151, 166
Klopp, Reid 48–50, 62
Kohistani, Israfeel 24
Kolarov, Aleksandar 207
Kosovo 168–9, 171–6
    FIFA recognition 169–70, 174–6, 178–82, 185–6, 188–9, 316
    international recognition 175, 179
    players in Switzerland 170–1, 183–5, 188, 316–17
    UEFA recognition 169–70, 174–5, 180–1
Kosovo War 169–70, 173, 197
Köves, Slomó 260

Lafrance, Kevin 47, 57–8
Lagerbäck, Lars 282, 283–4, 286, 289, 291, 307, 308, 312
Laos 37
Lebanon 112–18, 122–3, 219–20
    Camille Chamoun Sports City Stadium 114
    civil war 111, 115, 123, 124
    Iran match 217–18
    match fixing scandal 218–19
    political instability 111–12, 113
    Qatar match 217–20
    refugee camps 114, 118, 119
    religious groups 113, 114–15, 120
    South Korea match 113–14, 116
    UAE match 117–18, 123–7, 129–30
    Uzbekistan match 218
Leigertwood, Mikele 159, 160, 166
Liberia 277
Libya 277
Lichtenstein 290
Lithuania 290
L'Ouverture, Toussaint 44
Luani, Shalom 97

Lui, Tunoa   90, 104–5, 110
Luvu, Tala   102

Maamaaloa, Timote   97
Maatouk, Hassan   127
McCoy, Marvin   163
Macedonia   197
Mahmoud, Younis   297
Malaysia   130
Mali   81
Mandžukić, Mario   194, 207, 310, 311
Maracanazo   236, 237, 245, 303,
Maradona, Diego   8–9
Marcelin, James   54, 56–7, 61
Marshal Tito Cup   190–3, 194–6
Martelly, Michel   42–3, 50–2, 53–4,
   55, 159–60
Mashriqi, Mohammad Yusef   31
match fixing   129, 218–19
Maurice, Jean-Eudes   47, 57, 61
Mazza, Giampaolo   313–14, 320
Mehmedi, Admir   183
Messi, Lionel   298
Mexico   273, 274–5, 307–8, 318
Mihajlović, Siniša   191–3, 194–7,
   198–203, 207–8, 306, 307
Modrić, Luka   194
Mogadishu   63
Mohammed, Hawar Mulla   297
Montserrat   5, 6–8
   Belize match   3–4, 10–13, 49, 315
   Bermuda match, 2006   5
   Surinam match   6
Moore, Craig   99
Morsi, Mohamed   140, 210, 212, 213,
   275–6
Mortagy, Khaled   216
Mozambique, Egypt match   138–9,
   145–7
Mubarak, Hosni   131, 139, 143, 147
Murtagh, Keiran   162
Muzurović, Fuad   270
Myanmar   37

Nasrallah, Hassan   117
Nationalism   246–9, 250–1, 261, 270–1
Nationality rules   159–60
Nepal   37
New Zealand   90, 128, 226, 244–5,
   307–8, 318
Nigeria, Tahiti match   229–32
North Korea   10
Norway, Iceland match   281–2, 282–3,
   286–7, 289–90

Nottingham, Norman Archer Memorial
   Ground   1–3
Nottingham Forest FC   2
Notts County FC   2
Ntagungira, Celestin   67–8

Oceania Football Confederation   90
OFC Nations Cup   225
Ogwel, Patrick   222
Olić, Ivica   207, 310
Olson, Egil   287
Oman   37, 217
Onyewu, Oguchi   166
Orbán, Viktor   260
Ott, Ramin   96, 108–9

Palestine   16–22, 23–5, 33–4,
   Afghanistan first leg match   15–17,
      28–9
   Afghanistan second leg match   33–6
   Faisal al-Husseini Stadium   23, 33–6
   FIFA recognition   17, 34, 177–8
   Israeli checkpoints   37–8
   Israeli occupation   23
   Israeli settlers   38
   Thailand match   36
   in Tursunzoda   25–8
Palestinian Authority   17, 33
Palestinian Liberation Organisation
   112
Panama   272–3, 275
Pelé   239
Pereira, Maxi   304
Petur (Iceland fan)   286–7
Pinto, Jorge Luis   274
Pjanić, Miralem   266
Placide, Johnny   155
Platini, Michel   174–5, 180–2
Podolski, Lukas   314
Portmore United FC   12
Portugal   290, 312
professionalism   12
prostitution   58–9
Puskás, Ferenc   253–6

Qatar   127–9, 181
Queiroz, Carlos   220

Rajoub, Jibril   33–4
Refugees   84–7, 114, 118, 119, 292–9,
   300–1
Resende, Igor   230–2
Reykjavik   281
Richards, Viv   164

Roche, Mickaël 227, 236, 237
Romania 312
    Hungary match 246–9, 250–2, 262–5
    nationalism 246–9, 250
    qualification play-offs 265
    relationship with Hungary 249–50
Romario 239
Romi (Uruguay supporter) 304
Ronaldo 239
Rongen, Thomas 88–9, 90–4, 95, 96–8,
    101, 101–6, 106–7, 108–9, 110, 225
Rousseff, Dilma 234, 244
Rufer, Shane 100–1
Rufer, Wynton 100
Russia 14, 29-30, 170, 175, 177, 179,
    189, 290
Rwanda 65–70, 221
    Amahoro Stadium 63, 64–5
    comparison with Eritrea 83
    diaspora 66
    Eritrea first leg match 70–2
    Eritrea second leg match 63–4,
    78–82
    genocide 64–5, 67–8, 70–2
    life expectancy 70

Sabri, Noor 297
Saddam Hussein 39–40
Saeed, Basheer 126
Saelua, Jaiyah (Johnny) 92–3, 96, 97,
    98, 102, 108, 109, 110, 315–16
Sahel, Mohamed 121
Saify, Oday Al 304
St Lucia 13
Salah, Husain Abu 16
Salah, Mohamed 143, 147, 220–1, 276
Salapu, Nicky 89–90, 91, 96, 97, 97–8,
    98–101, 102–3, 104, 108, 109, 110
Saleh, Ramzi 26
Salihu, Eroll 168–9, 172, 173–4, 175,
    182–3, 185–6, 188–9, 317
Samad, Ziad Al 126
Samin, Xavier 229
Samoa 89, 90, 103, 225
    American Samoa match 103–6,
    106–10
    Tahiti match 110
San Marino 313–14, 319–20
Sanabria, Daniel 233, 234–5
Saudi Arabia 297
Seattle 99–100
Senegal 277
Serbia 170, 171–6, 179, 196–203
    Croatia match 194, 203–8, 306–7

sex-trafficking 58–9
Shafi, Amer 301
Shaqiri, Xherdan 183, 184, 186, 188,
    290, 317
Sharityar, Djelaludin 32, 33
Shbair, Mohammed 16
Shehata, Hassan 133–4
Sigþórsson, Kolbeinn 282, 285, 289,
    308, 311
Sigurðsson, Gylfi 282
Silva, Martin 304
Šimunić, Josip 197, 306, 311
Sium, Ambes 86
Skepple, Kerry 155
Slovakia 290
    Bosnia and Herzegovina match
    270–2, 279–80
Slovenia 282, 289
Solomon Islands 90, 225, 226
Somalia 63, 81
Soria, Sebastián 217
South Korea 113–14, 116, 219–20
Spahić, Emir 266
Spain 236–7, 245, 290
Spencer, Baldwin 161
Sponsorship 50, 70, 115
Srebrenica massacre 268
Sredojević, Milutin 'Micho' 66–7, 72,
    78, 80, 81, 82, 221, 277
Srna, Darijo 311
Stade Sylvio Cator, Haiti 41, 42–4
Štimac, Igor 192–3, 193–8, 200–1,
    202–3, 207–8, 269, 306, 307
Su'a, Alex 92
Suárez, Luis 298, 301, 304
Šuker, Davor 204–5, 208
Suleiman, Professor Yasir 295–6
Surinam, Montserrat match 6
Sušić, Safet 266, 269, 272
Sweden 284, 312
Switzerland
    Albania match 168, 182–9
    Iceland match 282
    Kosovar players 170–1, 183–5, 188,
    290, 316–17
    Kosovar population 168, 179
    Slovenia match 289
Syria 37
Syrian civil war 119, 132, 292, 294
Szilárd, Szabó 258–9

Tabarez, Óscar 298
Tahiti 90, 110, 223–4, 244–5
    Confederations Cup 224–32, 236–7

Nigeria match   229–32
   Spain match   236–7
Tajikistan   37
Tapui, Rambo   107
Tavares, Edson   43–4, 45–8, 56, 57,
   61, 62, 154–5, 156, 316
Taylor, Peter   128, 129
Teklehaymanot, Daniel   83–4
Teklit, Negash   72–3, 74, 75–6, 78, 79,
   81–2, 82–3, 221, 222
Tel Aviv   40
Temarii, Reynald   226–7
Thailand   36, 113
Thompson, Archie   9, 89–90
Thonglao, Datsakorn   36
Togo   277
Tonga   90, 103, 107
   American Samoa match   91, 93,
      94–8, 107
Torres, Fernando   236
transgender players   91–3
Trinidad and Tobago   3, 10
Tripoli   118–23
Tulkarem, West Bank   37–40
Tunisia   278
Turks and Caicos Islands   3
Tursunzoda, Tajikistan   15–17, 21,
   22–3, 25–8

Uganda   221–2, 277
Ujkani, Samir   188
United Arab Emirates   10, 37, 116, 309
   Al-Nahyan Stadium   125–6
   Lebanese population   117–18, 123–4
   Lebanon match   117–18, 123–7,
      129–30
United States of America   150–1, 153,
   156–7, 275
   Antigua and Barbuda match   151–2,
      164–7
   Costa Rica match   274
   Honduras match   273–4
   Mexico match   273
Uruguay   240, 243, 298, 315
   Jordan match   297, 302, 302–5,
      314–15
US Virgin Islands   13, 48–50, 62, 154
   British Virgin Islands match   3–4,
      48–9
   Haiti first leg match   42–4
   Haiti second leg match   53–5
Uzamukunda, Elias   66, 72, 79–80

Uzbekistan   218
   Jordan match   271–2, 298

Varela, Fernando   278
Vasconcelos, Lena   278
Venezuela   298
Vidić, Nemanja   199
Vidmar, Tony   99
Vokrri, Fadil   168–9, 171–6, 182–3,
   185, 188–9, 199, 200
Vukovar   190–1, 201–2

Wadi, Hussam   35
Wahl, Grant   275–6
Warshaw, Andrew   180
Willemstad, Curaçao   55–60
Williams, Chris   95, 107
World Cup   9, 13
   1930   9
   1934   9
   1950   235–6
   1954   254–5
   1966   10
   1974   10, 45, 309
   1986   8–9, 10
   1990   10, 141–2, 309
   1998   10, 196, 205
   2006   10, 19, 100
   2010   3, 5, 133, 142, 154, 215, 267
   2014   3–4, 10–13
   2018   14, 189
   2022   127–8, 181

Xhaka, Granit   183, 184–5, 186, 188,
   189

Yugoslavia   171–2
Yugoslavia, Federal Republic of   197
Yugoslavia, former   168, 178–9
Yugoslavia, Socialist Federal Republic of
   196
   Hajduk-Red Star match   190–3,
      194–6

Zaatari refugee camp, Jordan   292–9
Zaire   10, 309
Zico   127
Zidan, Mohamed   143, 146, 147–8
Zimbabwe   215, 220–1
Ziqawe, Khaled   302
Zreik, Ahmad   117, 121–2, 126–7,
   218–19

A NOTE ON THE AUTHOR

James Montague is a journalist from Chelmsford, Essex, who writes for the *New York Times*, *World Soccer* and *Delayed Gratification* as well as appearing regularly on the BBC World Service's *World Football Show*. He is the author of two books; *When Friday Comes: Football, War and Revolution in the Middle East*, which won him best New Writer at the British Sports Book Awards, and *Thirty One Nil: On the Road With Football's Outsiders*.